VITAL
OLD TESTAMENT
ISSUES

THE VITAL ISSUES SERIES

VITAL ISSUES SERIES

VITAL OLD TESTAMENT ISSUES

Examining Textual and Topical Questions

ROY B. ZUCK
GENERAL EDITOR

Grand Rapids, MI 49501

Vital Old Testament Issues: Examining Textual and Topical Questions by Roy B. Zuck, general editor

Copyright © 1996 by Dallas Theological Seminary

Published by Kregel Resources, an imprint of Kregel Publications, P.O. Box 2607, Grand Rapids, MI 49501. Kregel Resources provides timely and relevant resources for Christian life and service. Your comments and suggestions are valued.

Cover design: Sarah Slattery
Book design: Alan G. Hartman

Library of Congress Cataloging-in-Publication Data
Roy B. Zuck
Vital Old Testament issues: examining textual and topical questions / Roy B. Zuck, gen. ed.
p.   cm. (Vital Issues Series; v. 7)
1. Bible. O.T.—Criticism, interpretation, etc. 2. Bible. O.T.—Language, style. I. Zuck, Roy B. II. Series.
BS1171.2.V57   1996   221.6—dc20   96-10338
                                                              CIP

ISBN 0-8254-4073-4 (paperback)

1 2 3 4 5 Printing / Year 00 99 98 97 96

Printed in the United States of America

Contents

Contributors

Robert B. Chisholm, Jr.
Professor of Old Testament Studies, Dallas Theological
Seminary, Dallas, Texas

Charles H. Dyer
Assistant to the President and Professor of Bible Exposition,
Dallas Theological Seminary, Dallas, Texas

Charles R. Gianotti
Pastor, Auburn Bible Chapel, Peterborough, Ontario

Reg Grant
Professor of Pastoral Ministries, Dallas Theological
Seminary, Dallas, Texas

Tom R. Hawkins
President of Restoration in Christ Ministries, Altoona,
Pennsylvania

Homer Heater
President, Capital Bible Seminary, Lanham, Maryland

Harold W. Hoehner
Director of Ph.D. Studies and Chairman and Senior
Professor of New Testament Studies, Dallas Theological
Seminary, Dallas, Texas

Greg A. King
Assistant Professor of Biblical Studies, Pacific Union
College, Angwin, California

J. Carl Laney
Professor of Biblical Literature, Western Conservative
Baptist Seminary, Portland, Oregon

Eugene H. Merrill
Professor of Old Testament Studies, Dallas Theological
Seminary, Dallas, Texas

Mark F. Rooker
Professor of Old Testament and Hebrew, Criswell College, Dallas, Texas

Allen P. Ross
Professor of Old Testament Studies, Trinity Episcopal School for Ministry, Ambridge, Pennsylvania

Jeffrey L. Townsend
Senior Pastor, Woodland Park Community Church, Woodland Park, Colorado

Edwin Yamauchi
Professor and Director of Graduate Studies, History Department, Miami University, Oxford, Ohio

Preface

Old. Antiquated. Out of date. Irrelevant. Unnecessary. These words depict the way some people view the Old Testament. How could these books, written hundreds of years before Christ, have any relevance or meaning to Christians today? How could books dealing with ancient cultures, long-ago events, and individuals who lived in bygone times be pertinent to today's fast-paced, computerized society?

Actually, the Old Testament is remarkably relevant, even stunningly significant. It reports how God worked in creating the world, in selecting and guiding a chosen nation, in rewarding obedience and punishing sin, and in predicting the coming of His Son, the Messiah, to provide redemption from sin. The Hebrew Scriptures stand like a giant backdrop to the redemptive drama that unfolds in the New Testament. The Old Testament vividly portrays the way God uses, blesses, and nourishes those who follow Him, and how He disciplines and rejects those who disregard and disobey Him.

This volume of sixteen chapters, reprinted from the theological journal *Bibliotheca Sacra*, addresses numerous topics of continuing interest to believers today. God's creative work in Genesis 1:1–3; the debated date of Israel's exodus from Egypt; literary features in the books of Ruth, Isaiah, Lamentations, and Amos; the social concern of the prophets; Daniel's prophecy of Israel's "seventy weeks"; Zephaniah's prophecy of the day of the Lord—these and other topics call for study and reflection on the Old Testament, which Jesus said spoke "concerning Himself" (Luke 24:27).

ROY B. ZUCK

About *Bibliotheca Sacra*

A flood is rampant—an engulfing deluge of literature far beyond any one person's ability to read it all. Presses continue to churn out thousands of journals and magazines like a roiling, raging river.

Among these numberless publications, one stands tall and singular—*Bibliotheca Sacra*—a strange name (meaning "Sacred Library") but a journal familiar to many pastors, teachers, and Bible students.

How is *Bibliotheca Sacra* unique in the world of publishing? By being the oldest continuously published journal in the Western Hemisphere—1993 marked its 150th anniversary—and by being published by one school for more than six decades—1994 marked its diamond anniversary of being released by Dallas Seminary.

Bib Sac, to use its shortened sobriquet, was founded in New York City in 1843 and was purchased by Dallas Theological Seminary in 1934, ten years after the school's founding. The quarterly's one-hundred-and-fifty-three-year history boasts only nine editors. Through those years it has maintained a vibrant stance of biblical conservatism and a strong commitment to the Scriptures as God's infallible Word.

Each volume in the Kregel *Vital Issues Series* includes carefully selected articles from the thirties to the present—articles of enduring quality, articles by leading evangelicals whose topics are as relevant today as when they were first produced. The chapters have been edited slightly to provide conformity of style. We trust these anthologies will enrich the spiritual lives and Christian ministries of many more readers.

ROY B. ZUCK, EDITOR
Bibliotheca Sacra

For *Bibliotheca Sacra* subscription information, call Dallas Seminary, 1-800-992-0998.

CHAPTER 1

Genesis 1:1–3:
Creation or Re-Creation?

Mark F. Rooker

An issue that has taunted mankind through the ages is the question of origins. Since ancient times people have been keenly interested in understanding and explaining their provenance. The ancient creation mythologies of Mesopotamia, Egypt, China, India, Iran, Japan, or Mexico,[1] or a child's question to his parents about who made the world shows that this concern is intrinsic to human nature.

The Bible clearly portrays God as the Creator of all that exists. In fact this issue is so important in the biblical revelation that it is the first issue addressed, for it is mentioned in the opening lines of Scripture. However, these opening verses have not been understood unilaterally in the history of interpretation. In his book *Creation and Chaos,* Waltke, after thoroughly investigating existing views, argues that there are three principal interpretations of Genesis 1:1–3 open to evangelicals. He designates these as the restitution theory, the initial chaos theory, and the precreation chaos theory.[2] Of primary importance in distinguishing these views is the relationship of Genesis 1:2 to the original creation: "And the earth was formless and void, and darkness was over the surface of the deep; and the Spirit of God was moving over the surface of the waters." As Waltke stated, "According to the first mode of thought, chaos occurred after the original creation; according to the second mode of thought, chaos occurred in connection with the original creation; and in the third mode of thought, chaos occurred before the original creation."[3] This chapter examines the theory of a period of chaos after creation (often called the gap theory), the initial chaos theory, and the precreation chaos theory, the view endorsed by Waltke and other recent commentators on Genesis.[4]

The Gap Theory

The restitution theory, or gap theory, has been held by many and is the view taken by the editors of *The New Scofield Reference Bible*.[5] This view states that Genesis 1:1 refers to the original creation of the universe, and sometime after this original creation Satan rebelled against God and was cast from heaven to the earth.[6] As a result of Satan's making his habitation on the earth, the earth was judged. God's original creation was then placed under judgment, and the result of this judgment is the state described in Genesis 1:2: The earth was "formless and void" (תֹהוּ וָבֹהוּ). Isaiah 34:11 and Jeremiah 4:23, which include the only other occurrences of the phrase תֹהוּ וָבֹהוּ, are cited as passages that substantiate the understanding of "formless and void" in Genesis 1:2 in a negative sense, because these words occur in both passages in the context of judgment oracles.

Waltke points out that this view conflicts with a proper understanding of the syntactical function of the וְא conjunction in the phrase וְהָאָרֶץ, "and the earth" (Gen. 1:2). The construction of וְא plus a noun does not convey sequence but rather introduces a disjunctive clause. The clause thus must be circumstantial to verse 1 or 3. It cannot be viewed as an independent clause ("And the earth became")[7] as held by the supporters of the gap theory.

Furthermore Waltke rejects the proposal that the occurrence of "formless and void" in Jeremiah 4:23 and Isaiah 34:11 proves that Genesis 1:2 is the result of God's judgment. Scripture nowhere states that God judged the world when Satan fell.[8]

In view of these objections, the gap theory should no longer be considered a viable option in explaining the meaning of Genesis 1:1–3. The view is grammatically suspect, and Scripture is silent on the idea that the earth was judged when Satan fell. Waltke's critique of the gap theory is devastating.[9]

The Initial Chaos Theory

Proponents of the initial chaos theory maintain that Genesis 1:1 refers to the original creation, with verse 2 providing a description of this original creation mentioned in verse 1 by the use of three disjunctive clauses. This is the traditional view held by Luther and Calvin, and it is the position mentioned in the renowned Gesenius-Kautzsch-Cowley Hebrew grammar.[10]

Waltke argues that this view is unacceptable because it requires that the phrases "the heavens and the earth" in verse 1 and "without form and void" in verse 2 be understood differently from their usual meaning in the Old Testament.[11] In the initial chaos theory "the heavens and the earth"[12] in verse 1 were created without form and void. However, as Waltke observes, this "demands that we place a different value on 'heaven and earth' than anywhere else in Scripture . . . Childs concluded that the compound never has the meaning of disorderly chaos but always of an orderly world."[13]

A second objection proceeds from the first. If verse 2 describes the condition of the earth when it was created, then the phrase "without form and void," which otherwise appears to refer to an orderless chaos, must be understood as referring to what God produced along with the darkness and the deep, which likewise have negative connotations.[14] But this would not be possible in a perfect cosmos. As Waltke argues, "Logic will not allow us to entertain the contradictory notions: God created the organized heaven and earth; the earth was unorganized."[15] It is also argued that Isaiah 45:18 states explicitly that God did not create a תֹהוּ.

THE HEAVENS AND THE EARTH

In reference to Waltke's objection concerning the use of the phrase "the heavens and the earth" in Genesis 1:1 one may ask, Must the expression "the heavens and the earth" have the same meaning throughout the canon, especially if the contextual evidence explicitly refers to its formulation? It is a valid question to ask whether the initial reference to the expression in question would have the meaning it did in subsequent verses *after* the universe had been completed. It should be emphasized that this is the first use of the phrase and one could naturally ask how else the initial stage of the universe might be described. The phrase here could merely refer to the *first stage* of creation. This idea that Genesis 1:1 refers to the first stage in God's creative activity might be supported by the context, which clearly reveals that God intended to create the universe in progressive stages. Furthermore early Jewish sources attest that the heavens and the earth were created on the first day of God's creative activity.[16] Wenham nicely articulates this position in addition to replying to the objection raised by Waltke and others:

> Here it suffices to observe that if the creation of the world was a unique event, the terms used here may have a slightly different value from elsewhere. . . . Commentators often insist that the phrase "heaven and

earth" denotes the completely ordered cosmos. Though this is usually the case, totality rather than organization is its chief thrust here. It is therefore quite feasible for a mention of an initial act of creation of the whole universe (v. 1) to be followed by an account of the ordering of different parts of the universe (vv. 2–31).[17]

This is also Luther's understanding of the meaning of the phrase in Genesis 1:1: "Moses calls 'heaven and earth,' not those elements which now are; but the original rude and unformed substances."[18]

If the phrase "the heavens and the earth" does not refer to the completed and organized universe known to subsequent biblical writers, the premise on which Waltke rejects the initial chaos theory is seriously undermined.

Formless and Void

As previously mentioned the words תֹהוּ and בֹהוּ occur together in only three passages in the Old Testament. The word בֹהוּ occurs only in combination with תֹהוּ, while תֹהוּ may occur by itself. The most current and comprehensive discussion of the phrase in reference to cognate Semitic languages as well as biblical usage is given by Tsumura:

> Hebrew *tōhû* is based on a Semitic root **thw* and means "desert." The term *bōhû* is also a Semitic term based on the root **bhw*, "to be empty." . . . The Hebrew term *bōhû* means (1) "desert," (2) "a desert-like place," i.e. "a desolate or empty place" or "an uninhabited place" or (3) "emptiness." The phrase *tōhû wābōhû* refers to a state of "aridness or unproductiveness" (Jer. 4:23) or "desolation" (Isa. 34:11) and to a state of "unproductiveness and emptiness" in Genesis 1:2.[19]

Thus both the etymological history and contextual usage of the phrase fail to support Waltke's view that the situation described in Genesis 1:2 is that of a chaotic, unorganized universe. He overstates the force of the phrase "formless and void."

But what about the evidence from Isaiah 45:18? Does not this imply that God was not responsible for creating the state described in Genesis 1:2? The verse reads, "For thus says the Lord, who created the heavens (He is the God who formed the earth and made it, He established it and did not create it a waste place [תֹהוּ], but formed it to be inhabited)." Does not this passage explicitly state that God did not create a תֹהוּ? Waltke and others argue that this parallel passage substantiates the claim that God did not bring about the state described in Genesis 1:2 by His creative powers.[20] The answer to this objection appears to be found in the purpose of God's creation as seen in the context of Isaiah 45:18. It could be argued from the context that God created the earth to be inhabited,[21] not to leave it in a desolate תֹהוּ condition. Rather than contradicting the initial chaos theory, Isaiah 45:18 actually helps clarify the meaning of תֹהוּ in Genesis 1:2. Since תֹהוּ is contrasted with לָשֶׁבֶת, "to inhabit,"[22] one should conclude that תֹהוּ is an antonym of "inhabiting."[23] The earth, immediately after God's initial creative act was in a condition that was not habitable for mankind.[24] Tsumura nicely summarizes the contribution of Isaiah 45:18 to the understanding of Genesis 1:2:

> *tōhû* here is contrasted with *lāšebet* in the parallelism and seems to refer rather to a place which has no habitation, like the term *š?māmāh* "desolation" (cf. Jer. 4:27; Isa. 24:12), *ḥārēb* "waste, desolate" and *'azûbāh* "deserted." There is nothing in this passage that would suggest a chaotic state of the earth "which is opposed to and precedes creation." Thus, the term *tōhû* here too signifies "a desert-like place" and refers to "an uninhabited place.". . . It should be noted that *lō'-tōhû* here is a resultative object, referring to the purpose of God's creative action. In other words, this verse explains that God did not create the earth so that it may stay desert-like, but to be inhabited. So, this verse does not contradict Gen 1:2, where God created the earth to be productive and inhabited though it "was" still *tōhû wābōhû* in the initial state.[25]

The early Jewish Aramaic translation Neophyti I provides an early attestation to this understanding in its expansive translation of תֹהוּ וְבֹהוּ "desolate without human beings or beast and void of all cultivation of plants and of trees."[26] Tsumura writes, "In conclusion, both the biblical context and extra-biblical parallels suggest that the phrase *tōhû wābōhû* in Gen 1:2 has nothing to do with 'chaos' and simply means 'emptiness' and refers to the earth which is an empty place, i.e. 'an unproductive and uninhabited place.'"[27] This understanding of verse 2 fits well with the overall thrust and structure of Genesis 1:1–2:3.

> As the discourse analysis of this section indicates, the author in v. 2 focuses not on the "heavens" but on the "earth" where the reader/ audience stands, and presents the "earth" as "still" not being the earth which they all are familiar with. The earth which they are familiar with is "the earth" with vegetation, animals and man. Therefore, in a few verses, the author will mention their coming into existence through God's creation: vegetation on the third day and animals and man on the sixth day. Both the third and the sixth day are set as climaxes in the framework of this creation story and grand climax is the creation of man on the sixth day. . . . The story of creation in Gen 1:1–2:3 thus tells us that it is God who created mankind "in his image" and provided for him an inhabitable and productive earth.[28]

The structure of Genesis 1 shows that God in His creative work was making the earth habitable for man. He did not leave the earth in the initial תֹהוּ וָבֹהוּ state. This is seen clearly from the following table, which shows the six days of creation can be divided into two parallel groups with four creative acts each. The last day in each group, days three and six, have two creative acts each with the second creative act on these days functioning as the climax of each. This intentional arrangement shows that making the earth habitable for man is the purpose of the account by improving on the earth's initial status as desolate and empty.[29]

THE SIX DAYS OF CREATION

Waste	*Empty*
Day	Day
1. Light	4. Luminaries
2. Sky	5. Fish and fowl
3. Dry land	6. Land creatures
Vegetation	Humankind
(Lowest form of organic life)	(Highest form of organic life)

This supports the claim that תֹהוּ וָבֹהוּ is restricted to the earth's unlivable and empty condition before these six days. God converted the uninhabitable land into a land fit for man. He was not seeking to reverse it from a chaotic state. This is the point Isaiah 45:18 supports by presenting habitation as the reverse of תֹהוּ. The sequence in Isaiah 45:18 parallels that of Genesis 1. There is movement from an earth unfit to live in (Gen. 1:2 = Isa. 45:18a) to the finished product, to be inhabited by man (Gen. 1:3–31 = Isa. 45:18b).

However, what of Waltke's objection that a perfect God would not make a world that was "formless and void?" This charge loses its force when one considers the creation account itself. For one could also ask why God did not make the universe perfect with one command. He surely could have done so. And yet there was a progression, for He spent six days changing the state described in Genesis 1:2 into the world as it is now known. As Sarna has stated, "That God should create disorganized matter, only to reduce it to order, presents no more of a problem than does His taking six days to complete creation instead of instantaneously producing a perfected universe."[30]

Summary

Waltke's criticism of the gap theory is legitimate, as this theory conflicts with principles of Hebrew grammar. On the other hand Waltke objected to the initial chaos theory based on his understanding of the phrases "the heavens and the earth" and "formless and void." However, as has been shown, these phrases can be understood differently from the way Waltke understands them, so that the so-called initial chaos theory should not be dismissed on the basis of Waltke's objections to it.

Precreation Chaos Theory

The first feature of the precreation chaos view advocated by Waltke[31] concerns the grammatical understanding of Genesis 1:1–3. The opening statement, "In the beginning God created the heavens and the earth," is viewed as an independent clause[32] that functions as a summary statement for the narrative that ends in Genesis 2:3.[33] The first line of evidence Waltke puts forth for this rendering is the parallel structure in the subsequent Genesis narrative, Genesis 2:4–7.[34] Waltke argues that the narrative account of Genesis 2:4–7 is parallel to the construction of Genesis 1:1–3 in the following way: (1) Introductory summary statement (Gen. 1:1 = 2:4). (2) Circumstantial clause (1:2 = 2:5–6). (3) Main clause (1:3 = 2:7).[35] In addition, a similar structure is employed in the introduction to *Enuma Elish,* an important cosmological text from Mesopotamia. Waltke concludes, "The evidence therefore, seems overwhelming that we should construe verse 1 as a broad, general, declaration of the fact that God created the cosmos, and that the rest of the chapter explicates this statement. Such a situation reflects normal Semitic thought which first states the general proposition and then specifies the particulars."[36]

A second important tenet for the precreation chaos theory concerns the meaning of the verb בָּרָא, "to create," in Genesis 1:1. Waltke argues that בָּרָא does not necessarily mean "creation out of nothing" and that the ancient versions did not understand this to be the meaning of בָּרָא.[37] Thus Waltke concludes, "From our study of the structure of Rev. [*sic*] 1:1–3 I would also conclude that *bārā'* in verse 1 does not include the bringing of the negative state described in verse 2 into existence. Rather it means that He utilized it as a part of His creation. In this sense He created it."[38] In addition, "no mention is made anywhere in Scripture that God called the unformed, dark, and watery state of verse 3 [*sic*] into existence."[39]

The third interpretive feature proceeds from and is intrinsically linked with the immediate discussion of the meaning of בָּרָא. Because Waltke dismisses the possibility of *creatio ex nihilo* in Genesis 1:1, he says God was not responsible for the state of affairs described in verse 2. Waltke argues that verse 2 seems to depict something negative, if not sinister. "The situation of verse 2 is not good, nor is it ever called good. Moreover, that state of darkness, confusion, and lifelessness is contrary to the nature of God in whom there is no darkness. He is called the God of light and life; the God of order."[40] A perfectly holy God would not be involved in creating or bringing such a condition into existence. Furthermore other passages such as Psalm 33:6, 9 and Hebrews 11:3 refer to God creating by His word, which in the Genesis narrative does not begin until verse 3. No mention is made in Scripture of God's calling the chaotic state described in Genesis 1:2 into existence.[41] Deep and darkness "represented a state of existence contrary to the character of God."[42] Moreover, in the eschaton the negative elements of Genesis 1:2, the sea and the darkness, will be removed in the perfect cosmos (Rev. 21:1, 25). This transformation that will occur at the world's consummation substantiates the fact that the darkness and the sea are less than desirable and hence not the result of God's creative activity.[43] The existence of this imperfect state in Genesis 1:2, Waltke says, reinforces the view that verse 2 is subordinate to verse 3 and not to verse 1:

> It is concluded therefore, that though it is possible to take verse 2 as a circumstantial clause on syntactical grounds, it is impossible to do so on philological grounds, and that it seems unlikely it should be so construed on theological grounds, for it makes God the Creator of disorder, darkness, and deep, a situation not tolerated in the perfect cosmos and never said to have been called into existence by the Word of God.[44]

The fourth tenet of the precreation chaos theory concerns the distinctiveness of the Israelite view of creation in contrast with other ancient Near Eastern cosmogonies. While Waltke maintains that there is some similarity between the pagan cosmogonies and the Genesis account of creation, such as the existence of a dark primeval formless state prior to creation,[45] he maintains that the Genesis account is distinctive in three ways: (1) the belief in one God, (2) the absence of myth and ritual to influence the gods, and (3) the concept of God as Creator, which means that the creation is not coexistent and coeternal. This belief in God as Creator separate and above His creation "was the essential feature of the Mosaic faith"[46] and "distinguished Israel's faith from all other religions."[47] Waltke comments on the apologetic need to have a word from Moses about the origin of creation in the ancient Near Eastern setting. "If, then, the essential difference between the Mosaic faith and the pagan faith differed precisely in their conceptualization of the relationship of God to the creation, is it conceivable that Moses should have left the new nation under God without an accurate account of the origin of the creation?"[48]

Evaluation of the Precreation Chaos Theory

"GENESIS 1:1 IS A SUMMARY STATEMENT"

In relation to the first line of evidence for viewing Genesis 1:1 as a summary statement, it should be noted that while the correspondence between 1:1–3 and 2:4–7 is indeed similar, it is not exact. Not only is the relationship and correspondence between 2:4b and 2:7 different from the relationship and correspondence between 1:1 and 1:3, but also the lengthy circumstantial clauses in Genesis 2:4b–6 indicate that the styles of the two narratives are distinct.[49] Furthermore Waltke argues that beginning a narrative with a summary statement and then filling in the details is commonplace in Semitic thought. He does not, however, supply references to support this generalization. Beginning a narrative with a summary statement is, in any case, a literary device that is evident in Indo-European literature as well as in literature stemming from Semitic authors.[50] Pearson summarizes the evidence against the view that Genesis 1:1 should be taken as a summary.

> The first verse of Gen 1 cannot be regarded with Buckland and Chalmers as a mere heading of a whole selection, nor with Dods and Bush as a summary statement, but forms an integral part of the narrative, for: (1) It has the form of narrative, not of superscription. (2) The conjunctive particle connects the second verse with it; which could not be if it were a heading. No historical narrative begins with "and" (vs. 2). The "and" in Ex. 1:1 indicates that the second book of Moses is a continuation of the first. (3) The very next verse speaks of the earth as already in existence, and therefore its creation must be recorded in the first verse. (4) In the first verse the heavens take the precedence of the earth, but in the following verses all things, even sun, moon, and stars seem to be appendages to the earth. Thus if it were a heading it would not correspond with the narrative. . . . the above evidence supports the view that the first verse forms a part of the narrative. The first verse of Genesis records the creation of the universe in its essential form. In v. 2, the writer describes the earth as it was when

God's creative activity had brought its material into being, but this formative activity had not yet begun.[51]

In the summary-statement view of Genesis 1:1, grammatical structure is intricately connected to the interpretation of the phrases "heavens and earth" (v. 2) as the completed heavens and earth and "formless and void" as the antithesis of creation. These interpretations have been shown to be open to serious question. In addition Waltke asserts that the subordination of Genesis 1:2 to verse 3 should not be viewed as an anomaly, arguing that Young listed several illustrations of the circumstantial clause preceding the main verb.[52] This evidence is problematic, however, as none of the examples cited has the same structure as Genesis 2:2–3, that is, a *waw* disjunctive clause followed by *waw* consecutive prefixed form.[53] On the other hand it seems that such passages as Judges 8:11 and Jonah 3:3 are more helpful parallels to the grammatical structure reflected in Genesis 1:1–2, where a finite verb is followed by a *waw* disjunctive clause containing the verb הָיָה. This clause qualifies a term in the immediately preceding independent clause. The independent clause makes a statement and the following circumstantial clause describes parenthetically an element in the main clause. This would confirm the traditional interpretation that verse 1 contains the main independent clause, with Genesis 1:2 consisting of three subordinate circumstantial clauses describing what the just-mentioned earth looked like after it was created.

"בָּרָא IN GENESIS 1:1 IS NOT *CREATIO EX NIHILO*"

The second important feature of the precreation chaos theory is the assertion that the Hebrew root בָּרָא, "to create," should not be understood as creation out of nothing (*creatio ex nihilo*) in Genesis 1:1. This semantic understanding is critical for the precreation chaos theory, since it maintains that what is described in Genesis 1 is not the original creation but rather a recreation of the raw material that exists in Genesis 1:2.

The cognate of the Hebrew root בָּרָא is rare in the Semitic cognate languages, and thus its meaning in the Old Testament must be determined from its usage in the Old Testament corpus.[54] Finley has provided a thorough examination of the usage and meaning of the term.[55]

> The verb בָּרָא is applied to the creation of a nation, to righteousness, to regeneration, and to praise and joy. . . . Nearly two-thirds of the instances of בָּרָא refer to physical creation. . . . God's original creation encompassed

all of heaven and earth (Gen. 1:1). . . . Fully one-third of all the citations of physical creation refer to the creation of man (including Gen. 1:27; 5:1–2; 6:7; Deut. 4:32; Ps. 89:47 [Heb. 48]; Eccl. 12:1; Isa. 45:12. . . . In the Genesis 1 account of creation בָּרָא is used only five times, and of these occurrences three are in a single verse and refer to the creation of man (1:27). . . . The verb is also used of the creation of the great sea monsters (Gen. 1:21). The Israelites greatly feared these creatures, and it was reassuring to know that their God had created them and is Lord over them.[56]

In the examination of the occurrences of this verb some salient observations emerge. First, the only subject of the verb in the Hebrew Bible is God. Whereas God may be the subject for the semantic synonyms of בָּרָא, these synonyms have other subjects (creatures) in addition to God.[57] "A number of synonyms, such as 'make,' 'form,' or 'build,' are used of creation by God, but בָּרָא is the only term for which God is the only possible subject."[58] Usage supports the contention that the Hebrew verb בָּרָא is the distinct word for creation.

The Hebrew stem *b-r-'* is used in the Bible exclusively of divine creativity. It signifies that the product is absolutely novel and unexampled, depends solely on God for its coming into existence, and is beyond the human capacity to reproduce. The verb always refers to the completed product, never to the material of which it is made.[59]

Furthermore since the verb never occurs with the object of the material, and since the primary emphasis of the word is on the novelty of the created object, "the word lends itself well to the concept of creation *ex nihilo*."[60] This idea is reinforced by the fact that even when the context clearly indicates that what is being created involves preexisting material, that material will not be mentioned in the same sentence with בָּרָא.[61] Since this Hebrew verb has a semantic range, as do most other biblical Hebrew verbs, the context of any particular usage becomes determinative for meaning.[62] In Genesis 1 there is no explicit connection of this creative activity with any preexisting materials.[63] As Leupold aptly states, "When no existing material is mentioned as to be worked over, no such material is implied."[64] Thus this lexeme is distinct and is the best lexical choice to express the unprecedented concept of *creatio ex nihilo*.[65] As the Jewish exegete Nahmanides wrote, "We have in our holy language no other term for 'the bringing forth of something from nothing' but *bara*."[66] Waltke's argument that the verb does not inherently mean *creatio ex nihilo* is besides the point, as it is doubtful that any word in any language does.[67] The point is that while this is not the inherent meaning of this word or of any word, for that matter, בָּרָא would be the best candidate from the semantic pool of Hebrew verbs for expressing a creation that is unprecedented, namely, *creatio ex nihilo*. Sarna nicely summarizes the significance of the use of the verb בָּרָא in Genesis 1:1 as meaning *creatio ex nihilo* in the larger cultural context of the ancient Near East.

> Precisely because of the indispensable importance of preexisting matter in the pagan cosmologies, the very absence of such mention here is highly significant. This conclusion is reinforced by the idea of creation by divine fiat without reference to any inert matter being present. Also, the repeated biblical emphasis upon God as exclusive Creator would seem to rule out the possibility of preexistent matter. Finally, if *bara'* is used only of God's creation, it must be essentially distinct from human creation. The ultimate distinction would be *creatio ex nihilo*, which has no human parallel and is thus utterly beyond all human comprehension.[68]

Also the contextual joining of the verb בָּרָא, "to create," with the preceding phrase בְּרֵאשִׁית, "in the beginning," in the alliterative phrase בְּרֵאשִׁית בָּרָא (*bᵉrēʾšʾit bārāʾ*) clarifies the connotation of each and thus helps elucidate the meaning of בָּרָא.

> The word "beginning" is, of course, a relative term. It must imply the beginning of something. On that account, some say it refers only to the beginning of human history that we see unfolded round about us. But the content of the term is given to us by the word *bara'*, create, and vice versa. This is a beginning that is characterized by creation, and this is a creation that is characterized by the beginning. Here it means "the absolute beginning." . . . It refers to the absolute beginning, just as John, beginning his Gospel, takes over the phrase "in the beginning" and refers it to the absolute beginning.[69]

As noted, Waltke avoids attributing the meaning of *creatio ex nihilo* to בָּרָא in Genesis 1. Thus God's role as Creator in that chapter refers only to His reshaping preexisting matter. And yet if Moses wanted to refer to God as the Reshaper of existing matter, there were better lexical choices at his disposal to convey this idea. It does not seem that he would want to employ the distinctive verb for God's creative activity, the verb בָּרָא. In his attempt to play down the distinctiveness of the verb בָּרָא Waltke mentions that other verbs that are not as distinctive as בָּרָא may refer to creation out of nothing.[70] It almost seems that what Waltke really wants to say about the distinctiveness of בָּרָא is that it never means creation out of nothing.[71] The use of בָּרָא without any mention of preexisting matter in Genesis 1:1 conveys something stronger than Waltke's interpretation of the verse.[72]

"GENESIS 1:2 IS NEGATIVE"

The precreation chaos theory advocated by Waltke assumes that the chaotic state of Genesis 1:2 was in existence before God began His creative activity in Genesis 1:3.[73] The contention that the state described in verse 2 is negative and consequently not the result of the activity of God was addressed earlier in connection with the phrase תֹהוּ וָבֹהוּ ("formless and empty"). There it was shown that the phrase תֹהוּ וָבֹהוּ need not be understood as an orderless chaos as Waltke proposed but rather that the earth was not yet ready to be inhabited by mankind.[74] As Tsumura stated, "There is nothing in this passage that would suggest a chaotic state of the earth which is opposed to and precedes creation."[75]

But what of Waltke's objection that the darkness over the face of the deep also suggests the antithesis of creation and thus was not brought into existence by God? The significance of this occurrence of darkness is conveyed forcefully by Unger.

> Of special importance in the seven-day account of creation is the calling forth of light upon the earth about to be renewed. Sin had steeped it in disorder and darkness. God's active movement upon it in recreation involved banishing the disorder and dissipating the darkness. . . . Only when sin came, darkness resulted. Darkness, therefore, represents sin, that which is contrary to God's glory and holiness (1 John 1:6).[76]

Waltke maintains that the presence of the uncreated state with darkness over the deep in Genesis 1:2 is a mystery, since the "Bible never says that God brought these into existence by His word."[77]

The problems that arise with this view are more numerous and difficult than the theological problem its advocates are attempting to alleviate. First, the immediate question arises, To what should be ascribed the existence of the darkness over the face of the deep?[78] Who made the darkness and the deep if they were not made by God? The fact is noteworthy that God named the darkness in Genesis 1 without the least indication that there was something undesirable about its existence. "God gives a name to the darkness, just as he does to the light. Both are therefore good and well-pleasing to him; both are created, although the express creation of the darkness, as of the other objects in verse two, is not stated, and both serve his purpose of forming the day."[79]

Later in the same article Young addresses the theological tension felt by Waltke.

> In the nature of the case darkness is often suited to symbolize affliction and death. Here, however, the darkness is merely one characteristic of the unformed earth. Man cannot live in darkness, and the first requisite step in making the earth habitable is the removal of darkness. This elementary fact must be recognized before we make any attempt to discover the theological significance of darkness. And it is well also to note that darkness is recognized in this chapter as a positive good for man. Whatever be the precise connotation of the עֶרֶב of each day, it certainly included darkness, and that darkness was for man's good.[80]

Waltke states that the darkness and the deep were not brought into existence by God's word, and yet Isaiah 45:7 states that God created the darkness. In this verse חֹשֶׁךְ, the same word used for darkness in Genesis 1:2, is said to have been created (בָּרָא) by God.[81]

To disassociate the physical darkness mentioned in Genesis 1:2 from God because darkness came to symbolize evil and sin is to confuse the symbol with the thing symbolized. It is like saying yeast is evil because it came to represent spiritual evil.[82] The fact that a physical reality is used to represent something spiritual does not mean that every time this physical reality is mentioned, it must be representing that spiritual entity. Those who claim that darkness in Genesis 1:2 is evil have confused the spiritual symbol as used elsewhere with the physical reality in this passage.[83]

In addition the syntactical structure of verse 2 would seem to argue against understanding the verse in a negative tone. The three clauses in the verse each begin with a *waw* followed by a noun that functions as the subject of the clause. All the clauses appear to be coordinate. Waltke would not view the last phrase describing the Spirit of God hovering over the waters in a negative sense, and yet he does not offer an explanation for not treating all the clauses in verse 2 as parallel. As Keil and Delitzsch state, "The three statements in our verse are parallel; the substantive and participial construction of the second and third clauses rests upon the והיתה of the first. All three describe the condition of the earth immediately after the creation of the universe."[84] The presence of darkness illustrates, as does the preceding clause, "formless and empty," that the earth was still not ready to be inhabited by man.

As the first word in this clause חֹשֶׁךְ is emphasized, it stands as a parallel to הָאָרֶץ in the previous clause. There are thus three principal subjects of the verse: the earth, darkness and the Spirit of God. The second clause in reality gives further support to the first. Man could not have lived upon the earth, for it was dark and covered by water.[85]

Waltke's argument that the state in Genesis 1:2 was not created by God because passages like Psalm 33:6, 9 and Hebrews 11:3 state that God created everything by His word is not convincing.[86] Indeed, it should be observed that these passages do not in any way suggest that the universe was created in two distinct stages, a creation and a recreation, as Waltke must maintain.[87] Furthermore where is the evidence in these passages for the presence of preexisting matter before the recreation of Genesis 1:3? Verse 2 should be taken as a positive description, not a negative one.[88] And though the earth was not yet suitable for man to inhabit, "there is no reason, so far as one can tell from reading the first chapter of Genesis, why God might not have pronounced the judgment, 'very good,' over the condition described in the second verse."[89]

According to the traditional interpretation, however, Genesis 1:2 states the condition of the earth as it was when it was first created until God began to form it into the present world.[90]

"THE ISRAELITE VIEW OF CREATION IS DISTINCT"

In stressing the importance and significance of creation in Israelite theology Waltke wants to distinguish the Old Testament concept of creation from the creation mythologies of the ancient Near East. Because other accounts explaining the origin of the world were prevalent and would probably have been known to the Israelites, Waltke states that it would have been "inconceivable that Moses should have left the new nation under God without an accurate account of the origin of creation."[91] The essential difference between the pagan ideas and the Mosaic revelation is in the "conceptualization of the relationship of God to creation."[92] Numerous scholars have noted, for example, that the other cosmogonies of the ancient Near East have nothing so profound as the opening statement of Genesis 1:1, "In the beginning God created the heavens and the earth."[93] But why is this so unique? Part of the answer surely lies in the fact that these mythologies all assume preexisting matter when the god(s) begin to create. In other words the uniqueness of the phrase "in the beginning" is not primarily in its distinctiveness literarily but in the fact that no other creation account in the ancient Near East described the absolute beginning of creation when nothing else existed. Though Waltke would deny the eternality of matter, he opens the door to the idea of preexisting matter in Genesis 1 by saying the creation account in Genesis 1 assumes that physical existence is present at "the beginning."[94] Since Waltke does not believe that Genesis 1 refers to the initial creation before the existence of matter, his statement about the distinctiveness of Israel's view loses force, even though God as Creator is fundamental to the Israelite faith.[95]

What then is distinctive about the meaning of the Mosaic revelation of creation according to Waltke's interpretation of the passage? According to Waltke the account begins with a watery chaos already in existence, which God overcomes.[96] This is virtually identical to the sequence of events in the Babylonian *Enuma Elish.*[97] The creative activity of God described in Genesis 1 is limited to a sculpturing or reshaping of material that is chaotic and unorganized.

In distinguishing Israel's view of creation from the creation accounts of the ancient Near East, Waltke states, "The faith that God was the Creator of heaven and earth and not coexistent and coeternal with the creation distinguished Israel's faith from all other religions."[98] This theological deduction, however, cannot come from Genesis 1, according to the precreation chaos position. Such a credo could only result from a belief in *creatio ex nihilo*, a doctrine Waltke denies the Israelite consciousness until several hundred years later.

While the degree of distinctiveness should not be a controlling exegetical grid to impose on a passage (the interpreter should objectively investigate what the text is saying in its historical and literary context), it is fair to bring out that the traditional view of creation is more distinctive in the environment of the ancient Near East than is Waltke's precreation chaos theory. The key difference between pagan cosmogonies and Genesis 1 is *creatio ex nihilo* and the absence of preexisting matter.[99] Waltke can claim neither fact for Genesis 1, though he views Genesis 1 as the most significant text regarding the Israelite theology of creation.[100] Jacob brings into focus more clearly the distinctiveness of the Israelite account of creation in Genesis 1.

> It is the first great achievement of the Bible to present a divine creation from nothing in contrast to evolution or formation from a material already in existence. Israel's religious genius expresses this idea with monumental brevity. In all other creation epics the world originates from a primeval

matter which existed before. No other religion or philosophy dared to take this last step. Through it God is not simply the architect, but the absolute master of the universe. No sentence could be better fitted for the opening of the Book of Books. Only an all pervading conviction of God's absolute power could have produced it.[101]

Conclusion

The four primary features of the precreation chaos theory pose philological as well as theological difficulties. The conclusion should be drawn, therefore, that the traditional view[102] is the most satisfactory position regarding the interpretation of Genesis 1:1–3. According to this position, the Bible speaks with one voice about the creation of the universe. Genesis 1:1–3 describes the same events as other passages such as Psalm 33:6, 9; Romans 4:17; and Hebrews 11:3, and they describe *creatio ex nihilo*.[103] This understanding of Genesis 1:1–3 prevailed among the early Jewish and Christian interpreters.[104] Genesis 1:2 describes the initial stage of what God created, the state He then transformed (vv. 3–31) to make the earth into a place that could be inhabited by man.

The question that is asked by both ancient and modern man alike—the question that cannot be ignored—is answered adequately only from the revelation of Scripture. God created all that exists and He created out of nothing.

The Bible is unified on this issue. God is the Creator who existed before all His creation and who brought forth from nothing all that exists. The only biblical event that might rightly be called a recreation begins with the experience of the new birth and is consummated in the realization of the new heavens and the new earth (Rev. 21:1–2). This work from beginning to end is brought about by the One who was there "in the beginning," who creates and brings light and life through the redemption victoriously proclaimed on the first day of the week.[105]

CHAPTER 2

The Meaning of the Divine Name YHWH

Charles R. Gianotti

Without doubt the tetragrammaton, YHWH,[1] is the most significant name in the Old Testament. As one writer observed, "no single word in Hebrew has ever evoked such a torrent of discussion as . . . YHWH, the personal name of the Hebrew god [sic]."[2] In distilling the vast amount of literature on the subject, five popular views rise to the surface. But before discussing these, certain observations should be made.[3]

For the biblicist, the divine name YHWH was known as early as the time of Enosh (Gen. 4:26) and was used not infrequently during the patriarchal period (Gen. 12:1, 4; 13:4, etc.). Yet Exodus 6:2–3 seems to indicate that the name was not known until the time of Moses hundreds of years later: "God spoke further to Moses and said to him, I am the Lord and I appeared to Abraham, Isaac, and Jacob, as God Almighty [אֵל שַׁדָּי], but by My name, Lord [יהוה or YHWH], I did not make Myself known to them."

But this tension is resolved by a correct understanding of the passage. Motyer offers an excellent exegesis, translating it as follows: "And God spoke to Moses, and said to him: I am Yahweh. And I showed myself to Abraham, to Isaac, and to Jacob *in the character of* El Shaddai, but *in the character expressed by* my name Yahweh I did not make myself known to them. . . . "[4] He concludes that "it was the character expressed by the name that was withheld from the patriarchs and not the name itself. . . . to know by name means to have come into intimate and personal acquaintance with a person."[5] Mowinckel concurs in reference to the burning bush incident that

> Exodus 3 does not support the theory that the name of Yahweh was not known to the Israelites before Moses. . . . A name may have deeper meaning than the one discernible at first glance and recognizable to everybody . . . a man who knows the "real" deeper meaning of the name of a god, really "knows the god" in question.[6]

Thus though the name YHWH existed well before the time of Moses, the *meaning* of that name was not revealed until the time of Moses. To understand the meaning of the divine name is to understand the character of God revealed by that name. Clearly Exodus 3:14 provides the beginning point for this discussion. To Moses' first concern about his own inadequacies God responded, "Certainly I will be with you [אֶהְיֶה עִמָּךְ] (Ex. 3:12). Moses' second concern was stated in this way: "Behold, I am going to the sons of Israel, and I shall say to them, 'The God of your fathers has sent me to you.' Now they may say to me, 'What is His name?' What shall I say to them?" (Ex. 3:13). In verse 14 God addressed this second concern. Motyer well asks why Moses should suppose it likely that he would be faced by such a question from the captive Israelites?[7] Moses was not seeking information for his own benefit, but apparently he felt the answer to this question would in some way validate his mission.

Moses anticipated that the question pertained not to the recitation of God's name but to His character. The Hebrew term מַה introducing the question indicates a concern for quality. Abba points out that in biblical Hebrew "when the interrogative pronoun מַה which occurs in the question refers to substantives, it frequently expresses an inquiry concerning quality . . . and may be rendered, 'What kind of?' And in Biblical Hebrew it is never used in asking a person's name; for this מִי is employed."[8] Exodus 3:14 is God's response to Moses' concern about validating his mission to the Israelites with newly revealed information about God's character.

God's answer obviously involves a pun on the first person imperfect of הָיָה. Punning in the Bible is common (cf. Matt. 16:18) and to the Hebrew ear the repeated assonance of אֶהְיֶה . . . אֶהְיֶה . . . אֶהְיֶה . . . יְהוָה (Ex. 3:14–15) would be unmistakable. McCarthy asserts that "the repeated sound has by mere suggestion tied Yahweh to hyh [i.e., הָיָה] irrevocably."[9] Though this does not necessarily mean that the name YHWH is sourced etymologically in the root word הָיָה, it does suggest that the meaning of הָיָה is meant to inform the meaning of the name YHWH. As Schild indicates, "it must be granted that the passage seeks to explain the meaning of the Divine name, no matter what its real original derivation, as a derivative of hayah. . . ."[10]

McCarthy points out that since הָיָה is not necessary as a copulative, its repeated use in Exodus 3:14–15 must be explained as emphasizing the connection between הָיָה and YHWH.[11] Also early Jewish exegetes such as Onkelos, and pseudo-Jonathan accepted this connection.[12]

Mowinckel observes in reference to God's answer, that "instead of the name we get an explanation of the name."[13] It seems better, though, to see God's answer as both a name and an explanation. In verse 14a, אֶהְיֶה אֲשֶׁר אֶהְיֶה could be the name in the form of an epithet with verse 14b containing a shortened form—אֶהְיֶה. Two other passages which clearly use אֶהְיֶה as a proper name are Psalm 40:21 and Hosea 1:9.[14] This would result in three forms of the name given to Moses: (1) אֶהְיֶה אֲשֶׁר אֶהְיֶה, (2) אֶהְיֶה, and (3) יְהוָה or YHWH (Ex. 3:15).

Motyer feels that the relative clause אֲשֶׁר אֶהְיֶה adds nothing to God's answer to Moses, for otherwise it would not have been readily dropped in Exodus 3:14b and subsequently in the divine name YHWH.[15] But can this be maintained in a passage of this import? Bernhardt maintains, "The major use of hayah in its finite forms is as an auxiliary verb. These forms serve primarily to fix the temporal sphere of the clause more precisely and to define its logical structure unambiguously."[16] He also observes that הָיָה is used with participles only when the temporal framework is important for the meaning.[17]

The repetition in verse 14a probably should be seen as an *idem per idem* statement similar to Exodus 33:19 ("I will have mercy on whom I will have mercy," meaning "I will have great mercy"). Certainly the repetition is not for content for in 3:14b אֶהְיֶה occurs alone. Thus the form in verse 14a is one of emphasis. The connection between אֶהְיֶה and YHWH can be seen by comparing verse 14b with verse 15 where the sending agent in the former is אֶהְיֶה and the sending agent in the latter is YHWH. Hebrew parallelism would strongly suggest a relationship between the two.

This analysis provides a backdrop for evaluating the various interpretations of the divine name.

The "Unknowable" View

Some see the name YHWH as reflecting the incomprehensibility of God. Proponents of this view see in God's answer a rejection of Moses' question on the grounds that His name constitutes a mystery, since it is impossible, they argue, to define God (cf. Rev. 19:12). Zimmerli states:

> In this figure of speech resounds the sovereign freedom of Yahweh, who, even at the moment he reveals himself in his name, refuses simply to put

himself at the disposal of humanity to comprehend him. We must also take into account God's refusal to impart his name to Jacob in Genesis 32:30, "Why do you ask about My name?"[18]

Then Zimmerli adds, "In the only passage where the Old Testament itself attempts to provide an explanation of the name 'Yahweh' it refuses to explain the name in a way that would confine it within the cage of a definition."[19] In other words God answered, "You ask who I am; I simply am. There is no way to define Myself." Truly no mortal can ever comprehend fully the character or nature of God.

In response to this view, Exodus 3:14–15 gives no hint that Moses asked amiss or that God rebuked him for asking. Verse 14b ("Thus shall you say to the sons of Israel, 'I AM [אֶהְיֶה] has sent me to you . . .) seems clearly to use אֶהְיֶה as a name. And as pointed out earlier, אֶהְיֶה parallels YHWH in verse 15. Moses was to give them אֶהְיֶה or YHWH as God's name. This does not necessarily assert that the name fully reveals God's character, but it does make a statement about God's character being used as a name by God Himself.

The "Ontological" View

Lockyer maintains that the name YHWH in Exodus 3 "reveals God as the Being who is absolutely self-existent, and who, in Himself, possesses essential life and permanent existence."[20] This view is held in varying degrees by many other writers such as Unger, Stone, Jukes, and Montgomery.[21] Among Jewish scholars, Maimonides and Jacobs represent this view.[22] McCarthy points out that Exodus 3:14 "served as the proof text for Christian ontology in the early centuries of the church and later . . . at times [it has] led to an emphasis on static being. . . ."[23]

This view seems to rest on the Septuagint translation of Exodus 3:14 (ἐγώ εἰμι ὁ Ὤν). On the face of it, the use of εἰμι seems to support his view.

Schild supports this view with an extended exegesis of the passage, concluding that "the syntax of the sentence compels us to render 'hyh [= אֶהְיֶה , first person singular] as third person in English: I am (the) One who is. . . ."[24] Though this results in a difficult syntactical problem of agreement of antecedent, Schild produces a revision of GKC's rule of relative clauses: "If the governing substantive is the subject of a relative clause and is, in the main clause, equated with, or defined as, a personal pronoun, then the predicate of the relative clause agrees with that personal pronoun."[25]

This view is untenable for a number of reasons. Though the Septuagint is a serviceable translation of the Pentateuch,[26] the Septuagint is not inspired; it is a human translation by Jewish scholars. The primary understanding of Exodus 3:14 should come, rather, from a contextual understanding of the passage as well as from an analysis of the meaning and usage of the Hebrew term הָיָה and its imperfect form אֶהְיֶה.

This view imports a foreign concept to the Old Testament. Bernhardt insists that in Hebrew "'being' is 'a dynamic, powerful, effective being,' in contrast to Greek thought, which understands being as something immutable. In Hebrew, too, 'being' refers to existence; but in the Hebrew view existence expresses itself effectually. Therefore, 'existence is identical with effectiveness.'"[27] A. B. Davidson agrees with Bernhardt. "Such abstract conceptions (e.g. essential existence) are quite out of keeping with the simplicity and concreteness of Oriental thought, especially in the most early times. . . ."[28]

The range of meanings of הָיָה includes "fail out, come to pass, become, be."[29] The meanings that concern this study are the last two. Davidson asserts that "הָיָה does not mean to be essentially, but to be phenomenally; it is not εἶναι but γίνομαι."[30] Mowinckel agrees: "He is the god who 'is,' haya. . . . But his being is not the abstract Greek εἶναι, the mere existence *per se*. To the Hebrew 'to be' does not just mean to exist—as all other beings and things do as well—but to be active, to express oneself in active being . . . ."[31] The full impact of the meaning of הָיָה will be commented on later under the "phenomenological" view. Suffice it here to say that it cannot support the "ontological" or "existence" view.

This view also assumes a present tense meaning which is unjustified in light of the imperfect form, אֶהְיֶה , used in Exodus 3:14. Bernhardt notes that the imperfect form of this verb never expresses the present tense; for this, the perfect form is used.[32] Significantly, most interpreters translate אֶהְיֶה in Exodus 3:12 as future (i.e., "I will be [אֶהְיֶה] with you"). Yet, two verses later, why should not the same translation suffice?

McCarthy argues that אֶהְיֶה is not a true future, for the clause "I shall be" used absolutely means that the speaker is not yet in existence.[33] But this falls back on the faulty view of seeing הָיָה as meaning simple existence, rather than effective existence. The future in this case can indeed refer to future activity or effectiveness of YHWH. It should be observed that even Aquila (A.D. 130), noted for his "slavishly literal translation,"[34] translated the tense as future.[35]

Finally, concerning the problem of agreement of antecedent, there exists a serious tension with this view, unless אֶהְיֶה (first person) and יְהוָה (third person) are identical, which of course would be difficult to sustain.[36] Albrektson responds to Schild's modified rule concerning agreement:

> . . . the unusual translation revived by . . . Schild presupposes that the sentence is construed in a way to which . . . there are no real parallels in the Hebrew of the Old Testament and which is the natural way of expressing in Hebrew the idea which is supposed to be found in the passage. The traditional rendering [i.e., seeing the antecedent as being first person] on the other hand regards the sentence as one of many examples of a common and characteristic Semitic mode of expression which is often found also in Hebrew and the translation [i.e., first person] is irreproachable from a grammatical point of view.[37]

One may safely conclude that Exodus 3:14 does not support an "ontological" or "existence" view; the name YHWH therefore is not rooted in that view, by virtue of its close relation to Exodus 3:14.

How then does one account for the Septuagint translation ἐγώ εἰμι ὁ Ὤν? It must be remembered that the Septuagint was compiled in Alexandria for Greek-speaking Jews. With Alexandria being thoroughly Hellenized, the Septuagint was probably influenced by a Greek "ontology." Maclaurin suggests possibly that this view of God, which is also found in the apocryphal Book of Wisdom, was an attempt to commend Hebrew thought to Greek thinking.[38] It is relatively easy to imagine the backslidden Jews, a few hundred years after the Exile, having lost touch with the character and nature of their God YHWH. In such a condition they would have easily been influenced by a popular view of the nature of deity as propagated in their environment.

The "Causative" View

The proponents of this view see in the name YHWH a causative form and meaning. Albright states, "Yahweh can only be derived from the verbal stem HWY but cannot be the ordinary imperfect (qal) of the verb, but must be causative (hiphil)."[39] Freedman accepts Albright's analysis (YHWH being hiphil, imperfect, third masculine). Based on the connection between YHWH and the verb הָיָה in Exodus 3:14 he concludes that אֶהְיֶה אֲשֶׁר אֶהְיֶה means essentially, "I cause to be what comes into existence."[40] Obermann similarly sees the passage as meaning "I sustain—I am He who sustains."[41] This view has the advantage of removing a difficulty concerning the phrase יְהוָה צְבָאוֹת. Because YHWH is a name, it must share the negative characteristics of a name, including the idea that it cannot be followed by a word in the genitive.[42] The words יְהוָה צְבָאוֹת would go against this understanding unless YHWH were a hiphil form and thus the phrase would mean: "He who causes the hosts to come into existence."[43] Such phrases as יְהוָה קַנָּא and יְהוָה יִרְאֶה would then mean "The Zealous One creates" and "He creates reverence," respectively.

Two objections may be voiced against this view. First, phrases such as the common יְהוָה אֱלֹהִים or יְהוָה יְהוָה (Ex. 34:6) would be extremely difficult to understand if YHWH is taken as a causative. Freedman arbitrarily assigns יְהוָה אֱלֹהִים to the category of title, but this seems to beg the issue.[44] Why not also see יְהוָה צְבָאוֹת as a title, then? Second, both Abba and Bernhardt observe that there is no known evidence that the verb הָיָה was ever used in the hiphil, the causative being expressed by the piel.[45]

So the causative view of the divine name YHWH is not acceptable.

The "Covenantal" View

This view sees in the name YHWH the God of the Mosaic Covenant. The repeated introductions to the commandments at Sinai "I am YHWH . . ." give credence to this view (e.g., Ex. 20:1, Lev. 18:2, 4, 21, 30). Specifically this is the divine name that should not be taken in vain (Ex. 20:7). Motyer connects YHWH with explicit references to the covenant with the fathers and with the verb "to redeem," concluding that "the heart of the Mosaic revelation of Yahweh was that He was going to redeem His people."[46] Even those of a more liberal persuasion see the connection between the name and the deliverance from Egypt.[47]

The verb הָיָה to which YHWH is connected occurs often in covenantal formulas (e.g.. Deut. 26:17–18; Jer. 7:23; 11:4, 24; 24:7; 31:33, 32:38; Ezek. 36:28; 37:27).

Isbell deals with the relationship between Hosea and the "Deuteronomic tradition," deeming Hosea as the coming to an end of the era of YHWH's covenantal relationship with Israel.[48] Hosea prophesied concerning the Northern Kingdom, but the shekinah glory departed not many years later from the temple (in the Southern Kingdom) according to Ezekiel 10–11. Hosea 1:9 picked up the vocabulary of Exodus 3:12–13: "you are not My people, I am not your God." This might be rendered: "you are not My people and I am not אֶהְיֶה to you." This follows Hebrew parallelism, with לֹא עַמִּי parallel to לֹא־אֶהְיֶה. Rather than seeing a formula of covenant in Exodus 3:14, Isbell sees a formula of divorce in light of Hosea's experience. In this sense God is no longer אֶהְיֶה to Israel, but as the people are לֹא עַמִּי, "God" is לֹא־אֶהְיֶה to them. With the coming to an end of the Mosaic Covenant, God ceased to be אֶהְיֶה to them!

This "covenant" view seems correct, insofar as it goes, though it may be debated whether YHWH ever "divorced" His people. But this view does not take into consideration the full ramifications of the meaning of הָיָה. The name YHWH takes on much wider implications.

The "Phenomenological" View

Proponents of this view understand the divine name YHWH to mean that God will reveal Himself in His actions through history. Implicit in this view is the "covenantal" view. Delitzsch calls this the active manifestation of existence. God is present in history, manifesting Himself to others and especially to Israel.[49] In reference to Exodus 3:14 Mowinckel says:

> He is the god who "is," haya, in the fullest meaning of the word. . . . But this "being" is not the abstract Greek εἰναι, the mere existence *per se*. To the Hebrew "to be" does not just mean to exist—as all other beings and things do as well—but to be active, to express oneself in active being, "The God who acts." "I am what in creative activity and everywhere I turn out to be," or "I am (the God) that really acts."[50]

Clearly the use of הָיָה in the creation accounts leads one to perceive God's active manifestation in the beginning of "history" (Gen. 1:3, 5–6). Davidson would see in אֶהְיֶה אֲשֶׁר אֶהְיֶה the idea of ὁ ἔρχομαι in the sense of YHWH coming in action—His active coming.[51]

With this understanding of Exodus 3:14, the significance of the imperfect form (i.e., אֶהְיֶה) becomes clear.[52] God's manifestation to Israel is yet future at the time of the burning bush incident. This אֶהְיֶה is God's promise that He will redeem the children of Israel. The people were in great need. They needed not so much to know facts about God's character or that He was simply a covenant God present in their time of need, but to be reassured that this God would meet them in their time of need, proving true His character and promises. This in fact constitutes what God promised Moses in Exodus 3:12, namely, that God would be present and working on Moses' behalf in the difficult task ahead. Surely nothing less would have encouraged Moses to go. In the case of the Israelites, God declared in absolute form, אֶהְיֶה אֲשֶׁר אֶהְיֶה. No predicate or prepositional phrase is present; the God who will deliver Israel is the God for whom "hayah can be fully predicated."[53] Whatever the situation or need (in particular, the redemption from Egypt, but also future needs), God will "become" the solution to that need.[54]

In Exodus 6:6, after God revealed that before Moses' time He was not known by this character as revealed in His name YHWH, He declared אֲנִי יְהוָה ("I am YHWH"). Following on this declaration He cited Israel's need which He would fill: "I am the Lord [יְהוָה אֲנִי], and I will bring you out from under the burdens of the Egyptians, and I will deliver you from their bondage. I will also redeem you with an outstretched arm and with great judgments. Then I will take you for My people, and I will be your God; and you shall know that I am the Lord [אֲנִי יְהוָה] your God, who brought you out from under the burdens of the Egyptians. And I will bring you to the land which I swore to give to Abraham, Isaac, and Jacob, and I will give it to you for a possession; I am the Lord [יְהוָה אֲנִי]" (Ex. 6:6–8).[55]

The phrase אֲנִי יְהוָה occurs three times in these three verses. In the first occurrence God identified His name in respect to what follows. The second occurrence constituted what the people would recognize about the God who would deliver them—that He is YHWH, the One who would meet their needs just as His name implies. The final occurrence again emphasized His name in relation to His work. Clearly the saving acts on behalf of His people will reveal YHWH's name.

In Deuteronomy 29:2–6 God's provision for the Israelites in the wilderness was "in order that you might know that I am YHWH [אֲנִי יְהוָה] your God." Robert Davidson summarizes this well:

> Instead of being given a character sketch of God, Moses is given a promise, "I am who I am" or "I will be who I will be," i.e., "I am the God who is and who will be active in whatever situations you are called to face." On the basis of this experience, Moses interpreted to the people the events of the exodus from Egypt as the mighty act of God. This is the pattern throughout the Old Testament. Events are interpreted through the

eyes of what we may call prophetic faith. The events may be dramatic, mysterious, or very ordinary, but all are seen in the context of belief in a God who is active in and through history.[56]

That this is true in reference to the Exodus, can be seen throughout the Old Testament (e.g., Ex. 29:46; 30:2–3; Lev. 11:45; 19:36; 25:38; 26:13; Judg. 6:8–10; Ps. 81:10; Hos. 12:9; 13:4; Ezek. 20:5–7). YHWH declares or identifies Himself in connection with redemption.

To verify this conclusion in relation to the non-Exodus activity of YHWH, the significant phrase אֲנִי יְהוָה must be examined. Often this phrase is used simply to identify YHWH as the speaker. For example, in the enumeration of laws in Leviticus 17–26 אֲנִי יְהוָה occurs about 20 times and "identifies the speaker so that no one may be misled into thinking that the preceding sentiments are of mere human origin,"[57] but that they proceed from YHWH. But being in the context of the Exodus experience, the full meaning of the name must surely have remained fresh in the minds of Moses and the people.

Of particular import, the name YHWH is also connected with the rewards and retributions of the Law. "If you walk in My statutes and keep my commandments so as to carry them out, then I will give you rains . . . peace . . . I shall also eliminate harmful beasts . . . you will chase your enemies, and they will fall before you by the sword. . . . I will . . . make you fruitful and . . . confirm My covenant with you. . . . I will also walk among you and be your God, and you shall be My people. I am the Lord [אֲנִי יְהוָה] your God, who brought you out of the land of Egypt so that you should not be their slaves and I broke the bars of your yoke and made you walk erect" (Lev. 26:3–13).

The character revealed in the name YHWH is connected here with God's blessing on those who obey Him and His commands. Leviticus 22:3 speaks of specific violations of the Law: "If any man among all your descendants throughout your generation approaches the holy gifts which the sons of Israel dedicate to the Lord, while he has an uncleanness, that person shall be cut off from before Me. I am the Lord [אֲנִי יְהוָה]." Thus the certainty of rewards or retribution is bound up in the character of God who indicates that He will manifest Himself in the way He says He will manifest Himself.

In Leviticus 26, YHWH, foreseeing that Israel will disobey and be judged, attached this unique declaration אֲנִי יְהוָה to His promise not to destroy them totally: "Yet in spite of this, when they are in the land of their enemies I will not reject them, nor will I so abhor them as to destroy them, breaking My covenant with them; *for* I am the Lord [אֲנִי יְהוָה] their God. But I will remember for them the covenant with their ancestors, whom I brought out of the land of Egypt in the sight of the nations, that I might be their God. I am the Lord [אֲנִי יְהוָה]" (Lev. 26:44–45).

The promise of God's "phenomenal" effectiveness is seen also in Israel's later history. For example Ahab received this assurance from the name of YHWH in the face of the Syrian army: "Now behold, a prophet approached Ahab king of Israel and said, Thus says the Lord, Have you seen all this great multitude? Behold, I will deliver them into your hand today, and you shall know that I am the Lord [אֲנִי יְהוָה]" (1 Kings 20:13).

Ezekiel is representative of the prophets who also saw the significance of the divine name in this light (in particular, YHWH will bring retribution): "Alas, because of all the evil abomination of the house of Israel which will fall by sword, famine, and plague: He who is far off will die by the plague, and he who is near will die by the famine . . . throughout their habitations I shall stretch out My hand against them and make the land more desolate and waste than the wilderness toward Diblah; thus they will know that I am the Lord [אֲנִי יְהוָה]" (Ezek. 6:11–14; cf. 7:27).

To summarize, the name YHWH points to God's relationship to Israel in both His saving acts and His retributive acts, manifesting His phenomenological effectiveness in Israel's history. What God says, He will do. His Name promises that. And He will act on behalf of His people. But YHWH does not ultimately limit the significance of His name to the children of Israel. As Eichrodt succinctly states, "it is in the person of Jesus that the function of the Name of Yahweh as a form of the divine self-manifestation finds its fulfillment."[58] Truly Jesus is the *par excellence* manifestation of God's active effectiveness in the history of the world!

CHAPTER 3

Jacob at the Jabbok, Israel at Peniel

Allen P. Ross

W
hy is it that many people of God attempt to gain the blessing of God by their own efforts? Faced with a great opportunity or a challenging task, believers are prone to take matters into their own hands and use whatever means are at their disposal. In it all there may even be a flirtation with unscrupulous and deceptive practices—especially when things become desperate.

Jacob was much like this. All his life he managed very well. He cleverly outwitted his stupid brother—twice, by securing the birthright and by securing the blessing. And he eventually bested Laban and came away a wealthy man—surely another sign of divine blessing. Only occasionally did he realize it was God who worked through it all; but finally this truth was pressed on him most graphically in the night struggle at the ford Jabbok.

By the River Jabbok, Jacob wrestled with an unidentified man till dawn and prevailed over him, and though Jacob sustained a crippling blow, he held on to receive a blessing once he perceived that his assailant was supernatural (Gen. 32:22–32). That blessing was signified by God's renaming the patriarch "Israel," to which Jacob responded by naming the place "Peniel." But because he limped away from the event, the "sons of Israel" observed a dietary restriction.

Gunkel, comparing this story with ancient myths, observes that all the features—the attack in the night by the deity, the mystery involved, the location by the river, the hand-to-hand combat—establish the high antiquity of the story.[1] It is clear that the unusual elements fit well with the more ancient accounts about God's dealings with men. To be sure, something unusual has been recorded, and the reader is struck immediately with many questions, some of which probably cannot be answered to any satisfaction.[2] Who was the mysterious assailant? Why was he fighting Jacob and why was he unable to defeat the patriarch? Why did he appear afraid of being overtaken by the dawn? Why did he strike Jacob's thigh? Why was the dietary taboo not included in the Mosaic Law? What is the meaning of the name "Israel"? What is the significance of this tradition?

Von Rad warns against the false expectations of a hasty search for "the" meaning, for he along with many others is convinced that a long tradition was involved in forming and interpreting the record.[3] A survey of the more significant attempts to understand the present form of the text will underscore the difficulties.

INTERPRETATIONS

Several interpreters have suggested that this is a dream narrative. Josephus understood it to be a dream in which an apparition (φαντάσμα) made use of voice and words.[4] Roscher followed the same basic idea, but said that it was a case of incubation, induced by the obstruction of the organs of respiration, producing a vivid dream of a struggle like that of mortals with Pan Ephialtes in antiquity.[5]

Others have given the story an allegorical interpretation. Philo saw a spiritual conflict in literal terms, a fight of the soul against one's vices and passions.[6] Jacob's combatant was the Logos[7]; it was his virtue that became lame for a season. This allegorical approach was accepted in part by Clement of Alexandria; he said that the assailant was the Logos, but understood that the Logos remained unknown by name in the conflict because He had not yet appeared in flesh.[8]

Beginning with Jerome, many have understood the passage to portray long and earnest prayer. Schmidt relates how Umbreit, reacting to the concept of a fight with the Almighty, expanded this view to say it was a prayer that involved meditation in the divine presence, confession of sin, desire for pardon and regeneration, and yearning for spiritual communion.[9]

Jewish literature, however, recognizes that an actual fight is at the heart of the story. R. Hama b. R. Hanina said it was a real struggle but with the prince or angel of Esau.[10] Rashi followed this explanation, and the Zohar (170a) named the angel Samael, the chieftain of Esau.

The passage has proved problematic for critical analysis as well. Schmidt explains, "The usual criteria fail. Yahwe [sic] does not occur at all, not even on the lips of the renamed hero. Elohim is found everywhere, but in a way that would not be impossible even to a writer usually employing the name Yahwe. The words and phrases generally depended on by the analysis are not decisive."[11] As a result there has been little agreement among critical scholars. Knobel, Dillmann, Delitzsch, and Roscher assigned the passage to E (Elohim sources in the documentary hypothesis). And DeWette, Hupfeld, Kuenen, Studer, Wellhausen, Driver, Skinner, Kautzsch, Procksch, and Eichrodt assigned it to J. Some of these, however, gave Genesis 32:23 and 29 to E, and verse 32 to a glossator. W. Max Müller tried to explain the confusion over the sources as being due to the disguising of the main features. He argued that the language of verse 25a was ambiguous—the low blow should have been struck by Jacob. The weeping in Hosea's account (12:4) should then be referred to the angel (according to Meyer). In short, a solution of sorts was found in the suggestion that the record had been revised in tradition.

Gunkel attempted to muster evidence from within the narrative to show that two recensions of an old story had been put together: (1) verse 25a records that the hip was dislocated by a blow, but verse 25b suggests that it happened accidentally in the course of the fight; (2) verses 26–28 present the giving of the name as the blessing, but verse 29 declares that the assailant blessed him; (3) verse 28 has Jacob victorious, but verse 30 records that he escaped with his life.[12]

Because of such tensions, and because Yahweh is not named in the narrative, modern critical scholars have attempted to uncover an ancient mythical story about gods fighting with heroes, a story that could have been adapted for the Jacob narratives. Fraser, Bennett, Gunkel, and Kittel thought that the old story included a river god whose enemy was the sun god which diminished the river with its rays (especially in summer). In other words the Hebrew tradition was "pure fiction" (Schmidt) based on an old myth about a river god named Jabbok who attempted to hinder anyone from crossing. Peniel was his shrine.[13]

The myth was also identified with the deity El, the God of the land of Canaan. McKenzie suggests that the narrative followed an old Canaanite myth in which the "man" was at one time identified. When Jacob became attached to the story, he argues, the Canaanite deity so named was deliberately obscured,[14] being replaced by a mysterious being who may or may not be taken as Yahweh. This, McKenzie suggests, was left vague because there was a hesitancy to attribute such deeds to Yahweh. Later the role was transferred to intermediate beings, such as the angel of Esau.

To say that the account gradually developed from some such ancient myth greatly weakens a very important point in the history of Israel and solves none of the tensions that exist. Gevirtz, combining a synchronic study of the text with its geopolitical significance, provides a more constructive approach:

> The passage cannot be dismissed merely as a bit of adopted or adapted folklore—a contest with a nocturnal demon, river spirit, or regional numen who opposes the river's crossing—to which "secondary" matters of cultic interest have been added, but is rather to be understood as bearing a distinct and distinctive meaning for the people who claim descent from their eponymous ancestor. Where, when, and how Jacob became Israel cannot have been matters of indifference to the Israelite author or to his audience.[15]

This ancient tradition about Jacob's unusual experience was recorded for Israel because the events of the patriarch's life were understood to anticipate or foreshadow events in Israel's history receiving the blessing of the land in this case.

ANALYSIS

Observations. Several observations give direction to the interpretation of the story. First, the geographical setting is important. The wrestling occurred at the threshold of the land of promise. Jacob had been outside the land ever since his flight from Esau, from whom he wrestled the blessing.

Second, the unifying element of the story is the naming, that is, the making of Jacob into Israel. The new name is not merely added to an old narrative; it is explained by it.

Third, the account is linked to a place name, Peniel. The names Peniel (Gen. 32:30), Mahanaim (32:1–2), and Succoth (33:17) are each given and etymologized by Jacob in his return to Canaan, and so are important to the narratives.

Fourth, the story is linked to a dietary restriction for the sons of Israel. This taboo was a custom that grew up on the basis of an event, but was not part of the Law. The event in the tradition both created and explained it.

Significance. The theme of the story is the wrestling—no one suggests anything else. However, one cannot study the account in isolation from the context of the Jacob cycle of stories. The connection is immediately strengthened by the plays on the names. At the outset are יַעֲקֹב, the man, יַבֹּק, the place, and וַיֵּאָבֵק, the action. These similar sounding words attract the reader's attention. Before "Jacob" could cross the "Jabbok" to the land of blessing, he must "fight." He attempted once more to trip up his adversary, for at that point he was met by someone wishing to have a private encounter with him, and he was forced into the match.

> Tripping his fellow-men by the heel (*'qb*) has for Jacob come to its extreme consequence: a wrestling (*'bq*) with a "man" which to Jacob is the most shocking experience of his life, as appears from the fact that thereafter he proceeds through life a man changed of name, and thus of nature, and under the new name he becomes the patriarch of the "Israelites." (This comes out even more strongly in Jacob's own confession in v. 31) [English v. 30].[16]

Ryle notes that the physical disability he suffered serves as a memorial of the spiritual victory and a symbol of the frailty of human strength in the crisis when God meets man face to face.[17]

Structure. The event recorded in the narrative gives rise to two names: God renames Jacob "Israel," and Israel names the place "Peniel." It is clear that these names reflect a new status because of the divine blessing. Therefore everything in the record leads up to the giving of the name "Israel"; the giving of the name "Peniel" reflects the significance of the entire encounter as it was understood by Jacob. These names together provide a balanced picture of the significant event.

In a helpful analysis of the structure of this passage, Barthes evaluates the namings as follows:[18]

1. The demand of a name, ___ The response ___ The result:
   from God to Jacob   of Jacob   name change
   (v. 27)   (v. 27)   (v. 28)
2. The demand of a name, ___ An indirect ___ The result:
   from Jacob of God   response   decision
   (v. 29)   (v. 29)

   └─ Name change:
   Peniel
   (v. 30)

This parallel arrangement is instructive: The direct response of Jacob to his assailant leads to his being renamed "Israel"; but the indirect response of the assailant leads Jacob to name the place "Peniel," for he realized that it was God who fought ("Israel") with him face to face ("Peniel"). One name is given by the Lord to Jacob; the other name is given by Jacob in submission to the Lord.

The passage may be divided into three sections with a prologue and epilogue. Of the three sections, the first (the event, vv. 24b–25) prepares for the second (the blessing, vv. 26–28), and the third (the evaluation, vv. 29–30) reflects the first two.

The Narrative

PROLOGUE (32:22–24a)

These opening verses record the crossing of the Jabbok by Jacob and his family. Because verses 22–32 provide an interlude in the return of Jacob to Canaan,[19] they can be understood as a unit with their parts treated accordingly. The first verse (v. 22) provides a summary statement of the crossing of the river by the entire clan. The crossing is then developed in verses 23–31. Verse 23 introduces the narrative; verse 31 completes it. Between the time Jacob sent his family across and the time he joined them, the wrestling and blessing occurred.

Jacob's being left alone (v. 24a) is not explained. One suggestion is that he intended to spend the night in prayer before meeting Esau. This harmonizes with the allegorical view of the wrestling. More likely, however, Jacob was anticipating an encounter with Esau, and so at night he began crossing the river to establish his ground in the land.[20] Whether he anticipated an encounter in the night or simply was caught alone, is difficult to say. If Jacob remained behind to make sure everything was safely across, then the meeting came as a complete surprise.[21] When he was alone, he was attacked by a man—he was caught in the match.

At any rate the narrative goes to great lengths to isolate Jacob on one side of the river. The question of his plans is irrelevant to the story. The important point is that he was alone.

THE FIGHT (32:24b–25)

Only four sentences in the Hebrew are used for the fight; no details are given, for the fight is but the preamble to the most important part—the dialogue. Yet the fight was real and physical. Dillmann says the limping shows it was a physical occurrence in a material world.[22] The memory of Israel's limping away from the night that gave rise to the dietary restriction attests to the physical reality of the event.

The verb used to describe the wrestling is וַיֵּאָבֵק, "and he wrestled." It is rare, being found only here in verse 24 and in verse

25. Since the noun אָבָק is "dust," this denominative verb perhaps carries the idea to "get dusty" in wrestling. Spurrell suggests that it might possibly be connected to חָבַק, or that it might be a dialectical variant of this for a word play.[23]

Martin-Achard concludes that this very rare verb was selected because of assonance with יבֹּק and יַעֲקֹב, the sounds b/v and k/q forming strong alliterations at the beginning of the story.[24] The verb plays on the name of the river as if to say יבֹּק were equal to יֵאָבֵק, meaning a "wrestling, twisting" river.[25] The word play employs the name of the river as a perpetual reminder of the most important event that ever happened there.

At this spot "a man" wrestled with Jacob. The word אִישׁ is open to all interpretations. It suggests a mystery but reveals nothing.[26] But this is fitting, for the "man" would refuse to reveal himself directly. The effect of the word choice is that the reader is transported to Jacob's situation. Jacob perceived only that a male antagonist was closing in on him. The reader learns his identity as Jacob did—by his words and actions.

The time of the match is doubly significant. On the one hand it is interesting that the struggle was at night. Darkness concealed the adversary's identity. The fact that he wished to be gone by daylight shows that he planned the night visit. As it turned out, had the assailant come in the daytime, Jacob would have recognized the man's special authority (v. 29) and identity (v. 30b). If Jacob had perceived whom he was going to have to fight, he would never have started the fight, let alone continued with his peculiar obstinacy.[27]

On the other hand the fact that the wrestling lasted till the breaking of day suggests a long, indecisive bout. Indeed, the point is that the assailant could not be victorious until he resorted to something extraordinary.

The turning point of the long bout is clear. After a long, indecisive struggle, the man "touched" Jacob. The "touch" was actually a blow—he dislocated his hip.[28] But the text uses a soft term for it, demonstrating a supernatural activity (cf. Isa. 6:7, he "touched" Isaiah's "lips").

The effect of this blow is clear. The assailant gave himself an unfair advantage over the patriarch, for he was already more than a match for Jacob. The one who might be expected to take advantage of the other was himself crippled by a supernatural blow from his assailant. In a word, like so many of his own rivals.

Jacob now came against something for which he was totally unprepared.

THE BLESSING (32:26–28)

The blow was revealing for Jacob. The true nature of the nameless adversary began to dawn on him as the physical darkness began to lift. He is the One who has power over the affairs of men! He said, "Let me go, for the day breaks!" (author's translation). But Jacob, having been transformed from a devious fighter into a forthright and resolute one,[29] held on for a blessing.[30] He said, "I will not let you go unless you bless me" (v. 26).[31] Fokkelman characterizes Jacob by stating that "from the most miserable situation he wants to emerge an enriched man."[32] Jacob may not have been aware of all the implications (the narrator certainly was), but he knew the source of blessing.

The blessing for which Jacob pleaded finds expression in a changed name. The assailant first asked the patriarch, "What is your name?" (v. 27)—undoubtedly a rhetorical question. The object was to contrast the old name with the new. When one remembers the significance of names, the point becomes clear: a well-established nature, a fixed pattern of life must be turned back radically! In giving his name, Jacob had to reveal his nature. This name, at least for the narratives, designated its owner as a crafty overreacher. Here the "heel-catcher" was caught and had to identify his true nature before he could be blessed.[33]

"And he said, 'Not Jacob shall your name be called from now on, but Israel, for you have fought with God and man and have prevailed'" (v. 28, author's translation). This renaming of Jacob is an assertion of the assailant's authority to impart a new life and new status (cf. 2 Kings 23:34; 24:17).

What is the meaning of the name "Israel"? Both Genesis 32:28 and Hosea 12:3 interpret the meaning of the name with a verb "to fight."[34] The meaning of "Israel" would then be defined as "God contends, may God contend, persist."[35] Based on the context in Genesis, the verb should be understood in the sense of fighting.

Coote analyzes Genesis 32:28b[36] and concludes that (a) the syllabic meter is 8:8; (b) the parallel pairs are *śry//ykl*, *'m//'m*, and *'lhym//'nšym*; (c) the archaic parallelism of the suffixed and prefixed conjugations is present; and (d) the arrangement is chiastic (*śry—twkl*). The last word is isolated to combine the clause:[37]

ky šryt 'm 'lhym	"for you fought with God
w 'm 'nšym wtwkl	and with men, and you prevailed"

Therefore the root שָׂרָה is used to explain the name יִשְׂרָאֵל because it sounds the same, is derived from the very story, and is otherwise infrequent.[38] The verb יָכֹל is used to explain the outcome of שָׂרָה.

So the narrative signifies that the name יִשְׂרָאֵל means "God fights." It is as if one were to say יִשְׂרָה אֵל; the idea is similar to the epithet יְהוָה צְבָאוֹת.[39] But the meaning of the name involves an interpolation of the elements: "God fights" is explained by "you fought with God." Thus the name is but a motto and a reminder of the seizing of the blessing which would be a pledge of victory and success.[40] Gunkel states that this explanation of the significance of the name was affectionately and proudly employed to show the nature of the nation to be invincible and triumphant; with God's help Israel would fight the entire world and when necessary would fight even God Himself.[41]

Many have been troubled by the difficulties with this explanation. First, if the name means "God fights," then how is it reversed to say Jacob fights with God? The name must be explained on the basis of Semitic name formations. Consequently the form is an imperfect plus a noun that is the subject, as Nestle pointed out long ago.[42] Thus any interpretation with El as object drops out of consideration as the morphological etymology of the name.[43]

Second, the verb שָׂרָה is very rare, making a clear definition difficult. It occurs only in connection with this incident. But the meaning of שָׂרָה may be "contend" and not "fight." Since God has no rivals, such a name is unparalleled and unthinkable.[44]

Third, the versions did not all understand the distinction between, שָׂרָה, "to contend," and שָׂרַר, "to rule." The Septuagint has ἐνίσχυσας, Aquila has ἤρξας Symmachus has ἤρξω, and the Vulgate has *fortis fuisti*. The problem may be traced to the pointing of the verb וַיָּשַׂר in Hosea 12:4, which seems to be from a geminate root שָׂרַר (Symmachus, Aquila, and Onkelos). As a result the versions and commentators follow either the idea of "rule" or "contend, oppose" (Josephus).[45]

Various other suggestions for the etymology of "Israel" have been made.[46] A. Haldar suggests that the root is *išr/'šr*, "happy," and that it could possibly be connected to the Canaanite god Asherah.[47] In this view the name change would represent the merging of the two religions.

E. Jacob connects the name with the root יָשָׁר, "just, right."[48] He finds confirmation for this idea in the noun "Jeshurun" (יְשֻׁרוּן, Deut. 32:15; 33:5; 33:26; Isa. 44:2), a poetic designation of Israel, as well as in the words "Book of Jashar" (סֵפֶר הַיָּשָׁר), the old collection of national songs (Josh. 10:13; 2 Sam. 1:18). This could be the book of Israel, the righteous one, the hero of God, according to E. Jacob.[49] The major problem with this interpretation is that it involves a change of the sibilant.

Albright takes the name from *yašar*, "to cut, saw," with a developed meaning of "heal": "God heals."[50] He finds Arabic *wašara*, "cut, saw"; Akkadian *šararu*, "shine" (cf. *šarru*, "king"); and Ethiopic, *šaráya*, "cure, heal, " to be the most plausible roots. In connection with the root *wašara*, he points out that the Arabic root *našara*, "revive," could be equated due to morphological contamination of I-Waw and I-Nun roots. Albright argues that the original name was *Yaśir-'el* from a verbal stem יׂשׁר, with the developed meaning of "heal" (supported by Ethiopic *šaráya*, and the equation/interchange in Arabic of *našara* for *wašara*). He states, "The fact that the stem *yašar* is not found in biblical Hebrew is rather in favor of the combination, since its disappearance would explain how the meaning of the name came to be so thoroughly forgotten."[51]

Coote, also using the strong letters *śr* (I-Yod, I-Nun, Geminate, reduplicated, or III weak), chooses the Akkadian root *wašaru* and traces a semantic development of cutting>deciding>counseling (Arabic *'ašara*, "counsel" and *mušîr*, "counselor").[52] He notes that the root *ḥtk*, "cut, " develops to mean "decide or determine." Coote's idea is that *ḥtk* and *śry* are parallel in root meaning and development.

Coote finds confirmatory evidence in Isaiah 9:6–7, where there is confluence of *śar* and *śry* as in Genesis 32. The word for "government" is the key there. He concludes that the name יִשְׂרָאֵל means "El judges and is from either *yśr* or *śry*. It has the meaning of govern by rendering a decree or judgment (Ps. 82:1)."

Noth, taking it to be from a third weak root *śārâ*, suggests the meaning "to rule, be lord over."[53] Through this, God takes action in the world and particularly helps His own. "Israel" then means "God will rule" or "May God rule."

It is certainly possible that one of these Semitic roots is etymologically connected to the name, and that the name meant something like "judge" or "heal" at one time (for the name occurred before this time, as the Eblaite material suggests).[54] The popular etymology in Genesis is giving the significance of the name.[55] But most of these other suggestions are no more compelling than the popular etymology given in the text of Genesis. The fact that the word is rare should not lead to the assumption that it means "contend" or "vie with" as a rival. The concept of God's fighting with someone is certainly no more a problem than the passage itself. And the reversal of the emphasis (from "God fights" to "fight with God") in the explanation is because of the nature of popular etymologies, which are satisfied with a word play on the sound or meaning of the name to express its significance.

The name serves to evoke the memory of the fight. The name ("God fights") is freely interpreted to say that God is the object of Jacob's struggle.[56] Hearing the name יִשְׂרָאֵל, one would recall the incident in which Jacob wrestled with God and prevailed. These words were full of hope to the Israelites. Dillmann says that ever after the name would tell the Israelites that when Jacob contended successfully with God, he won the battle with man.[57] Thus the name "God fights" and the popular explanation "you prevailed" obtain a significance for future struggles.

THE RESPONSE (32:29–30)

Jacob afterward attempted to discover his adversary's name. The "man" had acted with full powers and spoken with authority. He had gotten to the bottom of Jacob's identity; He could not be mortal. Thus Jacob sought to discover His name. But the answer was cautious: "Why do you ask my name?" (author's translation).

On the one hand it is as if He was saying to Jacob, "Think, and you will know the answer!"[58] But on the other hand He was unwilling to release His name for Jacob to control. The divine name cannot be had on demand nor taken in vain, for that would expose it to the possibility of magical manipulation.[59]

Jacob had to be content with a visitation from a "man" whom he realized was divine. Jacob might have recalled that Abram was visited by "men" (Gen. 18) with such powers. Lot also received those men in the night, and was saved alive when the sun arose (Gen. 19). Apparently this was the manner of manifestation of the Lord in Genesis.

Jacob named the place "Peniel" because he had seen God face to face and had been delivered. This is the second part of the basic structure. First, God demanded and changed his name. Here, Jacob was not given the divine name, but named the place to commemorate the event. He had power over that realm, but could not overreach it. The play on the name is clear: Having seen God "face to face" he named the place Peniel, "face of God."[60] The impact of the encounter was shocking for Jacob. Seeing God was something no man survived (Gen. 48:16; Ex. 19:21; 24:10; Judg. 6:11, 22; 13). But this appearance of the "man" guaranteed deliverance for the patriarch. God had come as close to Jacob as was imaginable. Jacob exclaimed, "I have seen God face to face and I have been delivered" (Gen. 32:30, author's translation). The idea is not "and yet" I have been delivered, but rather "and my life has been delivered" (נָצַל). His prayer for deliverance (vv. 9–12) was answered by God in this face-to-face encounter and blessing.[61] Meeting God "face to face" meant that he could now look Esau directly in the eye.

EPILOGUE (32:31–32)

Verse 31 provides the conclusion for the narrative. As the sun rose, Jacob crossed over Peniel with a limp. Ewald says that he limped on his thigh "as if the crookedness, which had previously adhered to the moral nature of the wily Jacob, had now passed over into an external physical attribute only."[62]

The final verse of the story is an editorial note that explains a dietary restriction that developed on account of this event. The wounding of the thigh of Jacob caused the "children of Israel" not to eat of the sciatic nerve "until this day." This law does not form part of the Sinaitic Code, and so according to some scholars may have been a later custom in Israel. This is argued from the fact that the reference is made to Israelites rather than the "sons of Jacob," suggesting that the custom is post-Sinaitic.

The expression "until this day" is usually taken as a sure sign of an etiological note. Childs concludes that in the majority of the cases it is the expression of a personal testimony added to and confirming a received tradition, a commentary on existing customs.[63] He concludes that this cultic practice was introduced secondarily into the narrative. It provided a causal relation for the customary taboo.[64]

Summary

THE NATURE OF JACOB

The special significance of Jacob's becoming Israel is the

purification of character. Peniel marks the triumph of the higher over the lower elements of his life; but if it is a triumph for the higher elements, it is a defeat for the lower. The outcome of the match is a paradox. The victor ("you . . . have prevailed," Gen. 32:28) wept (Hos. 12:4) and pleaded for a blessing; once blessed he emerged, limping on a dislocated hip. How may this be a victory and a blessing?

The defeat of Jacob. Because Jacob was guilty, he feared his brother and found God an adversary. Jacob prepared to meet Esau, whom he had deceived, but the patriarch had to meet God first. God broke Jacob's strength before blessing him with the promise of real strength (the emphasis is on God's activity).

When God touched the strongest sinew of Jacob, the wrestler, it shriveled, and with it Jacob's persistent self-confidence.[65] His carnal weapons were lamed and useless—they failed him in his contest with God. He had always been sure of the result only when he helped himself, but his trust in the naked force of his own weapons was now without value.

The victory of Jacob. What he had surmised for the past 20 years now dawned on him—he was in the hands of One against whom it is useless to struggle. One wrestles on only when he thinks his opponent can be beaten. With the crippling touch, Jacob's struggle took a new direction. With the same scrappy persistence he clung to his Opponent for a blessing. His goal was now different. Now crippled in his natural strength he became bold in faith.

Thus it became a show of significant courage. Jacob won a blessing that entailed changing his name. It must be stressed that he was not wrestling with a river demon or Esau or his alter ego, but with One who was able to bless him.

He emerged from the encounter an altered man. After winning God's blessing legitimately, the danger with Esau vanished. He had been delivered.

THE PROMISES TO JACOB

What, then, is the significance of this narrative within the structure of the patriarchal history? In the encounter the emphasis on promise and fulfillment seems threatened. At Bethel a promise was given; at the Jabbok fulfillment seemed to be barred as God opposed Jacob's entrance into the land. Was there a change of attitude with Yahweh who promised the land? Or was this simply a test?

In a similar but different story, Moses was met by God because he had not complied with God's will (Ex. 4:24). With Jacob, however, the wrestling encounter and name changes took on a greater significance because he was at the frontier of the land promised to the seed of Abraham. God, the real Proprietor of the land, opposed his entering as Jacob. If it were only a matter of mere strength, then He let Jacob know he would never enter the land.[66] The narrative, then, supplies a moral judgment on the crafty Jacob who was almost destroyed in spite of the promise. Judging from Jacob's clinging for a blessing, the patriarch made the same judgment on himself.

The Descendants of Jacob

On the surface the story seems to be a glorification of the physical strength and bold spirit of the ancestor of the Israelites.[67] However, like so much of the patriarchal history, it is transparent as a type of what Israel, the nation, experienced from time to time with God.[68] The story of Israel the man serves as an acted parable of the life of the nation, in which the nation's entire history with God is presented, almost prophetically, as a struggle until the breaking of day.[69] The patriarch portrays the real spirit of the nation, engaging in the persistent struggle with God until they emerge strong in His blessing. Consequently the nation is referred to as Jacob or Israel, depending on which characteristics predominate.

The point of the story for the nation of Israel entering the land of promise is clear: Israel's victory will come not by the usual ways nations gain power, but by the power of the divine blessing. And later in her history Israel would be reminded that the restoration to the land would not be by might, nor by strength, but by the Spirit of the Lord God who fights for His people (Zech. 4:6). The blessings of God come by His gracious, powerful provisions, not by mere physical strength or craftiness. In fact there are times when God must cripple the natural strength of His servants so that they may be bold in faith.

CHAPTER 4

The Date of the Exodus Reexamined

Charles H. Dyer

W hy reexamine the date of the Exodus? Some might object to such a reexamination of the evidence as simply "beating a dead horse." However, this type of objection fails on two counts. First, each generation needs to reexamine the problem to decide for itself the validity of' the possible solutions based on the most recent textual and archaeological studies. New evidence can help condemn or confirm previous hypotheses. Second, the problem must be reexamined because other options are continually being advanced which must be evaluated.[1]

The two views that currently hold sway in the Exodus problem are known as the "early date" view and the "late date" view. The early date places the Exodus in 1445 B.C. while the late date identifies the Exodus as having occurred about 1290 B.C.

The Late Date

The late date is held by nearly all liberal scholars and by a number of conservative scholars. Four lines of evidence are presented in favor of a late date.

THE CITIES OF PITHOM AND RAAMSES

A biblical argument used to support the late date of the Exodus is based on Exodus 1:11. "So they appointed taskmasters over them to afflict them with hard labor. And they built for Pharaoh storage cities, Pithom and Raamses." The thrust of this argument is this: (1) The Israelites built the city of Raamses just before the Exodus. (2) This city is to be equated with the city of Pi-Ramesse built by Pharaoh Ramesses II, who ruled from 1240 to 1224. (3) Therefore the Exodus must have occurred sometime in the 13th century during the reign of this pharaoh. Kitchen feels that this argument alone is determinative for dating the Exodus in the 13th century.[2]

Those who hold to this position have failed to prove two links in their chain of evidence. First, they have failed to *prove* that the city of Raamses mentioned in Exodus 1:11 should be equated with Pi-Ramesse built by Ramesses II. Rather they have *assumed* the connection solely on the basis of similarity of the words "Raamses" and "Ramesses." Second, they have failed to prove that a similarity of names requires a chronological unity between the two events. That is, even *if* the two cities are to be equated, this still does not by itself *prove* that the events occurred simultaneously. Those holding a late Exodus date must still demonstrate a chronological harmony.

Unger attempts to argue against the late date of the Exodus by using the second argument from the preceding paragraph. He argues that the reference to Raamses in Exodus 1:11 does not provide a chronological marker that can be used to date the Exodus. Instead it is a later "modernization" of the Hebrew text used to designate a city that was in existence before Ramesses II.[3]

While Unger's explanation is possible, it does raise some questions concerning the validity of the biblical text. And yet the possible validity of his argument *must* be allowed by those who attempt to use Exodus 1:11 to prove a late date. The reason for this can be explained as follows. If the Exodus took place about 1290 or 1280 B.C. and if Moses was 80 years old at the time of the Exodus (Ex. 7:7), then Moses was born in 1370–1360 B.C. The text of Exodus 1 indicates that the building of the cities of Pithom and Raamses *preceded* Pharaoh's command to kill all newborn males, which preceded the birth of Moses. Therefore the building of the city of Raamses had to begin sometime before 1360 B.C. This is over 45 years before the start of the Nineteenth Dynasty and the first Ramasside king![4] Thus either the city of Raamses did exist before the reign of Ramesses II (which would allow for a prior city in Ex. 1:11) or else the name is a later modernization (which would allow for Unger's argument). In either case those who hold to a 13th-century Exodus cannot argue against the early-date interpretation of Exodus 1:11 without destroying their own argument.

Because of the doctrine of inspiration, this writer feels more comfortable in adopting the *first* argument—the lack of evidence for associating the city of Raamses in Exodus 1:11 with the city of Pi-Ramesse built by Ramesses II. In fact, the biblical text provides some support for not making this identification. Genesis 47:11

clearly indicates that the name "Rameses" was in use before the time of Ramesses II. "So Joseph settled his father and his brothers, and gave them a possession in the land of Egypt, in the best of the land, in the land of Rameses as Pharaoh had ordered." Obviously no one would date the *entrance* of Israel into Egypt during the reign of Ramesses II on the basis of this verse. But since the presence of the term here does not indicate a chronological correspondence, then why does the presence of the term in Exodus 1:11 indicate such correspondence? Why could not Exodus 1:11 be referring to a city of this area called Rameses the name of which existed centuries before Ramesses II? Merrill argues cogently for this possibility.

> . . . it is by no means certain that the city of Rameses was named after the Pharaoh of that name. In fact, Genesis 47:11 states that Jacob and his family settled in the land of Rameses when they entered Egypt in the nineteenth century; unless we postulate an anachronism, for which there is not the slightest proof, we must conclude that there was an area by that name before there was ever a Pharaoh Rameses. It could well be that there had been an ancient Ramesside dynasty long ages before and the Ramessides of the Nineteenth Dynasty were named for them, the city also having taken this name. In any case, there is no need to assume that the mention of the city of Rameses proves that the Exodus must have taken place during the reign of Rameses II.[5]

Exodus 1:11 offers little proof for the late date of the Exodus. The city mentioned was founded and named at least 70 years *before* the reign of Ramesses II even if one assumes the late date. It was located in an area which had been designated as "the land of Rameses" 550 years before Ramesses II. Thus there is no compelling evidence for associating the city with Ramesses II solely on the basis of similarity of name.

THE STATUS OF EDOM AND MOAB

The second argument advanced in favor of the late date focuses on the status of Edom and Moab at the time of the Exodus. "From Kadesh Moses then sent messengers to the king of Edom. . . . 'Please let us pass through your land. We shall not pass through field or through vineyard; we shall not even drink water from a well. We shall go along the king's highway, not turning to the right or left, until we pass through your territory.' Edom, however, said to him, 'You shall not pass through us, lest I come out with the sword against you'. . . . And Edom came out against him with a heavy force, and with a strong hand" (Num. 20:17–20). "Then the sons of Israel journeyed, and camped in the plains of Moab and beyond the Jordan opposite Jericho. . . . And Balak the son of Zippor was king of Moab at that time" (Num. 22:1, 4). These verses indicate that Edom and Moab were populated during the period shortly after the Exodus. However, according to Glueck the Transjordan area was largely uninhabited from about 1800 to 1300 B.C.[6]

> Since the book of Numbers refers to established kingdoms in the Transjordan, namely, the kingdoms of the Moabites and Ammonites, through whose territories the Israelites had to cross, and since surface explorations carried on for two decades by Nelson Glueck showed little or no trace of sedentary life in that region until the thirteenth century, some see in this another evidence that the Exodus took place in the thirteenth rather than in the fifteenth century B.C.[7]

The Bible records the fact that Israel encountered the nations of Edom and Moab during its journey through Transjordania. And yet, according to Glueck no evidence of any nations inhabiting this area between 1800 and 1300 B.C. has been found. His archaeological work sought to prove that the Transjordan kingdoms encountered or avoided by the Israelites did not appear till the 13th century.[8]

Can this argument be answered? Merrill offers a simple explanation, which attacks the central weakness of Glueck's position.

> The answer is quite obvious from a careful study of the Old Testament record and even a superficial knowledge of Biblical geography. We are told that Moses wanted to take the King's Highway, a road which passed through an extremely narrow mountain pass into and out from the city of Petra (Sela). This pass could easily be defended by only a very few hundred well-trained troops, and they need not be sedentary peoples. Nomads or semi-nomads could well have occupied the area in such sufficient numbers that they precluded Israel's passing through their difficult land; yet the nature of their existence would explain the lack of any material remains such as permanent structures. . . . The absence of remains of a settled people need not militate against the early date of the Exodus if the people simply did not leave remains. *Argumentum ad silentum* is not sufficient to overthrow the Biblical position.[9]

Merrill's point is well taken. An argument based on negative evidence is always tenuous. Thus it is interesting to note Kitchen's inconsistency in this regard. He uses Glueck's survey as his first line of proof from Palestinian archaeology to argue against the early date and for the late date of the Exodus.[10] However, he offers a different explanation of the evidence when excavations at Dibon failed to find any support for a settlement there in the 13th century (which would be required according to the Book of Numbers).

> In Moab proper Dibon offers an equally instructive example. . . . Here, the excavations found virtually nothing of Late Bronze Age date, even though Dibon is mentioned in Numbers (21:30; 32:2, 34, 45–46, etc.), precisely like the "gap" at the Negeb sites. However, *in this case we have independent written evidence at first hand to prove the existence of Dibon* in the thirteenth century BC: the war-reliefs of Ramesses II depicting his conquest of Batora and of Dibon "in the land of Moab," these being shown as fortresses. . . . the archaeological data from Dibon (Dhiban) are clearly inadequate, as is so often the case with mute, uninscribed, time-worn, incompletely-dug, archaeological sites. *Such evidence is a very unsatisfactory basis from which to pass judgment upon the biblical or any other literary source.*[11]

Perhaps Kitchen should be more consistent in his application of the biblical and archaeological evidence. Glueck's surface explorations are hardly sufficient to pass judgment on the occupation of the Transjordan area. Archer provides the most complete attack on this position.

> But Glueck's investigations were largely in the nature of surface exploration, and could hardly have been called thorough. Moreover, there has come to light more recently a new line of evidence which seems to belie his deductions. In the *Biblical Archaeologist* for February 1953, C. Lankester Harding reported that the discovery of an ancient tomb in Amman containing numerous artifacts (including black pricked ware, button-base vases, oil flasks, scarabs, and toggle pins) dating from about 1600 B.C. In Harding's *Antiquities of Jordan* (1959) he also speaks of characteristic Middle Bronze pottery and other objects found at Naur and Mount Nebo. A sixteenth century tomb was discovered at Pella in 1967 (*ASOR* newsletter. Dec. 1967). A Late Bronze Age temple was uncovered under a runway at the Amman airport in 1955 (*CT*, Dec. 22, 1971, p. 26). Franken's excavations at Deir Alla and those of Siegfried Horn at Heshbon have shown that the pottery of Transjordan was quite dissimilar from that produced on the west bank of the Jordan at the same period. Yamauchi suggests that Glueck mistakenly assumed the homogeneity of pottery from both regions and thus may have introduced confusion into his interpretation of the data (ibid.). Further excavation will no doubt uncover more products of this intermediate period and demonstrate once again the fallacy of hasty conclusions from superficial investigations.[12]

Once again an argument for the late date of the Exodus must be rejected. The argument is primarily an argument from silence which can be explained in the light of the lack of archaeological evidence left by a nomadic or semi-nomadic people. Also, additional evidence has been trickling in, evidence which *does* seem to confirm the existence of people in the Transjordan area in the period from 1800 to 1300 B.C.

THE SITUATION IN WESTERN PALESTINE

Perhaps the strongest evidence in favor of the late date is found in the archaeology of western Palestine.

> Various Palestinian city-sites show evidence of clear destruction in the second half of the 13th century B.C., which would agree with the onset of the Israelites placed at roughly 1240 B.C. onward. Such sites are Tell Beit Mirsim (possibly biblical Debir/Kiriath-sepher), Lachish, Bethel and Hazor.[13]

The evidence in this section is too numerous to examine in detail. However, some material needs to be considered carefully. Two specific archaeological sites will be considered.

Jericho. The biblical account clearly indicates that the first city destroyed by the Israelites as they entered Canaan was Jericho. Since this occurred approximately 40 years after the Exodus, the dating of the fall of Jericho should provide a clue for the dating of the Exodus. Initial work by Garstang seemed to provide good support for the early date of the Exodus.[14]

While Garstang's position is still held by some conservative writers,[15] most have abandoned the position in favor of that proposed by Kenyon, who has done extensive work at Jericho. Her general conclusions vary from those of Garstang.

> The evidence of the published pottery makes it clear, in the first place, that none of the areas excavated were occupied in the thirteenth century, nor the tombs discovered used then. There is no trace of any of the comparatively well-known thirteenth century forms. On the other hand, it is clear that there was occupation within some part of the fourteenth century. Our knowledge of pottery makes it difficult to assign very exact dates. It would appear that most of the typically fifteenth forms are lacking. . . .[16]

The question, however, is this: Which date of the Exodus does the archaeological evidence from Jericho support? Actually the evidence from the ruins themselves is somewhat sketchy. Kitchen notes that "the Late Bronze Age levels appear to have been almost completely washed away during the four centuries that the mound lay desolate from Joshua until Ahab's time. . . ."[17] Thus much of the evidence has been lost or jumbled through erosion and weathering over the centuries. Still, Waltke believes that a date can be established through the use of other archaeological markers.

Now can the fall of the city be dated more precisely during the Late Bronze period? Garstang argued convincingly that the Conquest must have occurred before the reign of Akhenaten, who began to reign ca. 1375 B.C. because (1) not one of the distinctive, plentiful, and well-established archaeological criteria characteristic of Akhenaten's reign has been found in either the city or in the tombs; (2) there is no reference to Jericho in the Amarna letters dated to Akhenaten's reign, though numerous cities of Canaan are mentioned frequently: (3) there is no scarab after Amenhotep III (1412 B.C.–1375 B.C.) though there survived an abundant and continuous series of scarabs of the Egyptian kings from the Middle Bronze Age right on down through the reign of Hatshepsut, Thutmose III, and Amenhotep III of the Late Bronze I period. Confessedly these are all negative evidences and may be subject to other explanations than that the Canaanite city ceased to exist before 1375 B.C., but together they lead to the plausible suggestion that the destruction of the city previously established by the ceramic evidence between 1410 B.C. and 1340 B.C. occurred before 1375 B.C.[18]

While Waltke labels his evidence for a 1375 B.C. destruction "negative evidences," one item could be considered in a more positive sense as an answer to Kenyon's position. Kenyon has argued that there is *no* evidence of occupation suddenly ending about 1375 B.C. However, she is then forced to deal with a 15th-century royal scarab which was found in one of the tombs by proposing a concept that has no supporting evidence.

The suggestion put forward in the report that [the scarab] was the insignia of office of the person buried is tempting, but it is so much at variance with the lack of what we now know as fifteenth century pottery, that it can only be suggested that it was an heirloom. We have not sufficient evidence of how in Palestine such scarabs, which may in origin have been insignia, were treated, to allow such a find by itself to contradict other evidence.[19]

Kenyon seems to be guilty of manipulating her evidence to fit a preconceived idea. If evidence is found which contradicts her thesis she explains it away even though there is no warrant for doing so. Taken as a whole the evidence for Jericho is mixed. While Garstang's support for the destruction of the walls in 1400 has been challenged by Kenyon, she has not conclusively shown that her alternative is correct. Additional evidence points to a destruction sometime between 1400 and 1375 B.C. Still, the evidence is mixed.

Hazor. The site of Hazor has been extensively excavated by Yigael Yadin. He discovered evidence of 21 cities covering a span of 2,550 years from 2700 B.C. to 150 B.C.[20] Yadin accepts the late date for the Exodus and Conquest and associates the destruction

of the city "at the end of the Late Bronze Age II in the second half
of the 13th cent. B.C."[21]
However, Yadin does present some other interesting evidence.
He notes the discovery of a Late Bronze II period gate erected on
the foundation of the earlier Middle Bronze Age II gate.[22] He then
writes:

> This gate must have been destroyed in a violent conflagration, though the
> exterior walls still stand to a height of nine feet. Traces of the burnt
> bricks of its inner walls and the ashes of the burnt beams still cover the
> floors in thick heaps. *The evidence suggests that this destruction occurred
> before the final destruction of Hazor by the Israelites*, but this problem
> remains to be studied.[23]

While the point could easily be missed, it is significant. Since
Yadin accepts the 1250 B.C. destruction as being that of Israel, he
is saying that another earlier destruction also took place during the
Late Bronze II period. Walton dates both phases of the Late
Bronze II period as extending from 1400 to 1200 B.C.[24] Thus if
two destructions were in this period, how does one know which is
to be associated with the Exodus? The first would correspond to
the early date for the Exodus and the second would correspond to
the late date for the Exodus. But which destruction is correct? The
problem is even more complex because a third period of destruction
is also in evidence during this period.

> There are then from the Late Bronze Age Canaanite city, layers of
> destruction at *ca.* 1400 B.C., *ca.* + 1300 B.C. and *ca.* + 1230 B.C. Moreover,
> there is no occupation after 1230 B.C. on the Lower Canaanite City and a
> probable gap on the tell between 1230 B.C. and the era of Solomon. The
> interpretive problem then is: "With which of these strata shall one associate
> Joshua?" Most probably Yadin is correct in his suggestion that the
> destruction level at *ca.* + 1300 B.C. should be associated with the burning
> of the city by Seti I (*ca.* 1318 B.C.). So then one is left with the destruction
> levels at 1400 B.C. and 1230 B.C. Yadin opted for the 1230 B.C. level.[25]

Which date should be assigned to Joshua? The Bible itself
helps provide an answer. Judges 4:2–3 indicates that Jabin, king
of Hazor, oppressed the Israelites during the period of the Judges
for 20 years. Israel was finally delivered by Deborah and Barak
when they destroyed Jabin (4:23–24). Whitcomb places the defeat
of Jabin approximately 165 years after Joshua's destruction of
Hazor.[26] This passage argues strongly against the 1230 destruction
as that of Joshua since the city was uninhabited between 1230 and
the time of Solomon. As Waltke notes, "If the city ceased to exist
after 1230 B.C., and if it is still in existence at least three or four

generations after Joshua, then Joshua's destruction cannot be attributed to the destruction level dated at 1230 B.C. . . .''[27] Rather than arguing for the late date of the Exodus, the destruction at Hazor actually favors the early date. In fact, neither Hazor nor Jericho argue conclusively for the late date of the Exodus. The data are capable of harmonization with the early date and in fact sometimes fit better with that date.

THE LOCATION OF PHAROAH'S RESIDENCE

A fourth argument in favor of the late date for the Exodus centers on the location of pharaoh's residence during the time of the Exodus. Those who hold to the late date argue that during the Eighteenth Dynasty (1580–1314 B.C.) the capital of Egypt was in the south at Thebes. It was not until the Nineteenth Dynasty that it was moved to the north to Pi-Ramesses. Thus for the pharaoh to have been geographically close to the Israelites (as the Exodus account seems to indicate), the pharaoh must have been from the Nineteenth Dynasty since only the Nineteenth Dynasty capital of Pi-Ramesses is close enough to the land of Goshen.[28]

Kitchen concurs with this assessment when he notes, "The official building-works of the Ramesside kings in the E. Delta are usually found to be the first original works there since the Hyksos period four centuries earlier. . . ."[29] Obviously if this evidence is true, then one would be hard pressed to place the pharaoh of the Eighteenth Dynasty near the land of Goshen if his capital was located far to the south. However, does the evidence actually support these claims? This writer thinks not.

Davis has amassed several items of evidence which point to the pharaoh's presence in the Delta region during the Eighteenth Dynasty.

> However, it is well known both from archaeological remains and important inscriptions that the Eighteenth Dynasty pharaohs did have a keen interest in building projects in the northern part of Egypt. Along with the two red granite obelisks erected by Thutmose III in front of the Temple of Ra'-Heliopolis, a scarab has been discovered that refers to the birth of Amenhotep II as having taken place in Memphis just below Heliopolis. It appears that as a youth Amenhotep II spent considerable time in that area. It has also been demonstrated that in the Eighteenth Dynasty there were two viziers in Egypt, one in upper Egypt and one in lower Egypt. Since Eighteenth Dynasty pharaohs were very active in Palestinian campaigns, it would seem reasonable that they would have established garrisons and store-cities somewhere in the Delta region to facilitate movement between Syro-Palestinian sites and Egypt itself.[30]

Other archaeological evidence found in Egypt confirms Davis's statement. A stela from Amenhotep II was found in Memphis which recorded some of his military exploits. One section dealt with his victorious return to Egypt. "His majesty reached Memphis, his heart joyful. . . . Now the God's Wife, King's Wife, and King's [Daughter] beheld the victory of his majesty."[31] The text seems to imply that the king at least had a temporary dwelling in the Delta area where his family would at times reside and which he would use as his base of operation for excursions into Palestine.

The location of the pharaoh's residence has little bearing on the date of the Exodus since the pharaohs of both the Eighteenth and Nineteenth Dynasties had residences in the northern delta region. Thus the pharaoh could easily come from either dynasty and still meet the scriptural requirements.

CONCLUSION

Much of the evidence advanced in favor of the late date is based on archaeological data which are subject to different interpretations. None of the material offers compelling evidence in favor of the late date. Instead, all the data can harmonize with the early date.

The Early Date

The early date of the Exodus (ca. 1445 B.C.) is held by many (but not all) conservative scholars. Several lines of evidence, both biblical and archaeological, are often presented as support for an early date.

FIRST KINGS 6:1

Perhaps the strongest evidence in favor of an early date is the statement of 1 Kings 6:1, which dates the beginning of the construction of the temple. "Now it came to pass in the four hundred and eightieth year after the sons of Israel came out of the land of Egypt, in the fourth year of Solomon's reign over Israel, in the month of Ziv which is the second month that he began to build the house of the Lord." Whitcomb dates the fourth year of Solomon's reign to 966 B.C.[32] Thus 480 years before to the fourth year of Solomon would place the Exodus at 1445 B.C.

Since the statement of 1 Kings 6:1 is so straightforward, one wonders why the early date for the Exodus would ever be questioned. And yet questions are raised.

> Against this line of reasoning stands the plain statement of 1 K. 6:1 that there were 480 years between the Exodus and the building of the Temple. If the reasoning is correct, how can that figure be explained? Commonly it is seen as a round figure, the sum of twelve generations of forty years each. The presence of two stock numbers, twelve and forty, is enough to create some presumption in favor of this explanation. Although there is no direction in the text that the number should be interpreted as an approximation, neither is there any evidence that the Hebrew people during the judges period had any need for, or any inclination to keep, an exact overall chronology.[33]

This argument is very tenuous. First, Oswalt argues in a circle. He takes the 480–year figure, divides it into two figures (12 and 40), and then argues that the presence of these "stock numbers" points to the fact that the number is an approximation. But where in the text are the numbers 12 and 40? He produced these himself from the 480 figure (i.e., 12 x 40 = 480). Yet the text itself does *not* have these "stock numbers"; it simply has 480. Second, Oswalt, fails to account for the specifics of the text in which the "480" is couched. This was also "the fourth year of Solomon's reign," "the month of Ziv," and "the second month." These are hardly "approximations." Rather the author of 1 Kings was citing a specific date for the beginning of the temple's construction. Should not this "create a presumption" in favor of a literal interpretation of the 480–year figure? Third, Oswalt is arguing from silence when he intimates that the people during the Judges period did not keep accurate chronological records. Judges 11:26 indicates just the opposite. Jephthah knew the exact amount of time that Israel lived in Heshbon (300 years). Evidently he *did* have "an inclination to keep an exact overall chronology." Furthermore, 1 Kings 6:1 was *recorded* during the monarchy; and a glance at 1 and 2 Kings reveals that the writer was concerned with chronology. Based on his use of numbers elsewhere in the book it seems probable that he intended the 480 year figure to be interpreted literally.

Wood provides a telling critique of this position.

> This explanation, however, must be rejected by one who holds to a high view of inspiration. The text in no way states or implies the thought of twelve generations. It refers merely to the definite number 480, which means that any idea of generations must be read into the text, One is minded to say that if this plain number can be reduced so drastically by this manner of analysis, then many other biblical numbers can be similarly adjusted by parallel methods, making Scriptural numbers very uncertain indeed.[34]

Those who would seek to reinterpret 1 Kings 6:1 do so on the basis of external archaeological evidence. Thus they are seeking to reinterpret the biblical data to "match" the archaeological data. This is a very dangerous position because archaeology is a very inexact, changing science. Unless there is good textual or contextual evidence to the contrary, it is better to let the Bible stand on its own.

JUDGES 11:26

The second argument in favor of the early date are the words of Jephthah in Judges 11:26. "While Israel lived in Heshbon and its villages, and in all the cities that are on the banks of the Arnon, three hundred years, why did you not recover them within that time?" Jephthah was saying, in effect, that Israel had been occupying the city of Heshbon (and other villages) in Moab for 300 years. These cities were taken by Israel just before their invasion of Canaan (cf. Num. 21:25–35). The possession of Heshbon occurred approximately 340-years before Jephthah. The problem for those who hold the late Exodus date is obvious. If the Exodus took place in 1280 B.C., then Jephthah would have been a judge in 940 B.C.—during the reign of King Solomon! However, if the Exodus took place in 1445 B.C., then Jephthah judged in 1105 B.C., well within the period of the Judges.

How does one who holds to a late date for the Exodus answer this? Some use a mixture of agnosticism and circular reasoning,

They begin by assuming that the Conquest occurred around 1240–1220 B.C. Since Jephthah's remark (made ca. 1100) would mean the Exodus occurred about 1400, his remark cannot be interpreted literally since it does not square with the "evidence." That is, they must reinterpret Scripture to "fit" their archaeological scheme.

> But here again, we do not know the basis of Jephthah's figure—it could, again, be an aggregate of partly concurrent periods (e.g., for Reuben, Gad, and East Manasseh?), but we have no indications on which to build. . . . Empty speculation is profitless, and sound method would counsel one to await fresh light on matters of this type. No-one is compelled to produce a complete answer when there is simply not enough information to do so.[35]

Davis makes a notable observation on the context of Judges 11 in which Jephthah's statement occurs. It is a prose section involving talks between two nations, both of which are aware of the historical situation of Heshbon.

It is scarcely possible, however, that Jephthah should make such a blunder in the midst of important international negotiations. His knowledge of the Torah is evident from the context of Chapter 11 of Judges. It is doubtful that Jephthah could have exaggerated this number as it was used in the argument to the king and have gotten away with it. The King of Ammon had some knowledge of the historical precedence involved in Israel's occupation of the territory of Transjordan (cf. Judg. 11:13). Again it would be well to point out that numerical information given in the passage under question does not appear in a poetic section and therefore probably reflects sober fact.[36]

It seems best to accept the testimony of Judges 11:26 at face value. There is nothing in the context to argue against a normal interpretation. Thus the early date of the Exodus seems to accord better with the biblical data.

THE "DREAM STELE" OF THUTMOSE IV

A third argument advanced to support the early date for the Exodus is the "dream stele" of Thutmose IV. This stele records a dream of Thutmose IV in which he was promised the throne of Egypt.

> One of those days it happened that the King's Son Thut-mose came on an excursion at noon time. Then he rested in the shadow of this great god. Sleep took hold of him, slumbering at the time when the sun was at its peak. He found the majesty of this august god speaking with his own mouth, as a father speaks to his son, saying, "See me, look at me, my son, Thut-mose! I am thy father, Harmakhis-Khepri-Re-Atum. I shall give thee my kingdom upon earth at the head of the living. Thou shalt wear the southern crown and the northern crown on the throne of Geb, the crown prince (of the gods). Thine is the land in its length and its breadth, that which the Eye of the All-Lord illumines."[37]

The argument here is that had Thutmose IV been the firstborn son, he would have had no need for the god to promise him the throne since he would have already been heir. Thus he must have had an older brother who later died. This would harmonize with the death of the firstborn at the time of the Exodus.

> It is quite obvious that if Thutmose IV had been the eldest son of his father, Amenhotep II, there would have been no purpose in divine promise that he should some day become king. He would naturally have succeeded to the throne if he had survived his father. It is a necessary inference, therefore, that the oldest son of Amenhotep must have later predeceased his father, thus leaving the succession to his younger brother. This well accords with the record in Exodus 12:29 that the eldest son of Pharaoh died at the time of the tenth plague.[38]

While this argument sounds impressive, it has some serious difficulties. First, it is an argument from silence. Second, for it to be valid Thutmose IV would have had to be old enough to go hunting and to have such a dream before the death of his brother (once the older brother was dead the dream was unnecessary). However, as Aling notes, "This seems highly unlikely, since the prince was *at most* five years old at the time of the exodus. The events described on the Sphinx Stele should in all probability be dated some years after the exodus, and therefore the stele is definitely not evidence for the death of the Egyptian firstborn."[39]

While there might be some latitude on the exact date of Thutmose IV's birth, Aling has presented a strong case against using the dream stele as an argument for the early date of the Exodus. This does not argue *against* the early date; it merely indicates that the dream stele has no bearing either way on the debate. Thus unless evidence arises which shows that (a) Thutmose IV was old enough to have had this experience before 1445 and (b) Thutmose IV had only one older brother, it seems better to eliminate this argument from the evidence for the early date.

THE 'APIRU AND THE AMARNA LETTERS

A fourth argument for the early date of the Exodus focuses on two interrelated events. The first is a class of people who invaded Palestine in the 14th century, and the second is a series of letters written from Canaan to Pharaoh Amenhotep IV (Akhenaten), also from the 14th century.

> The important question is whether there is any such invasion of central and southern Palestine hinted at in contemporary records that would suggest the Israelite conquest under Joshua. That there is such an invasion of outsiders recounted in the famous Amarna Letters, which deal with this period from about 1400–1366 B.C., has been known virtually since their discovery in 1886. These invaders, called Habiru, are etymologically actually equitable with the Hebrews. . . .[40]

The letters of this period illustrate Unger's point. One example is EA, No. 271 written by Milkilu, prince of Gezar, to the pharaoh. He writes, "Let the king, my lord. protect his land from the hand of the 'Apiru. If not, (then) let the king, my lord, send chariots to fetch us, lest our servants smite us."[41] A second example is from 'Abdu-Heba, king of Jerusalem, who writes:

> As truly as the king, my lord, lives, when the commis [sioners] go forth I will say, "Lost are the lands of the king! Do you not hearken unto me?

All the governors are lost; the king, my lord, does not have a (single) governor (left)! Let the king turn his attention to the archers, and let the king, my lord, send out troops of archers, (for) the king has no lands (left)!" The *'Apiru* plunder all the lands of the king. If there are archers (here) in this year, the lands of the king, my lord, will remain (intact); but if there are not archers (here) the lands of the king, my lord, will be lost![42]

While this does seem to describe an invasion (a) at the same time as that of an early date conquest and (b) by a people with a similar name to the Hebrews, not all associate the 'Apiru or the Amarna Letters with the Israelite Conquest. Pfeiffer presents at least four arguments against this identification: (1) "A strong argument against identification comes from the fact that 'Apiru appear in a wide variety of places of which there is no hint in the Biblical narrative." (2) "There is considerable evidence that the 'Apiru were regarded as a social rather than an ethnic group. . . . The 'Apiru of the Amarna tablets are never described as invaders." (3) "Although the place names of the Amarna texts are parallel to those of the Old Testament, the personal names are totally different." (4) "Most contemporary scholars date the conquest of Canaan after the Amarna Age, suggesting some time around 1280 B.C., as the probable date of the Exodus."[43]

While Pfeiffer's points are well taken, his arguments are answerable. The first argument assumes a one-for-one correspondence between 'Apiru and Hebrew. If 'Apiru could denote a larger class of people of which the Hebrews were considered one segment, then the argument has been answered. Much as one today might use the larger designation "American" or "European" to denote an individual who is actually from El Salvador or France, so a Hebrew could have been designated by the larger term 'Apiru. Pfeiffer's second argument is also somewhat moot for it is difficult to distinguish social and ethnic traits from the limited material available. Also it is easy to see the invading Israelites as *both* a social group (with their own laws, patterns of conduct, etc.) and an ethnic group. Pfeiffer's third argument assumes that individuals had only one name. However, there are examples in the Bible of individuals who had two names (or more). It is possible that the two accounts are reflecting the two different names (cf. 2 Kings 23:34 where Eliakim's name was changed to Jehoiakim by the pharaoh to signify Egypt's control of Judah's king). Pfeiffer's fourth argument involved circular reasoning. He is assuming what he is trying to prove.

While Pfeiffer's arguments can be answered, he should cause one to think before indiscriminately applying archaeological evidence to biblical events. Actually the Amarna letters and the 'Apiru *by themselves* do not prove the early date for the Exodus. Apart from clear scriptural testimony placing the Hebrews in the same location during the same period of time the evidence would be incomplete. As it is, the Amarna letters and the 'Apiru can *confirm* the early date of the Exodus but they cannot *prove* the early date.

OTHER EVIDENCE

Other relatively minor arguments are offered in favor of an early date for the Exodus. The first of these is the argument from antiquity. Josephus quoted the Egyptian historian Manetho to show that his records mention the Exodus. Josephus quoted Manetho as saying that "Tethmosis was king when they went away." However, Josephus then chided Manetho for erring in later declaring that a king named "Amenophis" was the pharaoh at the time of the Exodus.[44] Could it be possible that Josephus was preserving a garbled tradition that was associating Thutmose III and Amenhotep II with the Exodus? One cannot say for sure but the similarity is striking.

A second minor argument offered in favor of an early date for the Exodus is based on the chronology of the life of Moses. Moses was 40 years old when he fled from the pharaoh after killing an Egyptian (Ex. 2:11–15; Acts 7:23–29). Moses was 80 years old when God told him to go back to Egypt "for all the men who were seeking your life are dead" (Ex. 4:19; cf. 7:7; Acts 7:30). Since the pharaoh had been seeking Moses' life (Ex. 2:15), one needs to find a pharaoh who reigned for approximately 40 years to fulfill the chronological gap. Only two kings lived long enough to fill this gap—Thutmose who reigned for 54 years (1504–1450 B.C.) and Rameses II who reigned for 66 years (1290–1224 B.C.). However Rameses II must be eliminated because the pharaoh following him would be Merneptah and it was during his reign that the stele was written which identified his victory over the Israelites in Palestine. Thus Thutmose III must have been the pharaoh of the oppression and Amenhotep II the pharaoh of the Exodus.[45]

The main argument against this position is that it *assumes* that the pharaoh must have lived for the 40 years Moses was in the wilderness even though the biblical text never says that.

Theoretically the pharaoh could have died years earlier. Thus the argument is interesting, but irrelevant. While it does not prove the early date, neither does it disprove it.

CONCLUSION

Two types of evidence have been presented—biblical and archaeological. The biblical evidence was seen to be very strong for the early date. Both 1 Kings 6:1 and Judges 11:26, when interpreted normally, point to an Exodus sometime around 1445 B.C. The archaeological evidence is interesting but not quite as strong. The "dream stele" of Thutmose IV, the 'Apiru and Amarna letters, the testimony of Josephus, and the historical setting provide interesting, but not incontrovertible, evidence in favor of an early date. Some of these arguments are stronger than others, but each of them is capable of another interpretation. Thus the primary support for the early date must still rest on the biblical testimony.

Conclusion

> The fact is that the available archaeological evidence simply does not square well with the biblical account of the conquest [and Exodus] regardless of what one proposes as a date. If the Bible and archaeology are to be correlated *vis-a-vis* the conquest, the claims of the biblical account will have to be modified in some fashion and/or some of the archaeological evidence will have to be explained away. This brings into focus a crucial methodological issue which divides biblical scholars (and Palestinian archaeologists) more than we generally admit. The issue is simply this: What sort of conclusion is to be reached when carefully excavated archaeological evidence does not seem to meet the minimum requirements of the historical implications of the biblical texts?[46]

Miller has hit the heart of the question as it relates to the Exodus. Is the archaeological evidence or the biblical text to be the primary source of information? Those who opt for the late date of the Exodus do so primarily on the basis of archaeological evidence. And yet that evidence is always colored by the presuppositions and prejudices of those interpreting the raw data. On the other side are those who opt for the early date of the Exodus. They do so primarily because of the biblical data. So what is the answer? All truth is God's truth; yet the only truth which can be known absolutely is that truth which God chooses to reveal in His Word. Thus the biblical evidence must be the primary evidence. For this reason the writer accepts the early date of the Exodus as being the better alternative.

CHAPTER 5

Literary Structure in the Book of Ruth

Reg Grant

The Book of Ruth is so profound in its structure that it has induced a flood of literary analyses. The purpose of this study is not to explore the book's many intriguing literary angles, but to consider just its plot structure. A presupposition of this study is that the book's plot structure is comic/monomythic. As such, it manifests four literary structural elements as the plot moves from tragedy through anti-romance, and then through comedy to romance.[1]

Another presupposition is that plot structure should inform (but not prescribe) exegesis. Where the structural elements occur in a strategic place (e.g., as central words, phrases, or sentences in chiastic structure), this study attempts to demonstrate the significance of the placement. Consideration is therefore limited to literary aspects of the book that contribute in some substantial way to the reader's understanding of the hermeneutical significance of the structural elements. Though each of the four elements will be examined, the focus will be on the transitional elements (the comic and tragic), since they are the loci of change in the story.

The Literary Element of Tragedy

The first scene is recorded in Ruth 1:1–7a. The element of tragedy is introduced in the first part of the scene (v. 1), in which the Lord used a famine to initiate the tragic element.[2] The tragic element itself (that which effects the transition between the ideal state and the unideal) occurred at some point between the cause ("famine") and the effect (expressed initially in Elimelech's decision to move his family to Moab). A consideration of the contextual link to the period of the Judges[3] reveals why the audience would expect that the famine mentioned in verse 1 would lead to tragic consequences for Elimelech and his family.

First, one may note the significance of Elimelech's departure from Bethlehem in light of the place of the Ruth narrative in the so-called Bethlehem trilogy.[4] In the first of these narratives (Judg. 17–18), Jonathan, a Levite and descendant of Moses, left his hometown of Bethlehem[5] to seek employment elsewhere (17:8). The results of his leaving were tragic for several individuals and groups, himself, the one he served at first (Micah),[6] the tribe of Dan, and eventually the entire nation (he established a cult center at Laish, which caused problems for Israel from that time on). The second narrative in the trilogy (Judg. 19–21) reinforces the message of the first by repeating the Bethlehem-Ephraim connection motif of the first narrative.[7] Another Levite (this time from Ephraim) retrieved his concubine from Bethlehem, which was her home (19:1) and to which she had returned (v. 2). They left Bethlehem to return to Ephraim by way of Gibeah of Benjamin. The tragedy that befell the concubine and her husband affected them personally (the woman was raped and killed) and then affected the tribe of Benjamin and the nation (all but six hundred Benjamite men were slaughtered by Israel in reprisal for the murder of the concubine). The nation was further affected in that daughters from Shiloh and Jabesh-Gilead had to be taken as wives for the surviving Benjamites to insure the continuance of the tribe of Benjamin.

In the first two narratives everyone suffered and everyone lost. By now the idea is fixed in the reader's mind that departure from Bethlehem will probably lead to trouble. This is exactly what one finds in the Ruth narrative, but with an important difference. In the previous two narratives the structure that tied the tragic events to their long-term consequences received the focus. In the Ruth narrative the tragic events and the consequences that followed on Elimelech's departure from Bethlehem are at their worst by 1:5. Following verse 5, the return motif (based on the good news that "the Lord had visited His people in giving them food" [v. 6]) and Ruth's faithfulness to Naomi (vv. 16–17) combine to suggest at least the remote possibility of comic resolution. The focus shifts subtly then from the tragic to the (potentially) comic with the introduction of this news.[8] Also by the end of the Ruth narrative, the reader is convinced of Yahweh's faithfulness to His covenant promises.[9] There is never a hint of comic resolution in either of the Judges narratives. The structures in the closing narratives of the Book of Judges are like a spiraling whirlpool that gradually sucks everything down to destruction. However, the narrative of the Book of Ruth surprises the audience by avoiding the inevitable (even though the initial archetypal "departure" motif coupled with Naomi's fatalism would lead the audience to expect otherwise). What should have been the worst of three tragedies turns out instead to be a romantic comedy.

The famine as a "natural" cause of tragedy launches a series of increasingly painful events in the human realm (also archetypal) that combine to establish one of the two primary motifs in the first act, that of emptiness. First, Elimelech died (1:3), leaving Naomi with her two sons. Then Mahlon and Chilion died (v. 5), leaving Naomi with her two Moabite daughters-in-law. Finally, she lost one of them, and so she was left with Ruth (v. 18). The descent into the unideal state was gradual (it actually took more than 10 years [v. 4]), but the narrator covers the downward spiral in just 18 verses. The remainder of the narrative covers approximately three months (from the beginning of the barley harvest to the end of the barley and wheat harvest, 1:22; 2:23).

The famine is a perfect archetype at this point in the narrative, for it introduces the concept of literal, physical barrenness. The land was barren, unfruitful, empty. The concept moves to the personal realm when the reader realizes that Ruth and Orpah are both apparently barren (1:5; 4:13).[10] Naomi is seen as barren as well. She has lost her husband, her sons, one of her daughters-in-law, and her hope (1:12). Even Ruth's statement of commitment (vv. 16–17), as beautiful as it is, seems to anticipate a tragic end with its closing focus on death: "Where you die, I will die, and there I will be buried. Thus may the Lord do to me, and worse, if anything but death parts you and me." Thus the emptiness motif is introduced and developed in verses 1–18. The major motif in this section, however, is not that of emptiness, but "return."

The return motif dominates chapter 1, the first act, which means that it spans all the tragic consequences as well as the unideal experience (vv. 19–22b). To have a return, one must have an initial departure. That departure and its immediate repercussions are outlined in verses 1–5. The return motif is introduced in verse 6 when Naomi decided to go home to Bethlehem, based on what she had heard concerning the Lord's provision of food. Here is the first hint of the possibility of comic resolution. There is further cause for hope in the fact that Naomi and Ruth emerged from a literal (and figurative) winter of barrenness into a potentially fruitful spring (the barley harvest began about the end of April in Israel).

Seasonal archetypes play a subtle but distinctive role in the development of the comic and romantic elements in the Book of Ruth. The archetypes of autumn (normally associated with the tragic element) and winter (the unideal experience) are noticeable only in that the arrival of Naomi and Ruth is coincident with the beginning of the barley harvest in April (which suggests that winter had come to an end). Their arrival at the beginning of the barley harvest was more than "coincidental," however.

The significance of this season extends beyond literary expression of hope for fruitful land, fruitful wombs, and fruitful lives, though this is certainly part of the author's design. The significance of the barley harvest relates also to the feasts that were celebrated at that time of year, the feasts of Passover, Unleavened Bread, and Firstfruits (Lev. 23:4–14).[11] The festal cycle in Israel corresponded to specific points on the agricultural calendar, which also happened to reinforce the emptiness (and fullness) motifs as developed in Ruth.[12] It is necessary to examine briefly those three feasts as they relate to the development of the structure of the Book of Ruth.[13]

In the Passover, Israel acknowledged her need of a redeemer and her fealty to Yahweh. The Lord honored the Israelites' obedience by redeeming them out of a foreign land and ultimately by bringing them to the land of promise. The Passover feast celebrated this redemption and the faithfulness of God in bringing them to the land He had promised to Abraham (Gen. 12; 15). Ruth, of course, had come from a foreign land to the land of promise just in time for the celebration of this feast.

The Feast of Unleavened Bread focused on Israel's willingness to cut herself off from her old life in Egypt. Leaven, in the context of this feast, symbolized continuity; it was a symbol of connection with the old life of bondage. In calling for the baking of unleavened bread, the Lord was calling, in effect, for a symbolic break with Israel's tie to the past. Similarly Ruth broke with her past life in Moab when she decided to accompany Naomi into whatever situation lay before them; and this decision by Ruth was made at the same time of year Israel had decided to leave Egypt hundreds of years before. Her break was no less complete, though her personal loss and anxiety may have been greater. She left her family, her home, and her people to live in a foreign land and to embrace a God her fathers had not known; and she had only a destitute widow to lead her rather than a miracle-working Moses. Perhaps the most significant of these feasts for this study, in light of the prominent agricultural motif, is the Feast of Firstfruits. The wave offering at that feast signified Israel's recognition of her need of divine provision. It was a wave offering of a sheaf of raw barley (Lev. 23:11). Surely the reader would see the significance of Ruth's gleaning among the sheaves of barley (she was certainly in need of divine provision) at the very time Israel celebrated a feast that focused on the nation's need for divine provision. And this is not to mention Naomi's earlier request to the Lord that He deal kindly with Ruth and Orpah (i.e., give them husbands, a home, and rest; Ruth 1:8–9). Of significance is the difference between the attitude that should have been expressed according to Leviticus 23 and the attitude expressed by Naomi. Leviticus 23 enjoins an attitude of acknowledged dependence coupled with faith that the Lord will provide, that He will remain faithful to His covenant promises by giving His people a full harvest. Naomi lacked the component of faith. She definitely recognized her need for divine assistance, and she recognized that that assistance was available for Ruth and Orpah (Ruth 1:8–9), but Naomi felt she herself was beyond the point of receiving help from the Lord (v. 13).

Resenting her lot in life, Naomi nourished a fatalistic resignation to live out the rest of her empty days in bitterness (witness her name change to Mara ["bitter"], v. 20). Ruth, on the other hand, moved out in faith ("Your people shall be my people, and your God, my God," v. 16), never complaining (as Naomi did, and as the Exodus generation did repeatedly) or looking back (as the Exodus generation did in longing for the leeks and onions of Egypt, Num. 11:5). By the Lord's design, it was Ruth who wound up holding the raw barley. It was she who unwittingly embodied the true spirit of the feast, even though the Feast of Firstfruits was never mentioned explicitly.

Besides the literary connections with the previous context and the overlapping archetypal images and motifs, the structure of Ruth 1:1–7a highlights the transitional element. The context of verse 1—there was a famine and Elimelech left Bethlehem for Moab—is matched by verses 6–7—Naomi set out to return because the Lord had provided food. The return motif is strengthened through repetition of the word שׁוּב, "return," in verses 6 and 7.

The second (1:7b–19a) and third scenes (1:19b–22a) also are

framed by narrative constructions that reinforce the return motif: "And they went on the way to return to the land of Judah" (v. 7b); "so they both went until they came to Bethlehem" (v. 19a). The passage includes several other references to the "return" theme, all in symmetrical relationship. Naomi's speech in verse 8a ("Go, return each of you to her mother's house") balances with her admonition to Ruth in verse 15b ("return after your sister-in-law"). At the center of this scene (vv. 10–13) the dialogue between Naomi, Ruth, and Orpah reflects the return motif: "And they said to her, 'No, but we will surely return with you to your people'" (v. 10); "But Naomi said, 'Return, my daughters. . . . Return, my daughters! Go, for I am too old'" (vv. 11–12).

The third scene continues to reinforce the return motif with another narrative bracket: "And it came about when they had come to Bethlehem" (v. 19); "so Naomi returned, and with her Ruth the Moabitess, her daughter-in-law, who returned from the land of Moab" (v. 22).[14]

The Literary Element of Anti-Romance

The unideal experience in its pure form (i.e., an existence devoid of joy) is evident in Ruth 1:19b–22a, the third scene. When Naomi arrived in Bethlehem (v. 19), immediately the city was "stirred." The word translated "stirred" (וַתֵּהֹם, a *niphal* form) is the same word used to express the excited joy in the Israelite camp over the ark of the covenant (1 Sam. 4:5, also a *niphal;* translated "resounded" in the NASB). The word is also used in 1 Kings 1:45 (also a *niphal*) to express joy over Solomon's anointing.[15]

The women of Bethlehem asked, "Is this Naomi?" "The reaction is certainly . . . more of delight than of pity; hence, the question which follows, 'Is it Naomi,' is not to be taken as expressing shock at what time and suffering have done to Naomi, but rather delighted recognition."[16] The emphasis on delight in again seeing Naomi ("pleasant," "delightful," or perhaps here, "sweet"; cf. Prov. 9:17; 2 Sam. 1:23; 23:1)—prepares the reader for the sharp contrast that follows in the name change in verse 20.

Verses 20–22a form the nadir of the Ruth narrative. Here all the negative elements are present in concentrated form. Naomi and Ruth were now physically present in Bethlehem, and Naomi was preparing to live out her days in bitterness. Perhaps the most significant word in this passage is the one that captures the mood of a woman who felt that she had lost everything, including her hope: "Mara" ("bitter"). Naomi's name change is also descriptive of the static quality of the unideal experience in its purest form. Naomi then recounted the reasons for her bitterness. She said, "The Almighty has dealt very bitterly with me" (v. 20). How so? He had allowed her to leave Bethlehem "full" (of love, hope, family, purpose) but had brought her back "empty" (v. 21). Naomi's emptiness and bitterness typify the spiritual "famine" that characterized the nation during the period of the Judges and was pictured in the natural famine that plagued the land. The scene comes to a close with a narrative bracket emphasizing the theme of return: "So Naomi returned [וַתָּשָׁב] and with her Ruth the Moabitess, her daughter-in-law, who returned [הַשָּׁבָה] from the land of Moab" (1:22a).

From this point the narrative builds on the difference between Naomi's perception of "things as they are" and actual truth. As the reader advances through the narrative he becomes increasingly aware of the comfort and assurance that came (to Naomi in particular) from the realization that there is a literal correspondence between what God had said concerning His character[17] and the way He actually demonstrates His character. In the first two scenes of the first act Naomi interpreted God in light of her circumstances. She looked at her situation and said in effect, "This bitterness is the only reality I know or that can be known. This is 'truth,' and by it I will redefine my concept of God."

In other words Naomi interpreted God in light of the phenomena rather than interpreting the phenomena in light of what she knew to be true of God. Naomi was on the verge of discovering that a phenomenological approach to life and to the interpretation of God's promises is both frustrating and inappropriate. Over the course of the next three months (the months between the Feast of Firstfruits, when Israel acknowledged her need of divine provision, and the Feast of Pentecost, when she thankfully acknowledged God's having provided) Naomi learned that there is a direct correspondence between God's revelation concerning Himself and reality.

The Literary Element of Comedy

The comic structure of the Ruth narrative begins to unfold in the first verse of the second act: "And they came to Bethlehem at the beginning of barley harvest" (1:22b). As already noted, the barley harvest had significance for the original readers of this narrative. Until this point, the narrative is preparatory in a sense. Now the story comes into full play. This study concentrates on the comic element itself, which appears between verses 5 and 6 of chapter 4. Boaz had just added a stipulation to the redemption contract he was negotiating with the unnamed kinsman: "On the day you buy the field from the hand of Naomi, you must also acquire Ruth the Moabitess, the widow of the deceased, in order to raise up the name of the deceased on his inheritance" (4:5). In the brief space of two Hebrew verses, the comic element occurred, the decision was made, and the kinsman-redeemer (הַגֹּאֵל) responded, "I cannot redeem it for myself, lest I jeopardize my own inheritance. Redeem it for yourself; you may have my right of redemption, for I cannot redeem it" (v. 6).

Again, as is always the case with the transitional elements, one notes the move from cause (4:5) to effect (v. 6). This "effect" is the apex of the action, the denouement of the narrative, and counterpoint to the nadir of 1:20. Here the audience breathes a collective sigh of relief and celebrates with Boaz in his acquisition of Ruth (and the land, 4:9–10). The blessing of the people in the court (vv. 11–12) is the blessing of the auditors or the reading audience as well. The action then settles into joyful celebration immediately following the recognition recorded in 4:5–6. All that remains for the audience is the brief falling action and the "curtain."

Regarding the structure itself, there is an amazing inversion of traditional archetypal images as they are normally employed in this kind of narrative.[19] Alter has combined a modified version of the Homeric scholarship of Walter Arend[19] and his own understanding of biblical literature[20] in an effort to construct a literary paradigm that reflects the patterns he sees in certain biblical narratives called "type-scenes."[21] While this study disagrees with Alter on some of his character designations (e.g., Alter views Ruth as the protagonist), his insights into the archetypal inversions in the Book of Ruth narrative have a direct bearing on the hermeneutical significance of the relationship between structure and archetypal content. A few of the structural parallels and archetypal dissimilarities between the Ruth narrative and three earlier biblical betrothal type-scenes[22] will now be examined briefly to demonstrate archetypal accommodation to a basically "fixed" comic structure.

First, the reader is confronted with the unusual situation of the protagonist (Naomi) functioning as the pivotal character, but not as the heroine. In two of the three betrothal type-scenes that precede this one, the pivotal character was also the protagonist. The exception among the three is in Genesis 24:10–61, where Abraham's servant functioned as the protagonist, while Rebekah was the pivotal character. Jacob was both protagonist and pivotal character (Gen. 29:1–20), and Moses too functioned as both (Ex. 2:15b–21).

Second, readers are surprised to discover a focus on the heroine (Ruth), rather than on the hero (Boaz). Even though Rebekah was the pivotal character in Genesis 24:10–61, the reader is acutely aware of the importance of the absent (and typically passive) Isaac in the person of his father's servant. There could be little argument about the focus of the other betrothal narratives. Both Moses and Jacob were constantly in the heroic spotlight.

A third surprise for the reader of the Book of Ruth turns on the distinctiveness of the geographical locus of the narrative. From previous narratives the reader would expect the protagonist to travel to a foreign land where he would obtain a bride. Isaac (through his father's servant), Jacob, and Moses all traveled to encounter the women they eventually married. Not so in the Book of Ruth. In this narrative Ruth (a foreigner) left her home to "return" (1:22) to the "foreign" soil of Judah, where she was discovered by the hero, Boaz (thus the thematic emphasis on "return"). But how is it that Ruth could "return" to a place she had never been before? Alter suggests that "we get a progressive sense that [Ruth] is actually coming back to the unknown homeland of her new destiny."[23]

Another small twist on the use of geographical conventions is evident in the location and use of the well. Typically the well was located on foreign soil. In Ruth the well was in Judah, near Bethlehem. Given the inversion of the traditional archetypal roles of men and women in the Ruth narrative, the fact that the men drew the water (2:9) was a consistent action. (Men as a group did not draw water in the other three betrothal narratives: Rebekah drew water for Abraham's servant [Gen. 24:45–46]; Jacob drew water [Gen. 29:10]; and Moses drew water [Ex. 2:17, 19]). As Alter points out, since the three men each chose a wife from among the women who gathered around the well, the reader might have even expected Ruth to have chosen a marriage partner from among the young men.[24]

Boaz's conversation with Ruth is expected, though there was a twist in the content of their discussion. In the previous betrothal narratives much attention was given to the genealogies of both Rebekah and Rachel. Abraham made it clear to his servant that Isaac's wife must come from his relatives and not from the Canaanites (Gen. 24:3–4).[25] Isaac did the same with regard to Jacob's choosing a wife (Gen. 28:1–2). Boaz, however, focused not on Ruth's lineage but on her selfless service to Naomi. His wording in 2:11 is so close to the wording of Genesis 12:1 as to make the connection of Ruth with Abraham unmistakable. Just as Abraham moved from the east to Canaan, so did Ruth. Her exhibition of courage and faithfulness was recommendation enough for Boaz; no genealogy was needed. Thus the physical link to Abraham was downplayed and the spiritual link was reinforced.

Following the drawing of the water and the conversation with the prospective bride, the prospective groom (or his representative, as in Gen. 24) enjoyed a meal, often with his future bride. Abraham's servant enjoyed a meal following his conversation with Rebekah (v. 54). The Jacob narrative lacks reference to a meal after the initial encounter with Rachel, but the Moses narrative includes a meal at the behest of Reuel (Ex. 2:20). Thus the meal in Ruth 2:14 fits the pattern established in preceding narratives.

The archetypal reversals in the Ruth narrative are not to be taken as "the technical manipulation of a literary convention for the sheer pleasure of play with the convention."[26] If the initial readers had grown to expect certain literary conventions (as a result of exposure to earlier type-scenes)[27] by the time of the Ruth narrative, it seems logical to conclude that in an extended betrothal type-scene (such as the Ruth narrative), the significance of the archetypes and their structure would assume an even greater magnitude. If the crucial archetypes are reversed, then even more attention would accrue.

In the Book of Ruth, the basic structure (that which is common to the betrothal type-scene) remains intact. The action progresses from one archetype to the next as expected. The surprises, therefore, do not come in the structure but in the archetypal inversions. While the significance of the archetypal inversions is dramatic enough in light of the already established type-scenes, it is heightened even further when seen against the contrasting structures of the two preceding narratives in the Book of Judges.[28]

Thus the narrative of Ruth stands out. It is archetypally unique to the traditional betrothal type-scene, and it is structurally unique to the preceding narratives (though it maintains the structural conventions associated with romantic comedy). The comic structure of Ruth is established; however, while the structure is consistent, the archetypes within that structure are fluid. The careful interpreter cannot, therefore, assume (and may certainly not impose) a structure based on archetypal content alone. An exegetically determined structure will reveal the significance of archetypes that are a part of that structure, but the archetypes must not be used (in any determinative sense) to reveal structure, since the same archetype can be employed legitimately in a variety of structural contexts.

The Literary Element of Romance

One discovers the romantic element in the Book of Ruth in the changes recorded in 4:13–22. The joy of the birth[29] of a son to Ruth and Boaz is immediate. The sense of fullness has returned. She who had been barren was made fruitful just as the land was emerging from a famine to yield its full harvest, which also coincided with the (unheralded) celebration of divine provision at the Feast of Pentecost. But this joy is heightened in the following verses when the reader is informed that Ruth and Boaz were in the direct line of David the king (vv. 17, 22).

As noted in the discussion of Boaz's first conversation with Ruth, Boaz downplayed Ruth's foreign ancestry. Why is attention suddenly given to her progeny in 4:17 and in 4:18–22? One begins to understand the answer to this question by considering the betrothal narrative of Genesis 24. There Abraham demanded that Isaac's prospective wife be a relative from his land and that she be brought to his son in Canaan. Genesis 24:7 states the reason for his demand: "The Lord, the God of heaven . . . took me from my father's house and from the land of my birth, and . . . spoke to me, and . . . swore to me, saying, 'To your descendants I will give this land.'" Abraham based his directive to his servant on God's promise of the land as stated in the Abrahamic Covenant (12:7; 13:15; 15:18).

Intermarriage with the pagan Canaanites would contaminate the spiritual purity of the Abrahamic line, which in turn would jeopardize the fulfillment of the promise. Also since the Lord had brought Abraham out of Mesopotamia to the land of promise, he did not want Isaac to live in the land that held no divine promise of inheritance (Gen. 24:6–7). Abraham wanted to keep the marriage in the family and in the land.

Of particular interest is Abraham's desire to maintain racial purity. The Ruth narrative closes on a strong romantic note with a genealogy of the chief names that will be associated with the new "society" (the monarchy) that emerged (by the time of writing) out of the dark period of the Judges. The last name—David— mentioned in the short list of Ruth 4:17 is the same name that occurs last in the longer list in verses 18–22. Thus David is seen to be the product of the union of an Israelite (Boaz) with a foreigner (Ruth). What Abraham feared would disallow the inheritance was used by God to secure it.[30] But the irony does not stop there. To appreciate the impact this concluding genealogy must have had on the original readers, it is necessary to look more closely at the list in verses 18–22.

The lineage that leads to David began with Perez, the illegitimate son of Judah and Tamar (Gen. 38:29). Tamar was almost certainly a Canaanite who, like Ruth, married into the covenant community (v. 6). Posing as a prostitute (v. 14), she seduced Judah because he had not fulfilled his levirate responsibility to her. The focus on levirate responsibility is clear in Ruth. Equally clear is the contrast between "the-end-justifies-the-means" attitude of Tamar and the purity of Ruth, as well as the lechery of Judah over against the dignity and self-control of Boaz. The author prepared his audience for a heightened sense of contrast between these two pairs in the way he recorded the night meeting of Ruth and Boaz (Ruth 3).

The provocative imagery in Ruth 3 combines with the reference to Perez in 4:18 to reinforce not only the contrast between Judah/ Tamar and Ruth/Boaz, but also to widen the gulf between the expectations of man and the ways of the Lord. Who would have expected the Lord to include the illegitimate product of a sinful union of a Jew and an ostensibly Canaanite prostitute in the messianic line? The historical parallels actually serve to heighten the contrasts.

Matthew 1:5 states that Salmon (Ruth 4:21) was the husband of Rahab (presumably the Canaanite prostitute of Josh. 2:1). Rahab was probably the "mother" of Boaz in the sense of being his ancestress, since she lived in Joshua's day, two hundred or three hundred years before Ruth and Boaz.[31] This connection with Rahab is especially interesting in light of the Judah/Tamar story. While Rahab was indeed a prostitute, the Joshua narrative emphasized her courageous service to the spies and her inclusion within the covenant community (Josh. 6:25; cf. Heb. 11:31). Her character was more nobly presented than that of the scheming Tamar. Again the reader is forced to admit that he would probably not have picked either Rahab or her descendant Boaz as participants in the covenant promises, much less as contributors to the messianic line.[32]

In establishing the spiritual link between Ruth and Abraham (Ruth 2:11) and the physical link from Perez through Ruth to David (4:18–22), the author reinforced the concept that one's physical relationship to the head of the Jewish nation was not the ultimate criterion for the Lord's fulfilling His covenant promises. Neither does one's spiritual relationship with the Lord depend on physical connection with Abraham. Ruth, Rahab, and even Tamar entered the spiritual (and for them the physical) blessings of covenant community by an act of faith. The ideal experience, the idyllic romance into which Ruth resolves, turns out to be the product not of human engineering and manipulation but of simple faith in the Architect of history. The curtain comes down on a joyful new society, a society that began with the cry of new life and that held the promise of continued blessing in the person of David, Israel's greatest king.

Conclusion

What benefit does the definition of plot structure afford the interpreter of the text? Once the reader discovers the type of structure(s) of the narrative, and the locus of the defining element(s) in those structures, then he can more accurately reflect on the dynamic movement (or development) of the narrative from one level to the next and then to its climax and denouement. This kind of literary analysis offers several practical benefits to the interpreter: (1) It reinforces and adds dimension to correct exegesis. (2) It highlights the artistry of the writer, and thereby the audience's appreciation for the aesthetic beauty of God's inspired text. (3) It prevents the interpreter's placing an improper emphasis on what may be only incidental to the development of the author's message. (4) It exalts the Lord by showing that He is the Master of history. (5) Once the structure is discovered[33] and is shown to be theologically consonant with the rest of Scripture, that structure becomes a source of truth in and of itself. That is to say, the reader can discover truth not only through structure, but also in structure.

Plot structures, as immutable forms, provide more than a grid through which the reader may filter narrative. They offer more than a series of predetermined literary pegs on which one may hang exegetical data in an effort to see some abstruse design. Rather, the design inherent in the structures is meaningful as a structure in that context.[34] In other words any of the plot structures in the Book of Ruth, or even the monomythic structure of the narrative as a whole may, when taken in context, yield a different truth from the same structure in a different context. All comedies do not teach the same lesson. Otherwise the reader would need only one in the Bible.

One of the primary lessons learned from the comic structure of the Ruth narrative is that "appearances are often deceiving." Very little in this narrative unfolded as either the audience or the characters involved in the action would have guessed initially. Out of this constant twisting and turning of conventional literary patterns one also learns that the Lord is faithful to His covenant promises, that He is in control of even the most mundane affairs of life, and that He is free to choose whomever He desires as the object of His gracious provision. He is not bound by man's finite understanding of His ways and will always act consistently with His character.

But all of this means nothing unless the interpreter clings (as Ruth clung to Naomi) to a correspondence view of truth. Unless the interpreter comes to the same realization that Naomi did in 2:20, namely, that Yahweh is in reality the covenant-keeping God that His name suggests Him to be, then his studies will ultimately prove as fruitless and barren as the Judean desert during the famine of Ruth 1. These highly poetic narratives are no less true for their beauty. In fact the events recorded in such high style reveal more accurately God's artistic design in history than would a dry and unliterary reporting of the events. The critic's hesitancy to embrace the events as historic reveal more about his pedestrian view of God than about any professed historical objectivity.

The truth revealed in plot structure will always enhance exegesis; it will never detract from it. Hopefully this brief study on plot structure in Ruth helps reveal the harmony of God's design of all history (as revealed in His inerrant Word), the artful symmetry of His working in human lives, and the absolute trustworthiness of His Person.

CHAPTER 6

The Purpose of 1 and 2 Chronicles

Jeffrey L. Townsend

Most works on 1 and 2 Chronicles emphasize the themes but not the purpose of this most sweeping of all historical perspectives in Scripture. The reason is given by Freedman: "It is not easy to answer the basic question: What was the underlying intention or primary objective of the Chronicler in compiling his work? At the same time it is not difficult to isolate the major themes which run through the history."[1]

This study seeks to work with the major themes of 1 and 2 Chronicles and other data to synthesize and support a purpose statement that subsumes the various particulars of 1 and 2 Chronicles. A number of factors must be considered, such as date, authorship, audience, literary genre, and the author's selection and arrangement of the material.

Analysis of Various Factors in Chronicles

DATE AND AUTHORSHIP

According to internal evidence Chronicles was written following the decree of Cyrus in 538 B.C. (2 Chron. 36:22–23) and the return under Zerubbabel in 537 B.C. (1 Chron. 9). In addition the mention of Zerubbabel's grandsons (cf. 1 Chron. 3:19–21[2]) dictates a date around 500 B.C. as the earliest possible time of composition.[3]

Many, including the Jewish Talmud (*Baba Bathra* 15a), hold that Ezra was the author of Chronicles and date the book around 450 B.C. shortly after his return to Jerusalem. Though appealing evidence can be gathered to support Ezra's authorship of Chronicles,[4] the proof is not airtight. In fact Harrison feels that "attempts to identify the Chronicler with Ezra appear inadvisable because of significant differences in style, historical and theological perspective, the treatment of source material, and the basic metaphysic of history as exhibited in the two compositions."[5]

Since with present knowledge the authorship of 1 and 2 Chronicles cannot be determined with certainty, the author is referred to as "the chronicler."

Although 1 and 2 Chronicles have been dated as late as the Maccabean period,[6] manuscript evidence from Qumran points to a date as early as around 400 B.C.[7] Thus it is best to conclude that the Chronicles were written (perhaps by Ezra) sometime during the century following the rebuilding of the temple (i.e., 500–400 B.C.).[8]

AUDIENCE AND SETTING

Who were the readers the chronicler had in mind as he wrote his account, and what factors helped shape their lives and outlook? According to internal evidence the chronicler was writing for all the returned remnant. Especially significant in this regard is the chronicler's repeated use of phrases such as "all the house of Israel" and "all the tribes of Israel." Over 40 times he employed the term "all Israel." Clearly the chronicler was appealing to (and for) a new united Israel.

While his appeal is broad, the chronicler's focus is certainly on Jerusalem and the temple. The returned inhabitants of the Jewish capital are specified in 1 Chronicles 9, and emphasis on the temple is found throughout Chronicles. The chronicler's audience then was the returned remnant which had its focal point at the temple in Jerusalem.

What was life like for the repatriates of the Exile? In the postexilic historical and prophetic books, life after the Exile is presented as a mixture of terror and celebration (Ezra 3:3–4), tears and triumph (3:12), fear and frustration (4:4–5), joy and encouragement (6:22), unfaithfulness and confession (10:10–11). It was an unstable time. All that remained of the once-powerful empire of David and Solomon was the province of Judah governed by an appointee of the Persian king. There was no Davidic king on the throne and though the temple had been rebuilt, there was no glory. It was enough to make old men cry.

> By anyone's standards, the fifth century was hardly a golden age for the people of God. Their future as a kingdom and a distinct people of God, in fact, seemed bleaker at that moment than perhaps ever before. To make matters worse, it followed on the heels of the excitement of the return from exile and the anticipation of the coming messianic kingdom that accompanied the return.[9]

LITERARY GENRE

Wellhausen claimed that the chronicler tampered with his sources, selecting, omitting, modifying, and adding in order to bend the story to his own views. Hence it has been customary for those who follow Wellhausen's negative assessment to designate 1 and 2 Chronicles as midrash.[10] Two factors militate strongly against this view. First, since Wellhausen's day textual evidence (especially from Qumran) has indicated that the chronicler employed a text of Samuel and 1 Kings more in line with the Septuagint than with the Masoretic text.[11] Thus many of the divergences of Chronicles from Samuel and 1 Kings have a textual rather than a midrashic basis.

Second, it is inconceivable that the chronicler attempted a whitewash or a cover-up in that he constantly assumed his readers were aware of the Samuel-Kings history. For example the mention of the Prophet Ahijah the Shilonite in 2 Chronicles 10:15 assumes the reader is aware of the rebellion in 1 Kings 11:26–29, which came as God's punishment of Solomon's disobedience. In addition the chronicler repeatedly referred his readers to other historical records for further information (cf. 1 Chron. 29:29; 2 Chron. 9:29; etc.).

Clearly the chronicler was not attempting to deny or cover up the historical record. Rather, in the manner typical of historical narrative, he arranged his material from various sources to make a point without denying other facts and lessons developed in Samuel and Kings.

Thus the literary genre of Chronicles is properly classified as historical narrative,[12] the goal of which is well stated by Sailhamer: "Though its concern is to recount past deeds and events, the writers of historical narrative are never interested merely in what happened. Their interest in the past stems from the significance those past events have for the present and future."[13]

ARRANGEMENT OF MATERIAL

Unquestionably the chronicler's selection and arrangement of historical material are keys to his purpose in writing. Therefore an analysis of the contents of Chronicles is necessary for determining a synthesis of the chronicler's purpose.

Structure of Chronicles. A comparison of the structure of Chronicles with that of Samuel-Kings (see figure 1) reveals a general agreement and several unique details in Chronicles. First, the starting point of the chronicler was different. His concern was genealogical. Second, the chronicler's focus was obviously on the Davidic line (especially David and Solomon). He mentioned Saul only as an introduction to David, and he excluded the accounts of the illegitimate kings of the Northern Kingdom. Third, Chronicles ends differently, indicating the unique postexilic perspective and emphasis of the chronicler.

Introduction to the Monarchy	The Reign of Saul	The Reign of David	The Reign of Solomon	The Divided Kingdom	The Surviving Kingdom	The Restoration
1 Sam. 1–7 (Judgeship of Samuel)	1 Sam. 8–31	2 Sam. 1–24	1 Kings 1–11	1 Kings 12– 2 Kings 17 (Judah and Israel)	2 Kings 18–25	
1 Chron. 1–9 (Genealogies)	1 Chron. 10	1 Chron. 11–29	2 Chron. 1–9	2 Chron. 10–31 (Judah only)	2 Chron. 32:1–36:21	2 Chron. 36:22–23

Figure 1
Comparative Structure of Samuel/Kings and Chronicles

Omissions in Chronicles.[14] The following is a sampling of the material in Samuel-Kings that is omitted by the chronicler: Samuel (1 Sam. 1–7); Saul's reign (1 Sam. 8–15); David's exile (1 Sam. 16–30); David's conflict with Abner and Ishbosheth (2 Sam. 1–4); David's adultery and murder (2 Sam. 11–12); Absalom's rebellion (2 Sam. 13–20); Adonijah's struggle for the throne (1 Kings 1–2); Solomon's marriage to Pharaoh's daughter (1 Kings 3); Solomon's royal palace (1 Kings 7); Solomon's wives and enemies (1 Kings 11); Northern Kingdom (1 Kings 12–2 Kings 17); Abijah's sinful character (1 Kings 15:3–5); Jehoshaphat's campaign with Jehoram (2 Kings 3); Hezekiah's tribute to Sennacherib (2 Kings 18:7–8, 13–16); Jehoahaz's evil character (2 Kings 23:32); Jehoiakim's rebellion and enemies (2 Kings 23:35; 24:1–4); siege of Jerusalem and Zedekiah's captivity (2 Kings 25:1–7, 18–21); Gedaliah's appointment and death (2 Kings 25:12, 23–26); Jehoiachin's release (2 Kings 25:27–30). Most of the omitted material is either derogatory to or in opposition to the Davidic line. The chronicler's burden was to present the endurance of the Davidic line, in spite of its faults.

Additions in Chronicles.[15] Material in Chronicles not found in Samuel-Kings includes the following: genealogies (1 Chron. 1–9); David's warriors (1 Chron. 12:23–40); details of the return of the ark (1 Chron. 13:1–5; 15–16); details of David's sinful census (1 Chron. 21); David's arrangements for the temple (1 Chron. 22); David's organization of temple and civil workers (1 Chron. 23–27); assembly at Solomon's accession (1 Chron. 28–29); Levites' loyalty to Rehoboam (2 Chron. 11:13–17); Rehoboam's fortifications and family (2 Chron. 11:5–12, 18–23); Asa's 10 years of peace, covenant renewal, and sin (2 Chron. 14:1; 15:1–7, 9–15, 19; 16:7–10); Jehoshaphat's fortifications, reforms, commissioning of Levites to teach, warning by Jehu, reforms, prayer, and deliverance from Moab (2 Chron. 17:1–18:1; 19–20); Jehoram's killing of his brothers, invasions, and illness (2 Chron. 21:2–4, 12–18); Jehoiada's death (2 Chron. 24:15–16); Joash's sins (2 Chron. 24:3, 17–19); Zechariah's stoning (2 Chron. 24:20–22); Hazael's defeat of Judah (2 Chron. 24:23–24); Amaziah's hiring of soldiers and sin (2 Chron. 25:5–10, 14–16); Uzziah's army and building program (2 Chron. 26:6–15); Jotham's defeat of the Ammonites (2 Chron. 27:5–6); Ahaz's punishment by Edomites and Philistines (2 Chron. 28:17–19); Hezekiah's cleansing and consecration of the temple, reviving of Passover, and other reforms, wealth and building of defences against Sennacherib (2 Chron. 29:3–31:21; 32:1–8, 23, 27–30); Manasseh's captivity, repentance, and return (2 Chron. 33:11–17); Josiah's early reforms (2 Chron. 34:3–7); Cyrus's decree (2 Chron. 36:22–23).

Most of these additions relate to the establishment of temple worship and/or the evaluation of the Davidic line. Obviously the chronicler's message revolves around these two great themes. It is significant that the chronicler began his history with David and ended with the temple.

SUMMARY

This section has briefly analyzed various elements in 1 and 2 Chronicles based on internal and external evidence. As a result the parameters of the purpose of 1 and 2 Chronicles may be summarized as follows. The purpose of Chronicles must fit with the setting of the unsettled restoration community during the century following the rebuilding of the temple, must correspond with the nature of historical narrative which seeks to present the significance of the past for the present and future, and must account for the structural and thematic dual emphasis on the enduring Davidic line and temple.

Synthesis of the Purpose of Chronicles

A purpose statement for Chronicles is now presented based on the foregoing analysis of various elements in Chronicles. This purpose statement is then related to each major section of Chronicles by means of an annotated synthetic outline.

PURPOSE STATEMENT

A purpose statement for a Bible book states both an effective purpose (the effect the author desires to have on his readers: "to. . .") and an expressive means (the means by which the author seeks to bring about the desired effect: "by . . .").[16] The purpose of Chronicles may be stated as follows: To rally the returned remnant to hopeful temple worship (effective purpose) by demonstrating their link with the enduring Davidic promises (expressive means).

"To rally" relates to the beleaguered physical and spiritual status of the repatriates as already mentioned in the analysis of the setting of the book (cf. Ezra 3:3; 4:4–5; 10:6; Neh. 1:4; 4–6; Hag. 1:2; 2:3; Zech. 1:4; 8:9; Mal. 1:6). The chronicler sought to motivate the remnant who had no king and whose temple was so much less glorious than Solomon's temple. Though released from exile, the people were still discouraged, and the chronicler wrote to encourage them.

The words "hopeful temple worship" in the purpose statement relate to the anticipated fulfillment of "the enduring Davidic promises" (i.e., the promises in the Davidic Covenant). The chronicler's method of motivating was messianic. He referred to the Davidic Covenant established in the past to motivate his present audience about their future.

> The Chronicler sets himself to the task of taking the data of redemptive history and organizing them in such a way as to answer the burning theological question of the post-exilic community. The basic question that must be answered if the faith of the restoration community is to survive is the question of continuity with the past: "After judgment and the imposition of the covenant sanctions in the exile, is God still interested in us? What meaning have the promises of God to David and to Jerusalem when we have no king and the city has been destroyed?" In answering this question the Chronicler [refers to] the David and Solomon of his messianic expectations.[17]

The dual emphasis on the temple and on David's line in Chronicles can be properly understood only when David's line is seen in connection with the temple because of the covenant. The key that unlocks Chronicles is the Davidic Covenant, which the chronicler referred to no fewer than seven times (1 Chron. 17:11–14; 22:8–13; 28:6–7; 2 Chron. 6:8–9, 16; 7:17–18; 13:5; 21:7). The Davidic Covenant connects David's line and the temple, since in the covenant it is David's descendant who will build a house for Yahweh (1 Chron. 17:11–12; 22:9–10; 28:6; 2 Chron. 6:9).

Though Solomon is specifically named as the immediate (model) descendant (1 Chron. 22:9; 28:6), the terms of the covenant point to the ultimate Son in relation to the Father (17:13; 22:10; 28:6) whose kingdom will be established forever (17:14). The Son will fulfill the one conditional aspect of the unconditional covenant, which is obedience (22:13; 28:7).[18] It is to this messianic temple-builder (cf. Ps. 69:9; John 2:17; Ezek. 40–48) that the chronicler desired to direct the hopes of the returned remnant. He did this by demonstrating that the Davidic promises were still valid for the restoration community. As Harton puts it, "First and Second Chronicles were designed to instill hope in God's covenant faithfulness in the hearts of some of the restored exiles who were discouraged."[19] How the chronicler did that is now seen in the following discussion of the synthetic outline.

ANNOTATED SYNTHETIC OUTLINE

The purpose of a synthetic outline is to elaborate on the expressive means of the purpose statement. This enables one to relate the parts of a book to the book's effective purpose. As stated earlier the chronicler sought to demonstrate the returned remnant's link with the enduring Davidic promises. This he did by showing the remnant's genealogical link with David and the priestly line (1 Chron. 1–9), by showing that David's line was established by promises that relate to the temple (1 Chron. 10–29), by presenting Solomon as the model Davidic temple-builder (2 Chron. 1–9), by recounting God's faithfulness to the Davidic promises throughout the reigns of his sons (2 Chron. 10:1–36:21), and by presenting Cyrus's decree as Yahweh's provision for the restoration of the temple (and therefore hope in the Davidic promises; 2 Chron. 36:22–23). Each of these five elements in the purpose statement will now be discussed.

The remnant was linked genealogically with David and the priestly line (1 Chron. 1–9). The issue of legitimate linkage to the covenant promises was a crucial question for the postexilic community. Were God's promises, especially the Davidic promises concerning the kingdom, still valid after the Exile? In the first nine chapters of his work the chronicler met this question directly by showing the remnant their roots. Since the chronicler's concern centered on the continuing Davidic line and temple, the genealogies of David and Levi are more detailed than are other genealogies.[20] The Davidic line is actually traced into the postexilic era. The clear implication is that the Davidic promises are still in effect in spite of the captivity. Though without a king, the remnant was not without the kingly line. Though the restoration temple was without glory, the remnant was not without the priestly line in preparation for future glories. In other words the stage was set for the Son of David. So the remnant should respond in hopeful worship at the temple in Jerusalem.

The genealogies of the 12 tribes are traced in 1 Chronicles 4–8.[21] Benjamin's tribe is emphasized in chapter 8 because it was the only tribe other than that of Judah to remain loyal to the Davidic line. Benjamin is also the territorial location of Jerusalem, the hub of postexilic activity.

Chapter 9 applies the genealogical roots to real life in postexilic Jerusalem. Once again the emphasis is on those related to the temple: the priests (9:10–13), Levites (9:14–16), and temple servants (9:17–34).

The message of 1 Chronicles 1–9 is expressed well by Harton: "Genealogical records for all Israel have been preserved through the exile, and the people have the ability to trace their roots back through their particular tribe to Abraham himself. . . . The promise to Abraham and the promise to David [which involves the temple] continues in effect for the chosen blood line."[22] In these chapters the chronicler has successfully linked the returned exiles with their kingly and priestly heritage.

David's line was established by promises that relate to the temple (1 Chron. 10–29). Twenty chapters, the largest segment of Chronicles, are devoted to David. Because this is the heart of the chronicler's argument, he took nearly a third of his work to detail it. Having established the remnant's genealogical link with the Davidic and priestly lines, he focused on the groundwork of the Davidic promises. His design was to show how the kingly and priestly concerns were connected in David. David is then seen as a model for the postexilic community as they look forward to One like David.

The history of David begins with Saul's death as a result of disobedience (1 Chron. 10:13) and the divine appointment of David as king (11:2). Without mentioning David's struggle in 2 Samuel 1–4, the chronicler immediately presented David as having moved to establish worship in Jerusalem by capturing the city and bringing the ark to the city (1 Chron. 11:4–16:43). In doing this David was blessed in many ways (11:10–12:40; 14). Thus David was set forth as a model king; he became the standard by which other kings of Judah could be measured.

The Davidic Covenant in 1 Chronicles 17 (echoed in chaps. 22 and 28) is the heart of Chronicles because it established David's kingly line by promises (17:11–14) that relate to the temple and priestly concerns, thus linking the two great themes of Chronicles. Though Solomon, not David, was to build the temple, a large section (1 Chron. 22–27) is devoted to David's preparations for the construction of and future worship at the temple. At the same time the detracting incidents of 2 Samuel 11–20 are omitted. Even David's sinful census in 1 Chronicles 21 eventuated in the selection of the temple site. The chronicler presented David as one whose zeal for Yahweh's house was great, in anticipation of the Greater David (cf. Ps. 69:9; John 2:17). Chronicles was saying, in essence, "when Messiah comes, He will come like the priestly King David. So look at David's preoccupation with the prospect of the fulfillment of the covenant promises." For the remnant whose hope had waned during the postexilic period, this emphasis would have brought encouragement and hope.

The final two chapters of the David narrative (1 Chron. 28–29) provide the basis for evaluating the remainder of 1 and 2 Chronicles. On the one hand, as David addressed all the officials of Israel, there stood before him in the person of his son Solomon the very embodiment of God's faithfulness to His promise. In stating that David died and Solomon began to reign (1 Chron. 29:28), the chronicler provided a fulfillment motif that he carried through his record of the rest of the kings of Judah, indicating God's faithfulness to the Davidic Covenant.

On the other hand Solomon's kingdom would be established only if he obeyed (1 Chron. 28:7). Only then would the Davidic king prosper on the throne (22:13). Of course Solomon did prosper as long as he obeyed. But even Solomon in all his wisdom and glory ultimately failed to remain obedient to God. So Solomon died. The message echoes clearly throughout the rest of Chronicles: another must come. Then as the readers note that each son of David died and a new son of David reigned, they are reminded indirectly of the Son of David who would come and who would obey and will build a glorious temple. Thus there was hope and the remnant was to hope in His coming.

Solomon was presented as the model Davidic temple-builder (2 Chron. 1–9). In the chronicler's day the rebuilt temple was the focal point of Israel's faith. But it was not the only link with past glories. The remnant was also linked initially by lineage to the Davidic and priestly lines (1 Chron. 1–9). In the next section (1 Chron. 10–29) the author of Chronicles pointed out the vital connection between king and temple in the messianic hope of the nation. Now the chronicler began a historical survey of the descendants of David up to the time of the Babylonian Capitivity. "He in effect asks: How did the promise to David fare? Did the promised seed come? Was God's promise [of a priestly, temple-building King who would reign forever] fulfilled?"[23]

Solomon is the first king to be considered and is given more than twice as much space as any other. This is because the chronicler desired to point out that Solomon modeled the ultimate, Davidic temple-builder. Solomon was wise and prosperous (2 Chron. 1; 8–9), he built and dedicated the glorious temple (chap. 2–7), and he received the wealth of the Gentiles who sought his wisdom (chap. 9; cf. Hag. 2:7; Isa. 2:3). Similarly David's later Descendant, the Messiah, is wise, will build a glorious temple, and will receive the wealth of the nations. The remnant should set their hope on this Promised One.

The chronicler assumed his initial readers knew of (1 Kings 1–4; 11) or could find out about (2 Chron. 9:29) the negative aspects of Solomon's history. Solomon's disobedience accounts for his death in 2 Chronicles 9:31. In the final analysis he was not the promised Son who would reign forever. However, these nine chapters (2 Chron. 1–9) function to show the remnant, by means of Solomon's genuine greatness, something of what the ultimate Davidic temple-builder will be like.

God's faithfulness to the Davidic promises is seen throughout the reigns of his sons (2 Chron. 10:1–36:21). With Solomon, the chronicler established a pattern that he followed throughout his record of all the kings of Judah. As any particular king obeyed (especially with regard for the temple, the most immediate element of the promises for the postexilic remnant), he prospered and so embodied the blessings of the Davidic Covenant. As any king disobeyed, he was disciplined and eventually died, thus indicating that he was not the ultimate Seed of David. This pattern is often referred to as the retributive method of the chronicler. The chronicler used retribution to evaluate the kings of Judah in relation to their fulfillment (or lack of fulfillment) of the Davidic promises.

Asa (2 Chron. 14–16) is a good example of the chronicler's retributive method. The account in 1 Kings 15 is devoid of retributive comment. Asa is presented as one of the better kings of Judah (though not without fault; 1 Kings 15:14, 18–19) in a span of 16 verses. His foot disease is mentioned in verse 23, but it is not related to his death referred to in verse 24.

The structure of the account in 2 Chronicles 14–16 is quite different.[24] The chronicler expanded his account to 48 verses and divided Asa's reign into chronological periods of obedience/ blessing and disobedience/discipline.

In chapters 14 and 15 Asa is seen as a model of Davidic covenantal blessing. In Asa's accession to the throne (14:1) Yahweh was faithful to His covenant with David's line. Asa was a man of rest like Solomon, the model temple builder (14:6; cf. 1 Chron. 22:9–10). Asa removed false worship (2 Chron. 14:2–5; 15:8a) and reestablished true worship (15:8b–19), thus showing Davidic zeal for genuine temple worship.

Perhaps Asa, the readers would have thought, is the ultimate Son promised to David. But in chapter 16 the chronicler showed that this was not the case. In the 36th year of Asa's reign things changed. Asa no longer sought Yahweh's help in battle (16:2–3; cf. 14:11) and so he was disciplined with loss of peace (16:9). When disease struck his feet, he sought help from physicians rather than from Yahweh (16:12) and "so Asa slept" (16:13).

Thus the chronicler showed that though Yahweh was faithful to the Davidic Covenant in Asa's reign, Asa was not the ultimate King of promise because of his disobedience. In like manner the chronicler dealt with each king of Judah to give the remnant a basis for hope in the coming of the One who would obey.

The chronicler's account shows that each king proved not to be the Promised One. Eventually "the wrath of the Lord arose against

His people, until there was no remedy. Therefore He brought up against them the king of the Chaldeans" (2 Chron. 36:16–17). Finally the sanctions of the Mosaic Covenant (Deut. 28–30) were imposed. Yahweh had been faithful to the enduring Davidic promises even though David's sons were unfaithful to Him, for which He removed them from the throne.

Cyrus's decree was Yahweh's provision for the restoration of the temple (and therefore hope in the Davidic promises; 2 Chron. 36:22–23). The chronicler did not end his account with the Exile lest questions be raised about the faithfulness of Yahweh to His promises. Instead the chronicler showed that it was Yahweh who moved Cyrus to decree the rebuilding of the temple. In His loyal love God took the initiative to restore His people under His covenant promises. "Now that Cyrus had decreed the rebuilding of the temple (36:22–23), here was prima facie evidence that God had not annulled His covenant with Israel nor the levitical system revealed at Sinai."[25]

With the covenant intact and the temple decreed, the readers are left to expect the One who will fulfill the abiding promise of a priestly Son of David to prosper on the throne and attend to the upbuilding of Yahweh's house eternally. The Davidic promises are yet valid for the returned remnant of the Exile. Therefore there is solid reason for hopeful temple worship in anticipation of the arrival of the Promised One in His temple (cf. Simeon in Luke 2).

OTHER PURPOSE STATEMENTS

The current status of opinion on the purpose of Chronicles is summarized well by Dillard:

> There is considerable debate about the Chronicler's messianism; it centers around the question of the relationship of the Davidic dynasty to the cultic establishment. Some scholars see no messianic expectation in Chronicles, finding that the post-exilic community with its rebuilt temple were [sic] treated as a fulfillment of David's expectations; others see messianism as important to varying degrees.[26]

Since the relationship of the Davidic line to the temple is seen in the chronicler's emphasis on the Davidic Covenant, Chronicles is strongly messianic in its message. Others who see a strongly messianic purpose based on the chronicler's development of the Davidic Covenant include Freedman,[27] Saebo,[28] and Sailhamer.[29]

Another approach with less messianic and more cultic emphasis is that of Johnson, who says the purpose of Chronicles is "to encourage faithful temple worship among the returned remnant by chronicling faithful worship of David's line which enjoyed God's blessing."[30] Similar in viewpoint are Newsome[31] and Zuck.[32] Actually the cultic and messianic views are quite similar. The messianic view, however, is distinctive in that the chronicler's development of the Davidic Covenant is the determining factor for the purpose of Chronicles. This moves the focus one step beyond David and the temple to the future David and temple.

Conclusion

The aim of this study has been to present and defend from the text a purpose statement for 1 and 2 Chronicles. The method of the study was to derive parameters of purpose based on the date, authorship, audience, literary genre, and the selection and arrangement of material. These parameters were then used to synthesize a purpose statement for Chronicles. The statement was verified by a consideration of the argument of Chronicles that related each of the major portions of the book to the purpose statement.

Based on this study the conclusion was reached that Chronicles has a decidedly messianic focus. The chronicler's purpose was to show the returned remnant the vitality of hope they ought to have in the ultimate fulfillment of the Davidic Covenant. The warp and woof of his argument is Yahweh's faithfulness to the Davidic promise of an obedient Son to build the temple. His message to the returned remnant gathered around the rebuilt temple in Jerusalem could be stated as follows: The heritage of the abiding Davidic promises provides motivation for hopeful temple worship by the returned remnant. The message is clear. The Davidic king is coming to His temple; therefore the remnant should look for Him as they worship.

CHAPTER 7

The Wife of Noble Character in Proverbs 31:10–31

Tom R. Hawkins

Proverbs 31:10–31, the closing pericope of the Book of Proverbs, beautifully describes and praises a woman who is said to be of "noble character" (NIV). However, interpreters differ on how to understand this passage. Does the description refer to a wife and mother who may have actually lived, or is the passage describing qualities every woman should aspire to attain, or is the "noble wife" a personification of wisdom, or is she the epitome of wisdom?

The Noble Wife as a Role Model

Proverbs 31:10–31 displays numerous qualities of the noble wife (אֵשֶׁת־חַיִל), including trustworthiness, resourcefulness, foresight, industriousness, generosity, domestic and business skills, and fear of Yahweh. Her husband's praise at the conclusion of the poem includes his evaluation that she surpassed all her contemporaries, even others who were described as "noble" (חַיִל, v. 29). This means that the main character of the poem is presented in superlative terms regarding her extraordinary character.

While some have elevated her to a type of Christ or the Holy Spirit, von Hoffmann views her as a diligent housewife.[1] He is correct in not ascribing to her any "supernatural" status. However, his limiting her to being *only* a housewife does not adequately explicate either the immediate passage or its place in the Book of Proverbs. She is at least a "role model" and in fact seems to be more, as will be shown.

Because the poem begins with a rhetorical question about finding a wife, some argue that the poem was written as a "paradigm for a prospective bride."[2] Crook goes even further and sees it as "a memorandum from a school answering to the needs of young women who will shortly be assuming positions of wealth and importance in their communities."[3] No evidence has been found, however, that such a school ever existed. Whybray takes a third option and says the passage was written from a man's viewpoint and hence is "a handbook for prospective bridegrooms."[4]

Some of these hypotheses rest on or would be strengthened by the assumption that the poem is related in some way to Proverbs 31:1–9. This connection would logically make the woman of this poem the ideal wife sought by Lemuel. It must be admitted, however, that Proverbs 31 gives no indication that Lemuel did seek or was commanded to seek such a wife. Further there is no indication that the אֵשֶׁת־חַיִל ("wife of noble character") was a queen or was to become a queen (31:1). Also the husband of Proverbs 31:11, 23, 28 is a nobleman or elder, not a king. In any case it seems clear, as Murphy suggests, that the poem "holds out an ideal which Israelite society held up for the woman herself."[5]

The word חַיִל has a number of shades of meaning, including, among others, physical strength (Num. 24:18), wealth (Job 20:15, perhaps suggesting wealth attained by one's strength or ability), and integrity or strength of character (Gen. 47:6; Ex. 18:21, 25).[6] But what does it convey when used of women in Ruth 3:11; Proverbs 12:4; and 31:10, 29?

The van der Sluises assert that in view of the occurrence of חַיִל in Proverbs 12:4,[7] this word should not "be diluted" by omitting the idea of "strength" just because it is used with the word for "woman" (אִשָּׁה). For example they argue that the only woman outside Proverbs of whom the word חַיִל is used is Ruth (Ruth 3:11), whom Boaz acknowledged as "a woman of strength who knew how to achieve the object she pursued. She is a woman who purposefully, forcefully knew how to shape the circumstances to suit her needs."[8]

Furthermore they claim that the woman of Proverbs 31:10–31 is viewed in her role "as a woman of strength, a woman with might; and somewhat of that strong, self-assured and purposeful action sounds throughout the whole song."[9] They see this impression confirmed by others mentioned in the poem, such as her husband and children, who focus on her. She is the one whose actions are characterized by such words as "rewards, searches, brings, makes, arises, gives, thinks, takes, plants, girds, strengthens, tastes, stretches out, understands, spreads out, is not afraid, makes, sells, gives, opens, considers, eats, excels."[10] They find additional evidence of her strength in the descriptions in verses 17 and 19–20, all of which radiate "strength" and "self-assurance" and indicate an almost "aggressive" approach to life.[11] While the meaning of חַיִל is broader than "strength" alone, the point is well taken that physical strength and strength of character are both evident in the poem and should not be omitted from an understanding of the אֵשֶׁת־חַיִל.

The strength of her character and her capabilities are in fact the opposite of the woman lacking in character who is a problem to her husband (Prov. 12:4b). Instead the אֵשֶׁת־חַיִל is a woman "who is capable of managing a fortune."[12] McCreesh notes, "She appears to be completely self-sufficient, rather wealthy, and also spends herself and her resources totally for others."[13] Camp says this woman and Eve in Genesis "provide literary models for women idealized as creative, authoritative individuals, very much in league with men for the well-being of the world in which they lived (though not, primarily, for its perpetuation through reproduction), but not defined by or dependent on them."[14]

While the woman in Proverbs 31:10–31 is depicted as having a certain degree of financial security, every attribute of character mentioned in the poem can be true of those without the wealth she seemingly enjoys. Character traits such as trustworthiness (v. 11), industriousness (vv. 11, 13, 15, 17–20, 24, 27), wise speech (v. 26a), and faithful instruction (v. 26b) all rise out of her "fear of Yahweh" (v. 30) and are not related to economic means. In fact neither the possession of great wealth nor the lack of it excludes one from emulating the qualities of this outstanding woman.

All the favorable feminine imagery in the Book of Proverbs reaches a climax in the final poem. The noble woman is the summation of all that has been said about the good woman or wife. She is the ultimate role model after whom any woman in any era or culture can pattern her life if she desires to live according to the principles of wisdom and the fear of Yahweh.

The Noble Wife as the Epitome of Wisdom

As the climactic culmination of the good woman/wife motif portrayed throughout the Book of Proverbs, how is the אֵשֶׁת־חַיִל of 31:10–31 related to the theme of wisdom? More specifically, as the main character of the final poem in Proverbs, which forms an inclusio with Proverbs 1–9, is she related in any way to the figure of Lady Wisdom in those opening chapters?

Hermanson maintains that the author of Proverbs is teaching wisdom through the entire book by contrasting two kinds of people under the figure of the wise and the foolish woman. He sees the woman of folly as the unfaithful wife and the noble wife in 31:10–31 as the faithful one. Hermanson identifies the skillful woman with wisdom and the unfaithful wife with folly.[15] These two figures in Proverbs 1–9 become "representative examples of wisdom and folly through implied comparison." In his view 31:10–31 becomes the climactic *personification* of wisdom.[16]

Hermanson argues that since 31:10–31 is never referred to as a pattern for the New Testament role of woman or wife, the early church "did not see its value for women" and did not believe the passage is primarily pointing out qualities a woman should have.[17] But this argument from silence overlooks the obviously feminine qualities referred to in the passage, such as the three references to the woman's husband. While the noble woman may not necessarily have referred to a specific (unnamed) individual, the passage, as already suggested, does seem to depict a typical industrious and noble woman. Although the cumulative effect of all the activities of this industrious woman may seem overwhelming, what is said of her could be true of a particular individual. What she is represented as doing is possible for an actual woman of the first millennium B.C. In this sense her existence is historically plausible.

Numerous verbal repetitions describe both Lady Wisdom in chapters 1–9 and the noble wife of the final poem, thus suggesting, as some argue, that 31:10–31 depicts a personification of wisdom. One such parallel relates to the value of "finding" both wisdom and the noble woman. Proverbs 8:35 reads, concerning Lady Wisdom, "for he who finds me finds life, and obtains favor from the Lord." Likewise 31:10 asks the rhetorical question about who can find this "wife of noble character," whose value is "far above jewels." Proverbs 3:15 and 8:11 describe the value of wisdom as also being "more precious than jewels."[18] Thus the search for wisdom and for the noble wife are both worth the time and effort.

Other possible parallels are found in wisdom's bringing favor and a good name to those who embrace her (3:4) just as the noble wife brings good to her husband all the days of her life (31:12), enabling him to enjoy respect among the elders in "the gates" of the city (31:23).[19] Wisdom brings a profitable yield (3:14; 8:19) while the noble wife too sees that her trading is profitable (31:18). Wisdom and the noble woman both have maids (9:3; 31:15) who do their bidding. Furthermore their character each earns a well-deserved reward. Wisdom's "reward" to those who "embrace" her is better than fine gold or choice silver (8:19). Likewise, though in a slightly different sense, the noble wife is "rewarded" by praise from her children, husband, and the entire community (31:31). Wisdom and the noble wife are also both found at the city gates. Wisdom calls there for followers to come after her (1:21; 8:3) while the noble wife there receives well-earned praise for all her works (31:31). The speech of the noble woman is also filled with "wisdom" and "faithful" instruction (31:26), which loosely echo the character of Lady Wisdom seen in 8:11–12 and 9:6.

Finally, wisdom is inseparable from the "fear of Yahweh" (8:13). In fact the "fear of Yahweh" is said to be the beginning of wisdom (9:10), and yet in a reciprocal manner wisdom enables those who embrace her to understand the "fear of Yahweh" (2:5). In the climax of the poem that concludes the book the basis of all the noble woman's character traits and works of her hands for which she is praised is her "fear of Yahweh" (31:30).[20]

McCreesh sees these parallels as supporting the idea that the woman of 31:10–31 is a personification of wisdom.

> Do not the two portraits complement one another? The portrait of Wisdom inviting those who heed her call to make their home with her in chapter 9 is completed by the portrait of the woman settled down with her own in chapter 31. And the security and peace promised by Wisdom in 1:33 is amply portrayed in 31:10–31. If the portrait in chapter 9 is that of Wisdom searching for companions, the portrait of chapter 31 must symbolize Wisdom finally settled down with her own.[21]

The picture given in 31:10–31, according to McCreesh, provides support for his view that because wisdom is personified in chapters 1–9 and the noble wife in chapter 31 is described in similar terms, she also is the personification of wisdom.[22]

On the other hand, though verbal and other similarities between these two outstanding female figures appear at opposite ends of the book, rather profound differences do exist. While Lady Wisdom is never clearly pictured as a wife or a mother in Proverbs 1–9, the noble woman is obviously both. Her role as a mother, though not strongly emphasized, is reflected in 31:28.[23]

The figure of Lady Wisdom seems to be something of a composite, that is, she seems to be presented as a preacher (feminine) in 1:20–23, a prophet (feminine) in 1:24–33, and a teacher (also feminine) in 8:4–11. She is also said to be seeking followers in 9:3–6 (and perhaps by implication in 1:21 and 8:3–11, 17), whereas the Proverbs 31 woman is too busy in her productivity to seek after followers. She sews (vv. 13, 19, 22), cooks (v. 15), gets up before daylight (v. 15), provides food for her family (v. 15), buys fields (v. 16), plants vineyards (vv. 16–17), engages in trading (v. 18), shares goods with the poor (v. 20), clothes her family in the finest of warm clothing (v. 21), makes retail goods and turns a profit (v. 24). She "provides for the various needs of her husband, children, and servants" (vv. 15, 21, 27).[24]

Zuck points out that since the noble wife "speaks" with wisdom (v. 26), it makes no sense to equate Lady Wisdom with her and thus have "Wisdom speaking with wisdom." It therefore seems better to see the Proverbs 31 noble woman as a "*wise* woman, not wisdom personified."[25] This finds further support, according to Zuck, in verse 30. As 1:7 and 9:10 have made clear, the fear of the Lord is the foundational essence of wisdom. The noble woman, then, as one who fears the Lord, is most certainly a wise woman. She represents the epitome of all that Lady Wisdom teaches.

> She is a model or example of a wise woman. In contrast to a foolish, adulterous woman (2:16–19; 5:20; 6:23–34; 7:4–27) this woman is faithful to her family and is therefore praised (31:30–31) by her children and her husband (v. 28) and the public (v. 31). As a wise woman, she is in contrast to "woman Folly" (9:13–18). Rather than a personification of wisdom, the woman in 31:10–31 is an embodiment or model of wisdom, a woman who is wise because she is living skillfully.[26]

Rather than limiting the woman in 31:10–31 to simply a personification of wisdom, Garrett, Ringgren, and Wolters see her as both personification and the presentation of an ideal woman.[27] She is "wisdom in action" and "her deeds are the practical and concrete incarnation of what it means to be wise."[28] The advantage of this view is that it sees the obvious references to both wisdom and the womanly role model. Only in this way is it possible to do "justice to the everyday and down-to-earth character of the Valiant Woman's mighty deeds as manager of a large estate."[29]

Manifesting many of the traits of wisdom, the אֵשֶׁת־חַיִל is similar in many ways to Lady Wisdom. The latter, however, is depicted much more as a figure through whom the concept of wisdom can be vocalized while the woman in Proverbs 31 is clearly a woman doing what women do, though admittedly idealized. Her activities in real life represent concrete applications of the wisdom that Lady Wisdom personifies.

One of the questions faced by the writer or final editor of

Proverbs was how best to impress indelibly on his readers a poetic ideal of wisdom. It is nothing short of a brilliant stroke to delay his most convincing portrait of how to live wisely until the very end of the book. He then pulled together the major themes and motifs about women and concretized the concept of wisdom into a final, summarizing statement by giving a word picture of a woman who embodies the essence of what it means to live wisely. Though she represents wisdom in a female form, the character traits she demonstrates serve as examples to both men and women. Neither wisdom nor folly is limited to a single gender.

The Application of Proverbs 31:10–31 to Today

Throughout the Book of Proverbs women are neither ignored nor treated as inferior to men; in fact the climactic conclusion found in 31:10–31 elevates womanhood to a position of supreme honor. The status accorded the אֵשֶׁת־חַיִל in this passage was not granted because of birth or riches but was earned through industrious productivity and diligent application of the principles of wisdom based on the fear of Yahweh.

The noble woman presents an image of superior achievement in every area of life. In an era in which industry is discouraged by emphasis on rights over responsibilities, get-rich-quick schemes, and preoccupation with goods acquired on credit, the אֵשֶׁת־חַיִל models an industrious and productive lifestyle that contributes to the prosperity of the home and of society at large. In keeping with descriptions throughout the Book of Proverbs, this culminating picture reinforces the thought that anyone whose character, commitment, godliness, and productivity replicate the qualities of this woman has learned to live wisely.

Following the rhetorical question "who can find?" the poem describes the noble woman as gaining the full confidence of her husband. Such a relationship of trust is possible in a marriage in which each mate loves the other in a way that consistently benefits the other person. While 31:11–12 focuses on the trustworthiness of the wife, the husband has a similar responsibility to seek to develop the character qualities described in this acrostic poem.

The poem effectively portrays that the noble wife had a strong work ethic and willingly carried her share of the household's work. Although she was privileged to have servants, she did not use them as an opportunity for laziness. She remained in complete oversight of all activities in her household (v. 27), even rising before dawn to involve herself personally in the allotting of food for the day (v. 15). She did not seem to allow for an idle moment. The help of her servants enabled her to expand her horizons and spread her energies further afield in providing for the needs of her household. She did not look for an easy way out but instead did what was necessary to ensure that her activities manifested the best quality, whether in the food she secured for the table (v. 14), the clothing she made herself and her family (vv. 21–22), or the garments she sold to the merchants (v. 24).

Her priorities were thus devoted to the good of her husband and her household. She also sought to help the needs of the poor in her community (v. 20). In addition she ran a profitable home-based business (vv. 17–18), selling garments she made to increase the income of the household (v. 24). She knew how to operate in the business world, selecting raw materials (v. 13), investing in property that would yield a profitable return, and selling finished products (vv. 16, 24).

Collins calls her a "capable wife" whose character makes her "no mere homebody but an efficient businesswoman" as well. He correctly insists that if this passage teaches anything about the role of women, "it is that they can exercise responsibility quite as widely and efficiently as their male counterparts."[30]

Such industrious productivity on the part of the אֵשֶׁת־חַיִל reaped many benefits for her husband, her family, and herself. They all were able to enjoy quality provisions (v. 21) as well as financial and emotional security concerning whatever the future might bring (vv. 21, 25). With his wife providing such apt leadership over the affairs of the household, her husband was able to direct his energies toward the leadership needs of the community, where he too was well respected (v. 23). Obviously both members of this couple were committed to deep-seated character qualities enabling them to excel in their individual areas. In addition to the wife's unfailing devotion to the needs of her husband and family and generosity to the poor, the poem specifically mentions the kindness and wisdom with which she spoke (v. 26). The foundation from which these qualities arise is given in the grand climax of the pericope as her "fear of Yahweh" (v. 30). The end result is that this woman and her works are praised by all whom her life touches: her children, her husband (vv. 28–29), and her community (v. 31).

In spite of the great beauty of this portrayal of the ideal woman and the honor given her, this passage is nevertheless often viewed by modern women as a harsh yardstick by which to measure their shortcomings. Many cringe at the mere mention of this woman. Therefore it is important to put into perspective certain aspects of the poem's message.

First, no young bride can possibly fulfill all that is pictured in this poem before developing the maturity that comes only with time. This portrait looks at the finished product, not at a young woman entering marriage. It reflects the cumulative effect of a life lived wisely. At any given point in life a person can only seek to move in the direction this superb and energetic woman has laid out for all to follow. She serves as a kind of pictorial mentor of the "ultimate" wife just as the qualities listed for church leaders in 1 Timothy 3 and Titus 1 describe the direction and focus a man's life should take if he aspires to be a church leader.

A second area in which perspective is needed is in seeing the complementary roles of the husband and wife. At first glance it might be easy to conclude from this passage that the woman is the dominant figure who is the major provider for the family. What must be remembered is that the purpose of the poem is to focus on the role of the wife, not that of the husband. The portrayal of this woman is in no way inconsistent with the New Testament principle of the husband being the head of the wife (Eph. 5:23). If the husband's role and daily activities were depicted to the same extent as the wife's in this poem, she could still be seen as fitting under his leadership and loving authority.

In an age when women often tend to feel demeaned, Proverbs 31:10–31 provides a liberating concept of marriage with both husband and wife making a valuable contribution to the family. The poem presents a picture in which the אֵשֶׁת־חַיִל is no slave to her husband but has ample opportunities to develop her own potential. She is involved in the textile industry, agriculture, real estate, and household management while her husband takes a place in what might be called "politics" in the modern era. Their lives are not lived totally separate, however. They are partners in marriage. Modern couples could benefit by a careful examination of the interaction between spouses suggested in this acrostic poem.

> Like some recurring refrain in a musical masterpiece, in the midst of this paean the ideal woman's husband is mentioned directly or by implication five times. She is said to be his most precious possession: "If you can find a truly good wife, she is worth more than precious gems" (Prov.

31:10). She interacts with him by supplying his needs and giving him grounds for trusting her . . . (Prov. 31:11). She efficiently cares for and establishes a good relationship with their children: "Her children stand up and bless her" (Prov. 31:28). Then he realizes what her needs are and gives her his unstinted praise: "There are many fine women in the world but you are the best of them all" (Prov. 31:29).[31]

Third, while the woman of noble character is seen as expanding her horizons beyond her home, all her outside business endeavors are focused on meeting the needs of her family, and her generating extra income is carried on from a home base.

In a modern society that has tried to declare marriage and the family useless relics of bygone days tied to irrelevant customs, Proverbs 31:10–31 stands like a literary Statue of Liberty welcoming all who have tried the sociological jargon about loose commitment and easy divorce and found it wanting. By contrast, the אֵשֶׁת־חַיִל models faithfulness to her marriage vows and the family unit. Her commitment to purity of life and morals contrasts with the loose living of the adulteress and the prostitute. As a role model for the modern age, the Proverbs 31 woman is "liberated" in the good sense of that word and is a model of the kind of person, man or woman, whose character forms the foundation stone of any healthy society.

Just as Proverbs 9 brings together the matter of choice before each person in regard to Lady Wisdom and Dame Folly, so the final picture of the אֵשֶׁת־חַיִל as the epitome of wisdom presents a personal choice for readers to become actively involved in determining the direction of their lives, seeking a quality of life that is positive, uplifting, and beneficial rather than drifting through life as a spectator. To be equipped for the demands of normal life (31:21), as well as the uncertainties of the future (v. 25) every person, male and female, needs wisdom. The qualities wisdom imparts benefit all mankind. It is a tragedy that so many have stumbled through life, despising those attributes or being unwilling to pay the price to obtain them.

The אֵשֶׁת־חַיִל is a concrete word picture of all that it means to live wisely. She exemplifies wisdom in her life by her proper alignment of values. She does not follow the world's standards of feminine achievement focused on physical beauty and womanly charm. Instead she has chosen to anchor her life on the "fear of Yahweh" (v. 30), the true basis of all wisdom. One cannot embrace true wisdom without entering into a personal relationship with God.

With this as her foundation the noble wife further demonstrates wisdom in ordering other priorities in her life. Her marriage vows are not taken lightly, but she consistently and diligently applies herself to meeting the needs of her husband and her household in the best way possible. Her genuine concern for others does not end with her family, however, as she also reaches out in generosity to the poor (v. 20) and speaks with kindness (v. 26), indicating the value she places on human life and relationships.

Her disciplined, industrious lifestyle shows foresight, efficiency, and resourcefulness, all evidences of the application of wisdom in her life. She has prepared for the worst of winter weather and other unforeseen contingencies (vv. 21, 25). She uses her time wisely, and she diligently oversees her household affairs in an orderly manner (v. 27). She demonstrates business acumen and makes wise decisions (vv. 16, 18). Wisdom has become so much a part of her life that it is naturally expressed in her speech (v. 26).

Lady Wisdom in chapters 1–9, and the wife of noble character as the epitome of wisdom in Proverbs 31:10–31, are looking for followers in any age or society. They are female mentors to be held up to all young women and men as worthy of emulation. In a society that honors and highly pays sports and entertainment figures, a tremendous need exists to hold up a new kind of model. This noble woman demonstrates that a proper spiritual orientation and the arrangement of one's life under the "fear of the Lord" is the only way to reach one's "full potential" as wise created beings made to live free of slavery and yet under divine authority.

CHAPTER 8

The Prophets and Social Concern

J. Carl Laney

The 19th century saw the flowering of the "social gospel"[1] in America. Leading proponents Washington Gladden (1863–1918) and Walter Rauschenbusch (1861–1918) called for reformation in society and emphasized the need for churches to be concerned about the poor and the oppressed.

The social gospel met opposition among many more traditional church leaders. There was widespread fear that participation in works of social improvement would lead to neglect of more traditional evangelistic activities. Some Christians, in effect, minimized the importance of social concerns and shared no interest in improving the conditions of suffering humanity.

Through the influence of liberation theology, the social aspect of the gospel message has gained greater prominence today, especially in poverty-ridden, third world countries. The social gospel question was prominent at the Lausanne II conference in Manila in July 1989.[2]

What are the social implications of biblical Christianity? Many suggest that the gospel should include greater attention to the physical needs of the lost. Others seek to avoid compromising the "pure and simple" gospel by social involvement and Christian activism. This chapter seeks to present a biblical balance between these two approaches. While not equating church leaders with the prophets nor the Church Age with Old Testament Israel, this study suggests that the prophets provide a scriptural pattern for addressing social concerns.

The Prophets and Society

The prophets of Yahweh were raised up by God from society (Deut. 18:15) and sustained a prominent relationship with society as political and religious leaders, preachers of the Law, predictors of future judgment, watchmen over the spiritual life of the nation, intercessors for the people, and prosecutors against covenant-breakers.

The prophets were concerned with international events and the future, while at the same time they were practical in dealing with the concerns of their own localities and generations.[3]

"The great Hebrew prophets were public men, mainly concerned with political and social questions of the day."[4] They had a definite concern for social justice as well as religious orthodoxy. As Beecher notes, "More prominently than anything else they rebuke unequal and unkind practices in the administration of justice, and inexorably demand reformation. It is largely for the purpose of reform that they engage in public affairs."[5]

Yet while the prophets were involved in social concerns, they were not primarily *social* reformers. They were "theological reformers," for "their basic motivation was generated within their commitment to the fundamental laws of God."[6] Their concern for the oppressed, the widow, the orphan, the poor, and the resident alien sprang from God's own compassionate nature (Deut. 15:11; 24:14–15; Ex. 22:21–27).

Heschel has stated that justice was important to the prophets because it pertained to God's status in human life.[7] The social concern of the prophets was grounded in theological reform with an expressed concern for elevating the reputation of God and His standards in society.

The prophets considered each citizen responsible to dispense justice (Mic. 6:8). Isaiah called for Israelites to "give rest to the weary" (Isa. 28:12). When the members of Israelite society failed to fulfill this responsibility, the prophets stepped in to intercede on behalf of those who had no intercessor. As Bullock notes, "Where the king and official, either because of apathy or inaccessibility, stepped out of their expected role, the prophets stepped in."[8]

The Prophets and Social Issues

The prophets of Israel were greatly concerned with social issues, both moral and religious. In fact, for the prophets, social and moral concern lay at the very heart of religion. Repeatedly they rebuked idolatry, formalistic worship, failure to support temple worship, oppression of the poor, murder, usury, and dissipation.

The origin of the social and moral concern so often expressed by the prophets is debated. Many scholars have noted a relationship between the Deuteronomic law and the prophets and suggest that Deuteronomy was an attempt to bring the teaching of the prophets into statute form.[9] In reality it should be viewed the other way around. As Kaufmann observes, "The prophetic demands for social justice echo, for the most part, the ancient covenant laws."[10] Shultz, who concurs with Kaufmann, writes:

> The ethical and social concern expressed by Moses was likewise repeatedly appealed to by the prophets. Having departed from the prescribed Mosaic standard, the Israelites were warned by the prophets of their shortcomings on the basis of the divinely revealed law of Moses.[11]

The prophets were not great innovators, presenting the Israelites with new responsibilities in the social and moral realm. Rather, they believed that the ideal for Israel's society was laid down in the covenantal legislation of the past. Justice and righteousness, the foundation of the Law and pillars of society, were viewed by the prophets as the order for every age.[12] The prophets' concern for society and social issues clearly originated with the Mosaic Law and with Yahweh Himself. The following chart illustrates that the preaching of the prophets was based on the Law:

Subject	Law	Prophet
The orphan and widow	Deut. 10:18	Ezek. 22:7
The return of the pledge	Ex. 22:26	Amos 2:8
The perversion of justice	Deut. 24:17	Hab. 1:4
Bribery	Ex. 23:8	Mic. 3:11
Usury	Lev. 25:36	Ezek. 22:12

Many other verses relating to social concerns in the Law could be cited (Ex. 22:21–23; Deut. 14:28–29; 16:11, 14; 24:19–21; 26:12–13; 27:19). Clearly the messages of the prophets were based on a common body of instruction. The prophets of God simply applied the Mosaic legislation to their contemporary situations.

The Pattern of the Prophets

The prophets' concern for social issues is reflected throughout their writings. A brief survey illustrates this emphasis.[13]

AMOS

Amos prophesied to Israel during the reigns of Uzziah (791–739 B.C.) and Jeroboam II (793–753 B.C.), when both kingdoms enjoyed peace and prosperity unequaled since the reign of Solomon. In spite of its healthy appearance, however, Israel was in an advanced state of decay—socially, morally, and religiously.

Jeroboam did evil in the sight of Yahweh and continued in idolatry (2 Kings 14:23–24). Uzziah, though a good king, failed to remove the high places and the people continued their pagan sacrifices (2 Kings 15:4).

The Prophet Amos raised his voice in protest against the religious and moral corruption of his day. And he warned of national judgment on those refusing to change their ways. Kaufmann observes that Amos was the first prophet to evaluate social morality as a factor in national destiny.[14]

The sins condemned by Amos include exploitation and oppression of the poor and needy (4:1; 5:11; 8:4, 6), corrupt and degenerate religious practices (2:4, 6, 8; 4:4), corruption of justice and honesty (5:7, 10; 6:12), excessive indulgence (6:4), and general disregard for the laws of God (2:8; 8:5).

In dealing with the sins of Israelite society, Amos warned of impending judgment (2:5, 13–16; 3:2, 11–15; 5:25–27), but he also called the people to repentance (4:12–13; 5:4–15). Amos insisted that true religion and a biblical morality are inseparable. He called the people to "let justice roll down like waters and righteousness like an ever-flowing stream" (5:24). "Justice" (מִשְׁפָּט) or "proper arrangement" may be defined as "the just claims of God" on society.[15] In its ethical sense "righteousness" (צֶדֶק), refers to what is in conformity with the divine standards of God.[16] The righteous person recognizes God's standard, treating others (rich or poor) equally before the Law. Amos appealed for people to let these two qualities characterize their dealings with God and other individuals. Only then would society function according to divine norms.

HOSEA

Hosea began his public ministry in the reign of Israel's King Jeroboam II (793–753 B.C.) and continued into the reign of Hezekiah (728–686 B.C.). Israel prospered in the early years of this period, but Assyria was in the ascendancy and moving west. The kingdom of Israel was at a spiritual low point during Hosea's ministry. At this time of spiritual declension God raised up Hosea to convince Israel that the nation must repent and turn to God in order to avert divine judgment. Hosea pointed out that the root cause of the problems of the Israelites was their spiritual apostasy. Their failure toward God resulted in a failure toward fellow Israelites.

The sins of Hosea's day included harlotry (4:11, 18), false dealings (4:2; 7:1), violence and bloodshed (4:2; 6:8–9), stealing (4:2; 7:1), drunkenness (4:11; 7:5), idolatry (4:12; 8:4; 13:2), and rebellion against God (9:15; 13:16).

The solution Hosea offered to the social sins of his day included both judgment and repentance. Because of the nation's sins and unfaithfulness to the covenant stipulations, Hosea pronounced judgment on her (5:1–14; 8:1–9:9). Under the covenant curses the Northern Kingdom was doomed to destruction (5:7–9; 7:13). Yet the people were exhorted to repent from their sinful apostasy (6:1–3; 14:1–3) and to receive God's healing and restoration (14:4). God desired that Israel cultivate loyalty (חֶסֶד, 6:6) and that knowledge of the Lord be increased (6:3, 6). Hosea exhorted the people to practice "justice" as a step along the path toward healing and restoration (12:6).

Hosea repeatedly lamented the people's lack of "knowledge" of God (4:6, 14; 5:4; 11:3). Hosea anticipated that after the evils of society had been remedied by divine judgment, the people would "know the Lord" (2:20). Paterson observes, "The remedial purpose of judgment is to bring about repentance, and the result will be a newness of life that consists of knowledge of God."[17] Israel's failure in understanding the character of God issued in wrong attitudes and evil conduct. The ultimate corrective presented by Hosea is a knowledge of God brought about through judgment and repentance.

ISAIAH

Isaiah began his ministry in the year of King Uzziah's death (739 B.C.) and continued prophesying until at least the death of Hezekiah (686 B.C.). Isaiah ministered during a time of spiritual degeneracy and apostasy, especially during the reigns of Ahaz and Manasseh. Hezekiah did bring much-needed reform, but his son offset his worthy efforts. In Isaiah's day Judah was faced with the same spiritual problems that had destroyed the Northern Kingdom.

The sins Isaiah rebuked included idolatry (2:8; 48:5), injustice (1:21, 23; 5:7; 10:1–2; 59:8), bloodshed (5:7; 59:7), religious formalism and hypocrisy (1:10–15; 29:13; 58:1–5), rebellion (1:5; 57:4), neglect of widows and orphans (1:23; 10:2), excessive indulgence in wine and strong drink (5:11; 28:1–7), and oppression of the poor (3:14–15; 10:2).

Isaiah condemned the citizens of Judah for failing to measure up to God's righteous norms in relationship to God and others. Yet he maintained a confident expectation of the establishment of social justice. He anticipated a day in which justice and righteousness would prevail among the Israelites. Isaiah suggested two solutions that would enable righteousness to prevail. One was the responsibility of the people to repent and do good (1:16–17). If they repented, they would receive forgiveness of sins. God would give them blessing for their obedience. But continued rebellion would result in judgment. The people's responsibility was also expressed in 58:6–7, where true piety involves ceasing oppression and helping the hungry, homeless, poor, and naked. The Lord asked the people to "preserve justice, and do righteousness" (56:1). Such human efforts at righting the wrongs of society must, however, be preceded by repentance and turning to the Lord (55:6–7).

The second solution Isaiah anticipated is the coming of the Messiah, who will establish social justice in the millennial kingdom. The Servant-Messiah will "bring forth justice to the nations" and establish "justice on the earth" (42:1, 4; cf. 2:1–4). He will establish righteousness and peace (60:17) and will effect a just rule in society through His princes (32:1). Messiah Himself will judge the poor with righteousness and decide the case of the afflicted with fairness (11:4). A full knowledge of the Lord throughout all the earth will be the basis for harmony in the millennial society (11:9).

MICAH

Micah carried out his ministry during the reigns of Jotham (750–731 B.C.), Ahaz (743–715 B.C.), and Hezekiah (728–686 B.C.). He is unique as a writing prophet, being the only one whose ministry was directed to both the northern and southern kingdoms (1:1). The Assyrian crisis brought days of unrest, insecurity, and hardship for the people of the land. Accompanying the political unrest was the low spiritual and moral situation in the lives of the people.

Micah addressed problems of the common people. He lay bare Israel's sins, presenting God's complaints against His people. Ellisen observes, "While Isaiah depicts the social crimes of his time from the standpoint of the townsman in the capital, Micah shows us them from the standpoint of the suffering countryman."[18]

The societal sins Micah rebuked are basically those against the common man. These include plundering and oppressing the poor and defenseless (2:2, 8–9), perversion of justice through bribery and dishonest business practices (3:11; 6:11; 7:3), idolatry and idolatrous practices (1:7; 5:13–14), violence and bloodshed (6:12; 7:2), and empty religious formalism (6:6–7).

Like the Prophet Isaiah, Micah offered a twofold solution to the moral and spiritual problems of society. The first is to "do good." God wanted the people to yield to the requirements of true religion, summed up so well in Micah 6:8, "to do justice, to love kindness [חֶסֶד], and to walk humbly with your God." Here God linked ethics with piety, duty toward man with duty toward God.

The second aspect of the solution is the coming of the Messiah. Micah understood that individuals are responsible to provide social justice. But he recognized that the Lord is the One who will ultimately execute justice and see that relationships in society are arranged according to His divine norm. The execution of justice will take place during the millennium when the word of the Lord will go forth from Jerusalem (4:2). Messiah will bring peace (v. 3), provide security (v. 4), and free Israel from idolatry (v. 5). The messianic kingdom, by virtue of Christ's rule, will yield social justice as its fruit.

ZEPHANIAH

Zephaniah ministered in the days of Josiah king of Judah (640–609 B.C.), before the great revival of 621 B.C. The spiritual and moral condition of the kingdom progressively worsened from the death of Hezekiah until Josiah's reform. The threat of Babylonian invasion provided the political background for Zephaniah's prophecies of judgment. He warned of impending judgment and called for the remnant of God's people to turn to the Lord (2:3).

Zephaniah was concerned about the spiritual degeneracy of the people, the priests, and the leaders. He condemned idolatry and syncretistic worship (1:4–5), rebellion and oppression (3:1), unbelief (3:2), immorality among leaders (3:3), and disrespect for the Law and holy things (3:4).

Repentance is the solution Zephaniah offered Judah. He exhorted the people to seek the Lord, righteousness, and humility (2:3). Such repentance would have a significant effect on the spiritual problems of the nation. Zephaniah's exhortation undoubtedly paved the way for Josiah's great reformation.

HABAKKUK

The ministry of Habakkuk probably took place early in the reign of Jehoiakim (609–597 B.C.), before the first invasion of the Babylonians (Chaldeans) in 605 B.C. (2 Kings 24:1–2). After Josiah, the great reformer, died, the spiritual conditions of the people of Judah rapidly degenerated. The sins of the people left the nation ripe for judgment that God would effect through the invasions of Nebuchadnezzar in 605, 597, and 586 B.C. Habakkuk condemned the sins of both the Judeans and Chaldeans. These included violence (1:2; 2:12, 17), oppression (1:4), disregard for the Law (1:4), perversion of justice (1:4), plundering (2:8), inhumanity to man (2:10–11, 15), and idolatry (2:18–19).

Standing on the threshold of judgment prophesied by Isaiah, Habakkuk offered no alternative to judgment (1:12). He did set forth, however, a principle of divine recompense that would function as an encouragement to the people: the upright man living in reliance on God will be preserved, whereas the proud and wicked will perish (2:4). Habakkuk anticipated a day after judgment when the knowledge of God's glory will fill the earth (2:14).

JEREMIAH

Jeremiah was commissioned as a prophet during the reign of Josiah in 627 B.C., and he continued his ministry in Judah through the fall of Jerusalem (586 B.C.). Josiah brought spiritual reform to the nation, but the rulers who followed him had no such spiritual inclinations. The religious and spiritual life of the people went into deep decline after his death.

Jeremiah was a prophet intensely interested in society and the religious condition of the people. The sins he rebuked included religious failure and apostasy among the people and priests (2:8, 13; 3:1; 5:31; 7:18; 17:2; 19:4–5), immorality (2:33; 3:8; 5:7–8; 7:9), oppression of the poor (5:28; 7:6), and perversion of justice (7:5).

Jeremiah exhorted the people to turn from evil (4:14). Repentance from injustice, oppression, and bloodshed would deter God's judgment and would enable the faithful to enjoy God's blessing in the land (7:5–7). Also Jeremiah, like most of the other prophets, anticipated the coming of Messiah, who will "do justice and righteousness in the land" (23:5). Through Messiah's millennial reign, the Lord will exercise loyalty, justice, and righteousness on earth (9:24).

In addition Jeremiah explained that the New Covenant would give the people a new basis on which to fulfill their responsibilities to God and their fellow man (31:31–34). With the Law inscribed on their hearts, and a knowledge of Yahweh, the people would have divine enablement for living according to God's divine order. Jeremiah viewed the New Covenant as the spiritual solution to the social and moral problems of the people of Judah.

EZEKIEL

Ezekiel began his prophetic ministry in 592 B.C. and continued to minister to the exiles in Babylon for at least 27 years (29:17). Ezekiel was a contemporary of Jeremiah, who prophesied in Jerusalem, and of Daniel, who ministered in the royal court of Babylon. Until the fall of Jerusalem, Ezekiel's ministry to the colony of exiles consisted primarily of preaching judgment against Judah. After 586 B.C. his ministry was one of consolation, predicting the future restoration of the nation with its temple and worship.

The sins of Israelite society condemned or rebuked by Ezekiel included spiritual apostasy and idolatry (5:11; 6:3–6; 8:3, 5, 10; 14:3; 18:15; 36:18), oppression of the poor, widows, and orphans (18:12, 16; 22:29), bloodshed (22:3–4), false prophecy (13:2, 16, 23; 22:28), and sexual immorality (18:11; 22:10–11).

Ezekiel said divine judgment was one means by which the wrongs of society would be corrected. God's judgment on Jerusalem would bring the people to a knowledge of the Lord. The phrase, "and you will know that I am the Lord," is used about 60 times in the book with reference to the expected outcome of divine judgment (6:7, 10, 13–14; 7:4; 11:10, etc.). Ezekiel anticipated a judgment that would purify Israel and bring the people to the Lord (14:9–11).

A second solution is personal repentance. Ezekiel exhorted the people to repent and live (18:30, 32). The one who turns from sin and practices righteousness "will surely live" (18:5–9; 33:14–16).

With Jeremiah, Ezekiel set forth the New Covenant as a means of bringing a new heart and understanding to the people (36:25–28). This change will serve as the spiritual basis for obedience and blessing, enabling the people to live in the righteous and just manner required by God.

ZECHARIAH

Zechariah entered his prophetic ministry in 520 B.C., just two months after Haggai's first oracle. His last dated prophecy is two years later (518 B.C.). When Zechariah ministered, the temple was incomplete and the city of Jerusalem was in ruins. The people were experiencing drought and adversity instead of divine blessing. To these despairing people Zechariah offered a message of messianic hope and promise.

The sins he condemned included a neglect of justice (7:9), oppression of widows, orphans, and strangers (7:10), refusal to respond to the prophet of God (7:11), and devising evil (8:17). The first solution Zechariah offered was repentance (1:3–4). He exhorted the people to dispense justice and practice loyalty and compassion. The people ought to speak truth, judge with truth, and love truth and peace (8:16–17, 19). Such changes in attitude and practice would help bring about social justice in Israelite society.

Like many prophets before him, Zechariah looked to the day when the Messiah will dwell in the midst of Zion, establishing a righteous and just rule in Israel (14:9–11).

MALACHI

Malachi probably prophesied between the first and second governorships of Nehemiah (ca. 432–431 B.C.). The Jews had been home from Babylon a little over one hundred years. Though the exile had cured them of idolatry, they had lost their enthusiasm for the worship of God in Jerusalem. After Nehemiah's revival (Neh. 10:28–29), the people again succumbed to religious indifference and moral laxity. Through Malachi the Lord called these wayward people to repentance and obedience.

The sins of Judah included corruption of religion and proper worship (Mal. 1:7–8; 3:8), perversion of justice (2:9), intermarriage with pagans (2:11), divorce (2:16), and oppression of the helpless (3:5).

The first solution mentioned by Malachi was repentance. He exhorted the people to return to God (3:7) and obey Him (3:10; 4:4). A second solution, Malachi pointed out, is the approaching day of the Lord, in which the Messiah will come and will purge evil and oppression from society (3:2, 17; 4:1, 3, 5–6).

The Application of the Study

The prophets of Israel spoke to the social issues that troubled Israelite society both in matters of religious orthodoxy and social justice. The sins the prophets rebuked included the following: (1) the exploitation and oppression of the poor, orphans, widows, and aliens, (2) corrupt and degenerate religious practices, (3) idolatry and pagan practices, (4) perversion of justice, (5) dishonest business practices, (6) excessive indulgence in wine and strong drink, (7) violence of all sorts, including bloodshed and plotting evil, (8) adultery, immorality, and sexual violations, and (9) general disregard for the Law of Yahweh. This list reads like a moral commentary on contemporary society!

In response to these problems the prophets offered four solutions. The first two relate to what man must do; the other two relate to what God will do. First, the prophets exhorted the people to repent of their evil and turn back to God (Amos 5:4–6; Hos. 6:1–3; Zeph. 2:3; Jer. 4:14). Second, the prophets exhorted the people to exercise justice, righteousness, and loyalty. They challenged the citizens of their day to take positive steps to right the wrongs of society (Amos 5:24; Isa. 1:16–17; Mic. 6:8). Third, the prophets, particularly Jeremiah and Ezekiel, looked to the establishment of the New Covenant, which will provide the spiritual power for people to walk in the manner required by God (Jer. 31:31–34; Ezek. 16:60–63; 36:25–28). Fourth, the prophets anticipated the coming of the Messiah, who will establish justice and righteousness during His millennial reign (Isa. 11:4; 42:1–4; Mic. 4:2–4).

The prophets of Israel and Judah did not cloister themselves from society and its problems. They were aware of the issues and were actively involved in speaking to the social and moral concerns of their day. They pointed out social injustice and rebuked it as sin. They called on the Israelites to do something personally to correct the evils in their society. They had confidence that the New Covenant would give God's people the power and resources to work actively toward the establishing of social justice, and yet they recognized that complete justice and righteousness would ultimately be established by the Messiah in His future kingdom. A survey of the Gospels indicates that Jesus adhered closely to this pattern (Matt. 4:17; 5:3–12; 26:20–29; Luke 3:10–14; John 5:14).

Some may object to setting forth the prophets as models for Christians in confronting social and moral issues. Admittedly the church is not Israel, and pastors are not biblical prophets. Yet what is modeled by the prophets is certainly underscored in the New Testament Epistles. Paul instructed the Galatians, "Let us not lose heart in doing good. . . . So then, while we have opportunity, let us do good to all men, and especially to those who are of the household of faith" (Gal. 6:9–10). The writer of Hebrews admonished, "Do not neglect doing good and sharing; for with such sacrifices God is pleased" (Heb. 13:16). James wrote of visiting "orphans and widows in their distress" (James 1:27) and he described good works as expressions of genuine faith (2:15–17). Therefore it seems that the principles reflected in the prophets are not limited to a particular dispensation.

The Old Testament prophets provide a splendid pattern and an impetus for confronting and dealing with the sins and injustices of modern society. Like the prophets, Christians today should (a) recognize and condemn sin, (b) call men and women to repent of their sin, (c) direct men and women to Christ for the regeneration of the human heart and the New Covenant empowerment to overcome sin, (d) exhort people to take positive steps to correct wrongs and injustice, and (e) anticipate the return of Christ, who will establish perfect justice and righteousness during His reign in the millennium.

The prophets balanced spiritual concerns with physical problems, recognizing both man's part and God's part in the ultimate solution to each. This balance is reflected in the words of Amy Carmichael. Speaking in response to criticism of her humanitarian work in India, she said, "One cannot save and then pitchfork souls into heaven. . . . Souls are more or less securely fastened to bodies . . . and as you cannot get the souls out and deal with them separately, you have to take them both together."[19]

Christians must not be content to be experts on what the Bible says about contemporary social and moral issues. Following the pattern of the prophets, they should actively engage in confronting sin and injustice, directing sinners to salvation in Christ. Seeking to right wrongs and help the oppressed, Christians may enjoy the assurance that Christ is coming again to complete the task.

CHAPTER 9

Wordplay in the Eighth-Century Prophets

Robert B. Chisholm, Jr.

A variety of literary and rhetorical devices fill the writings of the Old Testament prophets, lending vividness and emotion to their powerful messages. Through these devices the prophets often expressed their theological themes. One of the most common techniques they employed was wordplay.

Wordplay can be based on repetition, various meanings expressed by an individual word (polysemy), identity in sound between two or more words (homonymy), or similarity in sound between two or more words (paronomasia).

Various systems for the classification of wordplay have been proposed.[1] In this study the following categories will be used (though this list is not intended to be exhaustive or definitive by any means).

1. Wordplay involving a single word
   a. repeated in the same semantic sense
   b. repeated with a different sense (explicit polysemantic wordplay)[2]
   c. used once with two senses implied (implicit polysemantic wordplay)[3]

2. Wordplay involving two or more words
   a. identical in sound (homonymy)
   b. similar in sound (paronomasia), including similarity in consonants (alliteration) and/or vowels (assonance)

In this study each of these categories is illustrated, drawing examples from the eighth-century prophets Isaiah, Hosea, Amos, and Micah. In each of the examples recognition of the wordplay contributes to a fuller exegetical and theological understanding of the passage and thereby enhances interpretation of the prophetic message. Through such examples the reader, whose concerns may be more exegetical than artistic, should recognize that identifying wordplay can be more than just an exercise in aesthetic appreciation of the biblical literature. At times it proves to be crucial to understanding the full import of the prophetic message.

Wordplay Involving a Single Word

REPETITION OF A SINGLE WORD IN THE SAME SENSE

An example of wordplay involving repetition of a single word used in the same sense appears in Hosea 8:3, 5. According to verse 3, Israel had rejected (*zānah*) what is good by breaking her covenant with God (v. 1) and turning to idolatry (v. 4). Consequently the Lord rejected (*zānah*)[4] Samaria's calf idol (v. 5), which would be broken to bits when judgment fell (v. 6). The wordplay brings out the correspondence between the divine response and the sin that prompted it.

Amos 5:10, 15, and 21 provide another example of this type of wordplay. According to verse 10, the sinners addressed by Amos hated (*śānᵉʾû*) anyone who attempted to stand up for truth and justice in the courts. In verse 15 the prophet exhorted these same individuals to "hate" (*śinʾû*) evil. The repetition serves to contrast the sinners' actual attitude with God's ideal. In verse 21 God declared that He "hates" (*śānēʾtî*) the sinners' religious feasts. The repetition of the verb *śānēʾ*, "to hate," draws attention to the correspondence between the divine response and the sin that prompted it. The sinners hated/rejected social justice; so God in turn hated/rejected their hypocritical religion, which was a false substitute for ethical living.

REPETITION OF A SINGLE WORD IN A DIFFERENT SENSE

Wordplay can sometimes involve the repetition of a word in a different sense. A well-known example occurs in Isaiah 1:19–20. The Lord promised that obedience to His ethical demands (cf. vv. 16–17) would bring blessing in the form of agricultural prosperity (v. 19). The people would eat (*tōʾkēlû*) the good things of the land. However, rejection of Yahweh's demands would result in judgment (v. 20). In this case unrepentant sinners would be destroyed (lit. "eaten," *tᵉʾukkᵉlu*) by the sword (symbolic of enemy invasion and military might). The use of *ʾākal* in two distinct senses ("eat"/

"destroy") highlights the contrast between the promise and the threat, a contrast which corresponds to the opposite responses hypothesized in the protases of verses 19–20.

Another example of this type of wordplay is found in Isaiah 32:9, 11, and 18. In verses 9 and 11 the Lord addressed the "complacent" (*ša³ănannôt̲*) women of Jerusalem who "feel secure" (*bōt̲ᵉḥôt̲*) and announced that judgment was imminent. However, the tone of the message changes in verse 15, where the restoration following judgment is portrayed. When God restores His people, they will live "undisturbed" (*ša³ănannôt̲*, v. 18; note also *mibt̲aḥîm* earlier in the verse) in the land. The repetition of *ša³ănannôt̲* in the senses "complacent"/"undisturbed" (as well as the repetition of the root *bt̲ḥ*) highlights the contrast between the sinful condition of the people in Isaiah's time and the future situation to be created by the Lord. True security comes only from Him.

Wordplay involving repetition is not limited to individual speech units. Sometimes it can be observed over wider contexts, attesting to the unity of the prophetic message as a whole. For example in Hosea 7:13 the Lord accused His people of having "strayed" (*nād̲ᵉd̲û*) from Him. In Hosea 9:17, where the theme of disobedience appears again, the Lord warned that Israel would become wanderers (*nōd̲ᵉd̲îm*) among the nations. The repetition of *nād̲ad̲*, used in slightly different senses ("stray" or "wander off/from" in 7:13; "wander about" in 9:17), brings out the appropriate nature of Israel's punishment. Since Israel was so determined to wander from the Lord, He would make wandering their way of life.

Another example from Hosea highlights the reversal of God's judgment in the final salvation of Israel. In Hosea 13:7 the Lord compared Himself, in His role as Israel's Judge, to a vicious predator which "lurks" (NIV)/"lies in wait" (NASB) (*³āšûr*) for unsuspecting prey passing by. In the conclusion to the prophecy, which stresses the Lord's future restoration and blessing of His people, this same verb reappears. Now the Lord declared His intention to "care for" (*wa³ăšûrennû*, from *šûr*) His people and protect them (14:9; Eng. v. 8). The vicious leopard has become the beneficent protector. The reversal in the Lord's attitude toward His people is highlighted by the repetition of the verb *šûr*.

USE OF A SINGLE WORD WITH TWO SENSES IMPLIED

Wordplay sometimes involves a word being used once with two senses being implied. For example in Micah 4:11 the nations assemble (*neʾespû*) for battle against Jerusalem in anticipation of a great victory. Little do they know that the Lord has actually gathered them like grain to the threshing floor so that Zion might "thresh" them (vv. 12–13). From the nations' perspective they are "massed" for battle.[5] However, verses 12–13 suggest another sense for *ʾāsap*. From God's perspective the nations have been harvested or heaped up for threshing/destruction.[6] The double entendre here serves to contrast the nations' limited perception with God's sovereign purpose.

Amos 3:12 provides another example of implicit polysemantic wordplay. The covenant rebels addressed by Amos were anticipating a great deliverance by the Lord (cf. 5:18). One of Amos's major themes was that this expectation would not be realized. Because of Israel's sin, the Lord's "day" would be one of judgment, not salvation (5:19–20). This background is essential to understanding the use of the verb *nāṣal* in 3:12. This word frequently refers to deliverance from enemies (including death), appearing in this sense in accounts of Israel's salvation history (Gen. 32:12, Eng. v. 11; 32:31, Eng. v. 30; Ex. 12:27; 18:8, 10; 1 Sam. 17:37) and in its hymnic tradition (Ps. 18:1, Eng. title; 33:19; 56:14, Eng. v. 13; 86:13). It was this kind of deliverance Amos's generation anticipated. However, in Amos 3:12 the Lord made it clear that Israel's "deliverance" would in reality be only a "snatching away," comparable to a shepherd's salvaging bits and pieces of a devoured sheep from a ferocious predator. *Nāṣal*, used here in its basic sense of "snatch away," has the force of "salvage," while at the same time reminding one of the unrealized ideal of genuine salvation. Once again wordplay is used for purposes of contrast and irony.[7]

Wordplay Involving Two or More Words

HOMONYMY

Micah 2:5, 10 provides an example of homonymic wordplay. According to verse 5, the sinful real estate entrepreneurs, having been dispossessed of their holdings by the Lord (cf. v. 4), would have no representative in the future distribution of the land in the time of restoration. More specifically, they would have no one "to divide the land by lot" (*mašlîk ḥebel beḡôrāl*, v. 5, lit. "one casting a measuring-cord by lot"). In verse 10 these oppressors are urged to flee from their present land holdings because the land they had accumulated was contaminated by a destructive illness (*ṭomʾâ teḥabbēl weḥebel nimrāṣ*, v. 10, lit. "uncleanness which brings destruction, even irreversible destruction"), which is probably a reference to their sins, which make judgment imminent. The word translated "destruction" in verse 10 (*ḥebel*, from the verb *ḥābal*, "to destroy") is a homonym of *ḥebel*, "measuring-cord" (used in v. 5). The point of the wordplay is unfulfilled ambition and appropriate punishment. The sinners would receive the opposite of what they so fervently tried to acquire. They desperately wanted land (cf. vv. 1–2). However, there would be no "measuring-cord" (*ḥebel*, symbolizing landed property) for them; they would have a different type of *ḥebel* (i.e., destruction), which would make continued existence on the land they presently possessed impossible.

PARONOMASIA

Probably the most common type of wordplay used by the prophets is paronomasia, which is based on the similarity in sound between certain words. For example in the parabolic song of the vineyard (Isa. 5:1–7) the Lord denounced sinful Judah for failing to meet His ethical demands. He required justice (cf. *mišpāṭ* and *ṣedāqâ* in v. 7), which corresponds to the good grapes of verses 2 and 4. Instead He witnessed only bloodshed (*miśpāḥ*, v. 7)[8] and cries of distress (*ṣeʿāqâ*, v. 7), corresponding to the bad grapes mentioned in the preceding context. Instead of promoting social justice, the men of Judah had oppressed the poor. This perversion of the divine standard is highlighted by the very words employed to describe it. Just as *miśpāḥ* and *ṣeʿāqâ* are semantically significant phonological alterations of *mišpāṭ* and even when some of the consonants are changed), so Judah's treatment of the poor was an ethically significant alteration (in this case "perversion" is preferable because of the moral connotation) of God's requirements.

In Isaiah 24:17–18 the inescapability of the coming judgment is emphasized. Paronomasia is employed to highlight this fact and to stress the unified character of the instruments of judgment, designated here as "terror" (*paḥad*), "pit" (*paḥat*), and "snare" (*pāḥ*) (note the repetition of the *p/ḥ* combination). These three will act in concert to make escape impossible. Their similar sounding names draw attention to their relationship as "allies" against the sinful inhabitants of the earth.

In the covenant lawsuit of Micah 6 the Lord used paronomasia to contrast His people's warped perception of reality with His own correct assessment of their situation. They were apparently complaining that the Lord had "burdened" them (*ûmâ helʾēṭîkā*, "How have I burdened you," v. 3). In denying the charge, the Lord pointed out that He had actually delivered, not burdened, them (*heʿĕlṭîkā mēʾereṣ miṣrayim*, "I brought you up out of Egypt," v. 4).

Combinations of the Preceding Types

Often a passage will combine several types of wordplay. For example in Micah 2:1–5, a judgment speech against those who oppress the poor, the prophet employed repetition and paronomasia to emphasize the theme of poetic justice. A woe oracle is announced over those who plan (*ḥōšᵉḇê*, v. 1) evil (*rāʿ*, v. 1) schemes to rob the poor of their landed property. They take away the fields (*śāḏôṭ*, v. 2) of the poor and carry off (*nāśāʾû*, v. 2) their possessions. In the announcement of judgment against these oppressors (vv. 3–5), the Lord proclaimed that He was planning (*ḥōšēḇ*, v. 3) a calamity (*rāʿâ*, v. 3; cf. *rāʿ* in v. 1) against them. In the day of judgment they would be forced to watch helplessly as their conquerors parceled out their fields (*śāḏēnû*, v. 4) to others. At that time the enemy would ridicule (lit. "lift up a taunt song over"; cf. esp. *yiśśāʾ*, v. 4, with *nāśāʾû*, v. 2) them. In the taunt song, the words of which are recorded in verse 4b, the mockers quoted the words of the mourning rich, who lamented that they were "utterly ruined" (*śāḏôḏ nᵉšaddunû*, Qal infinitive absolute + Niphal perfect, from *śāḏaḏ*, v. 4; note the similarity in sound to *śāḏôṭ*, "fields," used in v. 2).

As noted above, the various forms of wordplay include repetition of a word in the same sense (*ḥāšaḇ* and *śāḏeh*), repetition of a word in a different sense (*rāʿ*/*rāʿâ* in the senses of "moral evil" and "calamity," and *nāśāʾ*, in the senses of "carry off/steal" and "sing"), and paronomasia (involving *śāḏaḏ* and *śāḏeh*). Poetic justice clearly emerges as the central theme of the oracle. The rich, who oppressed their fellow citizens, would be judged appropriately. The Lord would scheme against the schemers and would repay evil with evil. Those who stole the fields of the poor were about to learn how their victims felt by experiencing the loss of their own fields. Those who lifted up the possessions of others would have a taunt song lifted up over them. The very words of that song (specifically those words containing sibilants and dentals) would be a stark reminder of their unjust acts.[9]

In Isaiah 1:4–7 repetition (of *zûr*, "be a stranger") and homonymic wordplay contribute to the theme of poetic justice. In verse 4 the Israelites are accused of rejecting the Lord. The phrase *nāzōrû ʾāḥôr*, "they are estranged backward," describes their departure from the Lord. In verse 7 the same word (*zûr*) appears twice (in participial form), referring to the foreign armies that had already overrun the land of Judah. The repetition of *zûr* emphasizes the close relationship between sin and punishment. The people had treated the Lord as a "stranger," and so, appropriately, their judgment involved "strangers." In verse 6 the homonymic *zōrû* is used in a description of a badly beaten body (representing Judah here). Judah had been severely battered by the Lord's judgments and was covered, as it were, with sores that had not received medical attention. These wounds had not been "cleansed" (i.e., "pressed out," *lōʾ zōrû*), bandaged, or soothed with oil. Because of its similarity in sound to *zûr*, "be a stranger" (used in vv. 4 and 7), *zûr*, "press down,"[10] contributes to the theme of poetic justice by drawing one's attention to the correspondence between sin and punishment.

The Prophet Amos was also a master at combining several types of wordplay to emphasize the theme of poetic justice. In 6:1–7 he employed repetition (of the root *rʾš* and the word *sᵉrûḥîm*, "sprawled out") and paronomasia to demonstrate that the arrogant leaders of Samaria would be justly and appropriately punished by the Lord. In verse 1 these leaders are referred to as the "notable men of the foremost (*rēʾšît*) nation." According to verse 6, these individuals used the "finest (*rēʾšît*) lotions" to anoint their bodies. Appropriately they would be first (*rōʾš*, v. 7) in line when the roll call of exiles was given! In that day those who loved to "lounge" (*sᵉruḥîm*, v. 4) on their couches would find that their "lounging" (*sᵉrûḥîm*, v. 7) had come to an end. The verb translated "will end" (*sār*, v. 7) sounds like *sᵉrûḥîm*, further highlighting the correspondence between sin and punishment.[11]

Conclusion

While wordplay has numerous functions,[12] its most exegetically significant uses are to indicate correspondence and contrast (or reversal). The prophets frequently used wordplay to bring out the relationship between events that on the surface might seem unrelated or only loosely connected. This is especially true with respect to the themes of sin and judgment. The prophets used wordplay to draw attention to the appropriate or poetic nature of divine justice. A word used in the accusatory section of a prophetic message to describe the sin of an offender is repeated, or matched by a similar sounding word, in the accompanying announcement of judgment on that sin, impressing one with the fact that the punishment announced by God fits the crime committed.

The prophets also employed wordplay to draw contrasts between two or more phenomena. The precise nature of the contrast varies from context to context, as the examples cited in this chapter illustrate. Theologically speaking, wordplay often highlights the sharp distinction between the divine and human perspectives. God's erring people fell short of His holy standard (Amos 5:10, 15) and failed to evaluate properly His sovereign actions (Mic. 6:3–4). Consequently they failed to achieve their own ambitions (Amos 3:12; Mic. 2:5, 10). In spite of His people's sin, which brings harsh divine judgment, God still promised to restore Israel and reverse their situation, a fact highlighted by wordplay (Hos. 13:7; 14:9, Eng. v. 8; and Isa. 32:9, 11, 18). In this way one gains insight into the gracious character of divine salvation. The same God who appropriately judges sin promises to reverse completely the effects of that judgment.

CHAPTER 10

Structure, Style, and the Prophetic Message: An Analysis of Isaiah 5:8–30

Robert B. Chisholm, Jr.

I n her final, unforgettable adventure in Wonderland, Alice appeared as a witness at the trial of an unfortunate knave accused of stealing the queen's tarts. After listening to the White Rabbit present some cryptic, nonsensical verses as evidence against the defendant, Alice in exasperation challenged the jurors, "If any one of them can explain it, I'll give him sixpence. *I* don't believe there's an atom of meaning in it." In moments of absolute honesty every would-be interpreter of the Old Testament prophets, when confronted by their all-too-often impenetrable messages, has uttered words similar to those of Alice.

Why are these prophetic messages so difficult to comprehend? Often the reason is the major barrier the interpreter faces, the immense distance (chronological, geographical, cultural, and linguistic) that separates him from the prophetic author. Due to modern advances in textual criticism, philology, and archaeology, however, one is often able to cross the expanse. Yet even when this long, arduous journey is successfully completed, problems sometimes remain. Frequently the prophetic message defies attempts to discern its organizing principle(s) and summarize its theological theme(s). On occasion the prophet's words seem to be a disorganized collection of unrelated themes. To make matters worse, the prophets did not always express their ideas in straightforward, propositional statements. In fact their highly poetic, impassioned style frustrates efforts to theologize their messages.

Fortunately the situation is not as bleak as it seems. As the recent trend toward literary study of the Bible gains impetus,[1] significant breakthroughs in the understanding of Scripture are taking place. In particular, studies in the prophets are revealing that the prophetic messages are organized in a highly artistic manner. The force of the messages and their theological themes are linked to and at times veiled within their structure and style. As more is learned about the literary structures and rhetorical devices employed by the prophets, understanding of and appreciation for their profound messages grow. Even in texts whose organization and meaning have been reasonably clear for some time, this new emphasis is bringing greater precision and sophistication to interpretation.

The Method

Many scholars call this study of structure and style rhetorical criticism. However, proponents of this approach have yet to achieve unanimity in defining the discipline and outlining its method.[2] For some, rhetorical criticism is a rather loosely defined, all-encompassing analysis of a text's structure(s) and stylistic devices.[3] Others propose a more restricted definition and apply the categories of classical rhetoric to the biblical text.[4] Despite these differences in approach, it is possible to arrive at a basic working definition of biblical rhetorical criticism. Understanding "rhetoric" as "the art of speaking or writing effectively," one may define rhetorical criticism as "the study of a speaker's/author's communicative technique." Rhetorical criticism studies the dynamics of the author's/speaker's relationship to his audience via his message. It examines how the author/speaker has organized (structure) and expressed (style) his message in order to achieve maximum effectiveness in light of his purpose.

Some might object to applying the term "rhetoric" to the biblical message for at least two reasons. First, the word frequently has negative connotations in today's culture. "Rhetoric" makes one think of campaign speeches and political demagoguery. Second, "rhetoric" is usually associated with oral presentations. Since the Bible is a collection of *writings* in book form, the term "rhetoric" seems inapplicable.

Both of these objections are invalid. While the term does have a specialized meaning that conveys a negative idea, it can also carry the more general, neutral sense defined above. Also the term may be applied legitimately to written texts.[5] Even more importantly, one must recognize that the Bible, in the context in which it originated, was primarily intended to be read aloud. Before the invention of printing, it was impossible for copies of texts to be widely distributed. Consequently public readings of texts were the normal means of dissemination. One presupposes that texts would be composed with this form of communication in mind. This built-in oral orientation should leave no doubt that the biblical texts are valid objects of rhetorical analysis.[6]

Biblical rhetorical criticism has built on the foundation of form criticism. Despite the great value of form criticism,[7] especially in its identification of typical structural patterns in biblical texts, it has proven inadequate. Many have become dissatisfied with its inflexibility, overemphasis on the typical, and tendency to fragmentize texts.[8] Rhetorical criticism moves "beyond" form criticism in that it gives attention to a text's individuality and unique structural elements and focuses on the unity of the text in its present form. Its concern for stylistic devices takes it far beyond the scope of form criticism.

This brief study employs rhetorical criticism in analyzing Isaiah 5:8–30.[9] The purposes are (a) to illustrate the types of observations a rhetorical approach might include and (b) to demonstrate the benefits of such an approach to the interpretive-theological process. The study is intended to be illustrative and provocative, not exhaustive or methodologically definitive. A thorough rhetorical study of the passage would need to include an application of classical categories and a detailed treatment of figures of speech, both of which are beyond the scope of this study.

Isaiah 5:8–30: Audience and Purpose

The rhetorical situation or context of Isaiah 5:8–30 must first be determined. Several factors complicate this task. While the broad outlines of Isaiah's time are known, it is impossible to date this particular message precisely. The internal evidence of the prophecy indicates that Isaiah's purpose was to convince the sinful people of Judah that divine judgment was both necessary and certain. There appears to be no intent to motivate repentance. The prophet's role was to condemn sin and announce divine vengeance. An examination of Isaiah's commission at the time of his call (Isa. 6:9–13) supports this conclusion.

One cannot limit the scope of Isaiah's message, however, to the sinful audience addressed in the prophecy or to the context in which it was initially proclaimed. A righteous remnant also became recipients of the message (Isa. 3:10; 6:13b). For them the message was a reminder of the Lord's demand for covenant fidelity and a motivation to continued faithfulness (8:11–17). The prophecy's heavy emphasis on divine justice possibly even encouraged this group. If evildoers were punished in an appropriate manner, then the righteous could expect an appropriate reward from the divine Judge (3:10–11). The remnant would have interpreted the coming judgment as the first stage in the divine program of renewal and restoration (1:21–31).

Once the prophecy is viewed in the larger context of chapters 1–12, the major theme of which is restoration through judgment, this positive emphasis is apparent as well. In this canonical context Isaiah 5:8–30 became a warning to all who heard or read it that only the faithful would participate in the Golden Age to come.[10]

The Structure of Isaiah 5:8–30

FORM CRITICISM

One is immediately struck by the sixfold use of הוֹי (translated "woe" in the NIV and NASB) in verses 8–22. Its repetition suggests its function as a structural device. Most commentators, following this lead, have divided verses 8–24 into six individual units, each introduced by הוֹי.[11] Form critics, who have isolated the הוֹי (or "woe") oracle as a distinct prophetic speech form with a specific *Sitz im Leben*, usually support this arrangement.[12]

From a form-critical standpoint this outline is acceptable but inadequate. A more basic formal pattern, the judgment speech, into which the הוֹי pattern fits, is discernible. Westermann has shown that the prophetic הוֹי oracle is a subcategory or variant of the judgment speech.[13] The basic components of the judgment speech are an accusation and an announcement of judgment.[14] In the הוֹי type, the vocative of address following the interjection often contains, at least in part, the accusation. As will be seen, הוֹי itself suggests impending doom, but often a more developed announcement will appear.

At first glance verses 8–30 fit incompletely into the judgment speech pattern. Only the first, second, and sixth woe oracles follow the accusation-announcement scheme.[15] The pattern appears to break down in verses 18–21. Woes 3–5 (vv. 18–19, 20, 21) are only accusatory; in each case no announcement of judgment intervenes before the following הוֹי oracle. Form critics explain this inconsistency in various ways. For example Clements maintains that the expected announcements have fallen out in the course of transmission.[16] Kaiser, on the other hand, regards the announcements attached to the other woes as later additions.[17]

Once certain rhetorical features are recognized in verses 18–30, the apparent breakdown in the judgment speech pattern can be explained without resorting to such explanations. If one combines woes 3–6 (vv. 18–23), they constitute a lengthy accusation, to which verses 24–30 (v. 24b being an exception) form the concluding announcement. The clustering of woes with no intervening announcements has the rhetorical effect of heightening the accusatory tone of the section. The sequence of four הוֹי pronouncements delivered in rapid succession leaves one overwhelmed by and thoroughly convinced of the people's guilt. Thus rhetorical design led the author to depart from the usual formal pattern involving הוֹי. Nevertheless the typical judgment speech pattern was preserved.

This heightening or intensifying effect actually characterizes the entire passage as illustrated by the following form-critical outline of verses 8–30:

Section	Woe(s)	Accusation	Announcement
I	1	v. 8	vv. 9–10
II	2	vv. 11–12	vv. 13–17
III	3–6	vv. 18–23, 24b	vv. 24a, 25–30

The accusations increase in length from 2 lines of Hebrew text in I (following the arrangement in the *Biblia Hebraica Stuttgartensia*) to 4 (in II) to 10 (III). Likewise, the announcements of judgment increase in length from 3 lines (I) to 7 (II) to 15 (III). Consequently the three major sections as a whole increase from 5 lines (I) to 11 (II) to 25 (III). Through this snowballing effect the reader/listener becomes increasingly impressed by two facts: The people are indeed guilty, and their judgment is certainly impending.

"BEYOND" FORM CRITICISM

The form-critical approach utilized above, even though supplemented by rhetorical considerations, fails to reflect all the structural artistry of Isaiah 5:8–30. A more thorough rhetorical analysis yields the following outline, which fits into the form-critical framework presented above, but also reflects a chiastic pattern within the larger unit:[18]

(I)   A   Accusation: social injustice (v. 8)
      *   Announcement of judgment (vv. 9–10)
(II) B   Accusation: carousing (vv. 11–12a)
          C   Accusation: failure to recognize Lord's work (v. 12b)
      *   Announcement of judgment (vv. 13–17)
(III)   C' Accusation: failure to recognize Lord's work (vv. 18–21)
          B' Accusation: carousing (v. 22)
      A' Accusation: social injustice (v. 23)
      *   Announcement of judgment (vv. 24–30)

The outline reflects the chiastic arrangement of the individual elements in the three accusatory sections.[19] Two related examples of social injustice are condemned in verses 8 and 23. The condemnation of accumulation of properties (v. 8) is not a general criticism of real estate endeavor. Rather, economic exploitation (cf. Mic. 2:1–2), though under the guise of legality, is in view. As Kaiser states, greedy landowners were "taking advantage of the distress of small farmers and craftsmen which may have been caused by sickness, crop-failure, inflation, or excessive taxation." He explains, "Such people would be offered a loan; and if they were unable to pay it back at a later date, their movable possessions would be pawned, their children would be taken in payment and thus be made slaves, and finally their house and land would be seized."[20] This self-seeking and cruel practice reduced a large segment of the population to a level of inescapable poverty and represented a blatant practical denial of the covenantal principle that the Lord alone owns the land (cf. Lev. 25:23).[21] The legal corruption described in Isaiah 5:23 was one of the means whereby these wealthy individuals accomplished their purposes.[22]

Verses 11–12a and 22 contain accusations against those who lived only to carouse. From sunrise to sunset their time was spent in revelry. This group included the wealthy upper crust referred to in verse 8. They had both the time and the means to sustain such a lifestyle (cf. Amos 4:1; 6:1–7).

Insensitivity to the Lord's purposes is condemned in Isaiah 5:12b, 18–21. The references to the Lord's "work" in verses 12 and 19 (מַעֲשֶׂה—probably the impending judgment He had threatened through His prophet: 10:12; 28:21–22) tie the two sections together. The arrogant (5:21) perverters of all proper ethical standards (vv. 18, 20) failed to recognize the Lord's approaching "work" (v. 12b). In fact in mockery they urged Him to bring it to pass quickly (v. 19).

A closer examination of the substructure of verses 11–17 reveals two more chiastic patterns. In verses 11–12 carousing and insensitivity to the Lord's work are condemned, respectively. In the announcement of judgment in verse 13 these are taken up in reverse order. Insensitivity would be punished by exile (v. 13a) and the carousers would die, appropriately, of hunger and thirst (v. 13b).[23] The chiasmus can be outlined as follows:

A Carousing condemned (vv. 11–12a)
  B Insensitivity condemned (v. 12b)
  B' Insensitivity punished (v. 13a)
A' Carousing punished (v. 13b)

The judgment announcement in verse 13 is expanded in verses 14–17.[24] The carousers, besides dying of hunger and thirst, would themselves become the main course at another banquet—Sheol's.[25] Death, personified as a devouring enemy, was about to open its mouth wide and swallow up the revelers (v. 14).[26] At that time proud men would be abased (v. 15) as the Lord exalted Himself (v. 16). Thematically verses 15–16 present two sides of the same coin, a fact highlighted by the repetition of the root גבה (cf. גְבֹהִים in v. 15 and וַיִּגְבַּה in v. 16). The "eating" motif, used in verse 14, reappears in verse 17. Following the disappearance of the carousers, only sheep[27] would be left to graze on the ruins of the wealthy.[28] Once more a chiastic arrangement is apparent:

A Sheol *eats* the sinners (v. 14)
  B The *self-exalting* sinners are humbled (v. 15)
  B' God *exalts* Himself (v. 16)
A' Sheep *eat* on the ruins of the sinners' dwellings (v. 17)

The placement of verses 15–16 in the middle of this chiasmus is significant. The theme expressed in these verses is the dominant one for verses 8–30, namely, that the sovereign Lord was about to exalt Himself through His just judgment of arrogant rebels against His covenant. The announcement of judgment (vv. 13–17), which provides the context for verses 15–16, is the second of three in verses 8–30 and is therefore central to the overall structure of the passage. Thus the central place of verses 15–16 in the structure of this particular announcement highlights their thematic centrality in the passage. This is an example of form contributing in a significant way to the force and emphasis of the prophetic message.

The structure and function of verses 24–30 require special

attention. Verse 24a contains an announcement of judgment (cf. the introductory לָכֵן) complementing the accusation of verses 18–23. However, in verse 24b there is a movement back to accusation (cf. introductory כִּי). One gets the impression that verse 24b is designed to summarize and conclude the preceding message by clearly identifying the essence of Israel's sin (breach of covenant). Consequently verses 25–30 seem to be a rather awkward appendix or addition. Indeed many commentators regard verses 25–30 as a misplaced intrusion that really belongs with 9:8–21.[29] However, the matter is not this simple. Once again rhetorical considerations prove to be instructive.

The expansion of the announcement of judgment in 5:25–30 has an important rhetorical function in the development of the message. It was simply impossible for Isaiah to terminate his message with a reference to Judah's sin (v. 24b). Throughout the preceding context the movement has been from sin to judgment. The prophet emphasized that Judah's sin demanded and would receive appropriate punishment. A return to the reason for judgment (v. 24b) also required a return to the announcement of that judgment. The nature of the accusation in verse 24b, by which the essence of Judah's sin is exposed, demands an announcement of judgment that is commensurate with the transgression. The detailed and terrifying picture drawn in verses 25–30 satisfies this demand.

Also the brief announcement of verse 24a fails to bring to an appropriate conclusion the developing intensity that the prophet has created, especially through his heaping of the woes in verses 18–23. Something more is needed, a fact to which the text itself testifies in verse 25b. The expansion of the judgment announcement in verses 25–30 brings the developing pattern of the preceding verses to a powerful culmination. These final verses demonstrate beyond all doubt that justice would indeed be carried out in a most tangible way on the violators of the covenant.

Stylistic Devices in Isaiah 5:8–30

IRONY AND POETIC JUSTICE

The prophet employed several stylistic devices that contribute to the effectiveness of his message. Particularly prominent is his use of irony to express the theme of poetic justice.

Irony is present in each of the accusation-announcement cycles. Verses 9–10 describe the judgment about to come on the rich landowners of verse 8. Appropriately those who added "house to house" would see those same houses destroyed and left uninhabited. The fields they accumulated would yield only a fraction of their potential.[30] According to verse 13, the carousers described in verses 11–12 would die, ironically, of hunger and thirst. Even more appropriately, they were to become the main course at Sheol's banquet (v. 14), with only sheep being left to inhabit the banqueting halls (now in ruins) the carousers once frequented (v. 17). Verses 26–30 describe in vivid detail how the "warriors" of verse 22 (note גִּבּוֹרִים and אַנְשֵׁי־חַיִל) whose skill was solely in the area of mixing drinks, would be overwhelmed by true warriors, armed with all the destructive implements of warfare.

In this third cycle (vv. 18–30) word repetition contributes powerfully to the theme of poetic justice. In verse 19 the proud rebels challenge the Lord to hasten (יְמַהֵר) His work. They mockingly called for the plan of the Lord to come (וְתָבוֹאָה). According to verses 24–30 this work of judgment would indeed come hurriedly, in the form of the mighty Assyrian army. Appropriately the same roots employed in verse 19 are used in verse 26 to describe the Assyrians' swift approach (מְהֵרָה קַל יָבוֹא). The proud rebels would get just what they scoffingly requested.[31]

Another example of wordplay involves the use of חֹשֶׁךְ), "darkness," and אוֹר, 'light,' in verses 20 and 30. In the former verse the rebels' perversion of moral and ethical standards is compared to turning darkness into light and light into darkness. Darkness and light correspond to evil and good mentioned in the preceding line. According to verse 30 the "darkness" produced by the clouds of judgment would sweep over the sinners' land, blotting out the "light" (cf. esp. וְאוֹר חָשַׁךְ). While חֹשֶׁךְ) and אוֹר are used in different senses in verses 20 and 30, the repetition of the words is essential to the overriding theme of the judgment announcement, namely, that the coming judgment would be appropriate for the crime committed. Those who had brought "darkness" to the moral/ethical realm would find their sphere of sinful activity "darkened" by God's judgment.

הוֹי AND AN APPROACHING FUNERAL

By addressing the Judean sinners with הוֹי, the prophet compared them, by implication, to a dead man. While the background of the woe oracle has been debated by form critics, it is likely that it originated in the funeral lament.[32] In several passages הוֹי introduces a mourning cry. For example the old prophet lamented the death of the Judean man of God with the words הוֹי אָחִי, "Oh, my brother" (1 Kings 13:30).[33] Thus when the prophets prefaced their judgment speeches with הוֹי, they were suggesting that the sinners' demise was so certain that their death could be lamented proleptically.[34] Rhetorically this would have been a powerful device.[35] The prophet was figuratively acting out their funeral before their very eyes, reminding them in the process of the reasons for and manner of their death.

A WORD PICTURE OF THE ASSYRIAN ARMY

A vivid, detailed description, or word-picture,[36] of the invading Assyrian army (vv. 26–30) brings this prophecy to a powerful, terrifying climax. The fact that the campaign originated with the Lord (v. 26a; cf. 7:18–20) spells doom for Judah. The foreignness of the enemy (5:26a) creates an ominous atmosphere,[37] especially in light of the covenant curse of Deuteronomy 28:49, to which the prophet may have been alluding.[38] The army's approach is swift and unswerving (Isa. 5:26b–27). Its seemingly superhuman warriors (v. 27a) never rest (v. 27b). They are prepared for battle and equipped with the best of weapons (v. 28a). The Assyrians' horses gallop along without injury, while their chariots race toward their objective (v. 28b).[39] The invaders are comparable to a vicious, roaring lion that allows its prey no escape (v. 29). The deafening Assyrian roar is accompanied by the descent of the dark clouds of judgment (v. 30).

This preview of the forthcoming Assyrian invasion is immensely effective from a rhetorical standpoint. Invincible armies, roaring uncaged lions (cf. Amos 3:8), and ominous storm clouds are inherently fear-provoking. Also Isaiah's audience was certainly familiar with Assyria's military might, if not by firsthand experience, then by oral accounts of earlier or contemporary campaigns against neighboring states.[40]

The language used in Isaiah 5:29–30 resembles that employed by Assyrian kings contemporary with Isaiah to describe their military prowess and accomplishments. The comparison to lions was quite common. For example Sargon described his valor as follows, "In the anger of my heart I mustered the masses of Assur's troops and, raging like a lion, I set my face to conquer those lands."[41] The references to roaring (vv. 29–30) may allude to the king's powerful battle cry, a motif that appears as well in

Assyrian battle accounts. Sennacherib recalled, "I raised my voice, rumbling like a storm. Like Adad I roared."[42] On the other hand, Clements suggests that the roaring metaphor "makes allusion to the general noise and din of an army."[43] Sargon described a siege as follows: "Over that city I made the loud noise of my army resound like Adad, and the inhabitants . . . his people, the old men and old women, went up on the roofs of their houses and wept bitterly."[44] The darkness motif (v. 30b) may allude to the invading forces sweeping over the land. Sargon described an invasion in similar terms: "As with a dense cloud of the night, I covered that province, and all of its great cities."[45]

Of what significance are these points of contact between Isaiah's description and that of the Assyrians? Since the motifs are conventional in nature and widespread, in both biblical and other ancient Near Eastern literature, the similarity may be purely coincidental. In this case both Isaiah and the authors of the Assyrian annals drew on a common stock of conventional ancient Near Eastern warrior imagery. However, it is possible that Isaiah was familiar with Assyrian propaganda and purposely described the Assyrian army in Assyrian terms.[46] If the Judean populace, at least to some extent, was also aware of this propaganda, the rhetorical effect of Isaiah's description would have been greatly enhanced.

Conclusion

A form critical and rhetorical approach to the structure of Isaiah 5:8–30 enables one to move beyond a simplistic outline of the text (based on the succession of "woes") and reveals several overlapping structures that testify to the author's literary and rhetorical artistry. The overall structure of the message contributes to its rhetorical force and highlights its central theme (cf. vv. 15–16). Several literary devices enhance the power of the message and emphasize its themes. Especially noteworthy is the use of irony and word repetition to express the theme of poetic justice. In this way one gains greater insight into the character of the coming judgment and of the Judge Himself.

CHAPTER 11

Literary Genres in Isaiah 40–55

Eugene H. Merrill

Contemporary scholarly consensus recognizes four major genres (disputations, lawsuits, salvation oracles, and proclamations of salvation) and one minor genre (hymns/hymnic) in Isaiah 40–55.[1] Each of these will be grouped under the categories of hymns, polemic genres, and salvation speeches.

The Hymns and Hymnic Sections

It is virtually impossible to find any two scholars who agree on any list of hymns or hymnic passages in Isaiah 40–55, but the following will satisfy most: 40:12–26, 27–31; 42:10–13; 44:23; 45:8; 48:20–21; 49:13; 51:3; 52:9–10.

Only a brief review of the hymn/psalm genre can be presented here. Gressmann defined the hymn as fundamentally a praise of the deity.[2] He said that the hymns in Isaiah 40–55 enumerate Yahweh's great deeds through predications in the form of epithets. Any texts that use that characteristically participial construction should be considered hymnic. Gressmann saw four categories: (a) hymnic expansions of the introduction and conclusion formulae; (b) hymnic expansions of self-predication expressions (which he considered to be due to the Babylonian environment);[3] (c) concluding hymns;[4] and (d) larger hymns.[5] He has often been accused of finding too many examples of hymns, but in fact he sees no hymns at all independent of their contexts. That is, the prophet did not use the hymn as a separate genre but only to introduce, conclude, or tie together nonhymnic sections.

Mowinckel, in his monumental work *The Psalms in Israel's Worship,* divided Israelite hymns into two main types—general and specific.[6] The general hymn praises the deeds and/or attributes of Yahweh and is appropriate for any cultic occasion. The specific hymn, on the other hand, concentrates on a single deed or quality and has its origin in a particular cultic festival.

Structurally the hymn usually opens with an exhortation to

sing, praise, thank, and exalt the Lord, usually in the imperative plural. Next follows the person or persons who are so exhorted; this may even include inanimate objects such as heaven and earth, woods, and rocks, or the sea. Yahweh is always mentioned by name (in the Psalter, at least), frequently with a series of laudatory attributes or epithets.

The body of the hymn generally begins with the basis for exhortation introduced by כִּי or something similar. Then follow recitations of Yahweh's deeds and qualities sometimes augmented by appositional nouns or participles. In expanded form this body may consist of a series of sentences each mentioning something for which Yahweh is praiseworthy. They usually are made up of appositions, relative clauses, and nominal clauses. Frequently these laudatory clauses speak of Yahweh in relation to history and they do so with the verb in the perfect, imperfect, or preterite. There may also be the form of rhetorical questions, exclamations, or indicative statements.

Occasionally the hymn closes with a brief wish or prayer for God's blessing. In this connection the hymn may serve as an introduction to a lament or petition, exactly as is the case in the Assyrian and Babylonian cultic songs.

Mowinckel drew special attention to the "I-hymn," which, though lacking in the Psalter, is common in Job and Isaiah. "In this way," Mowinckel pointed out, the prophet "emphasizes the position of Yahweh as the only God, the creator of the world and the governor of history and the absolute superior of all strange gods."[7] This form in Babylonian hymnody consisted of the epiphany of the god who comes forth to tell his name and reveal his character in hymnal form, enumerating his deeds and qualities. This model was fully used by the prophet.

Muilenburg was struck with the frequent use of hymns and hymnic style in Isaiah 40–55, noting that the poet used characteristics of this form especially in his introductions or with the covenant asseveration "I am Yahweh."[8] Westermann, describing particularly the "eschatological hymns of praise" in Isaiah 40–55 (42:10–13; 44:23; 45:8; 48:20–21; 49:13; 52:7–10), drew attention to the ways these resemble the descriptive psalms of praise—his designation for hymns in the Psalter—in their introductions, the call of praise in the imperative, and the extension of this call by means of jussives. He pointed out a significant difference, however: Whereas the psalms celebrate the majesty and goodness of God, the prophet always, in his series of attributions, introduces an act or deed of God.[9] The prophet always roots his praises of God in historical activity. Crüsemann, contrary to Gunkel, rejected the distinction between collective psalms of thanksgiving and hymns.[10] He did, however, distinguish between the "imperative hymn" and "participial hymn," the latter closely related in both form and content to the Babylonian hymns. The imperative in Isaiah 40–55 is found in 42:10–13; 48:20–21; 49:13; and 52:9; while the participial is in 40:12–26, 28–30; 42:5; 43:16; 45:6b–7, 18; 51:15.

In a recent dissertation, Deming has traced the genre "call to praise" in Isaiah 40–55.[11] She used this term to describe the hymn proper, the form of which is as follows:[12]

1. A series of imperatives (or jussives)
2. Vocative
3. Substantiation introduced by a causal כִּי + divine name
   a. Verb in the perfect in the first clause(s)
   b. Verb in the imperfect in the second clause(s).

She limited the hymns to 42:10–13; 44:23; 49:13; 51:3; and 52:9–10, not all of which contain all the characteristics. Her typology seems sound, however, as her exhaustive dissection of each of the exemplars demonstrates.

In addition to the hymns are the passages with hymnic material, namely, 40:9–11; 45:8; 48:20–21; 54:1. These, she suggested, are in the structure of the call to praise but are technically not hymns since they omit essential characteristics of form and/or content. Deming described the participial constructions so typical of Isaiah 40–55 as expansions of the messenger formulae which provide introductions to prophetic oracles.[13] These include 42:5 (+ vv. 6–7); 43:16–17 (+ vv. 18–21); 45:1 (+ vv. 2–7); 45:18a (+ vv. 18b–19); and 49:5 (+ vv. 1–6). Shorter participial elements are in 43:1a; 43:14a; 44:2a; 44:6a; 44:24a; 45:11a; 48:17a; 49:7a.

The self-predication formulae, common to Isaiah and the Babylonian hymnic genre, are isolated by Deming as follows:[14] 44:24b–28; 45:6b–7; 46:9b–11a; 48:12b–13; and 51:12–16. Shorter units exhibiting the formula are 41:13; 43:3a; 43:15; 43:25a; 45:3b; 45:19b; 48:17b; 49:26b. As for 40:12–31, Deming (with Westermann) treated this as a special case. This is a larger unit consisting of four disputations held together by hymnic themes and grammatical features characteristic of the main sections of Psalter hymns.[15]

That the prophet employed hymns and hymnic material in his composition is, then, quite clear. And it is evident that he did so in ways that are unique to him. Though such characteristics as the "I-form," the participial attribution, self-predications, and sense of praise related to historical events may have roots in Israel's ancient hymnic traditions, they find their peculiar combinations and florescence only in Isaiah 40–55, a fact which may be explicable in that the prophet was sensitive to and deliberately utilized the Babylonian milieu which he anticipated and against which he undertook his labors.

The Polemic Genres[16]

Scholars have long noted that Isaiah, in defense of the majesty and integrity of Yahweh against both Israel and the nations, frequently employed language and imagery from the courtroom or (in the case of disputation) from a forensic setting. This is understandable, for, as Klein said, in spite of whatever other miseries the future exiles might encounter in Babylonia, their most serious problem would be theological. "How could they believe in a God who lost the latest war? Why not worship the gods of Babylon whose armies, after all, were the winners?"[17] To meet the problem, the prophet created or at least took up creatively the polemic speeches which, according to Klein, "are defenses of Yahweh's claim to rule history and a radical denial of the counterclaim of the gods (of Babylon)."[18]

As with the hymns, modern form-critical studies of the lawsuit genres must begin with Gressmann's famous article in 1914.[19] Again following up on Gunkel, Gressmann saw in Isaiah 40–55 the word of rebuke *(Scheltwort)* but in this prophet, as opposed to others, he said there was no close connection between rebuke and threat *(Drohwort)*. The reason, of course, is that there is no threat in this corpus; it is a book of promise and hope.

Gressmann identified the following passages as lawsuits: 41:1–13; 41:21–19; 43:8–13; 44:6–20; 45:20–21; and 48:12–16. He noted that the form was borrowed from secular law courts but that in Isaiah Yahweh Himself was on trial. The prophet argued that since Yahweh predicted all that happened, only He is God and the Babylonian gods were patent frauds.

Köhler also studied the lawsuit, which he designated *Streitgespräch* ("dispute").[20] With Gressmann he maintained a secular origin for the form, a legal process that included a presentation of the charge, entering of evidence, a challenge to the accused for his defense, and the judge's verdict and sentence. Köhler indicated the prophets took over this sequence intact and made it their own. From the nine examples Köhler adduced (40:12–16, 17–20, 21–26; 41:1–5, 21–24; 42:18–25; 43:8–13; 48:14–16; 49:14–21), he drew the following conclusions: The whole composition consists of two trials—Yahweh versus foreign gods and Yahweh versus Israel. In the first He is the Accuser and in the second He is the Accused. The results are that Yahweh put the Babylonian gods to rout but was able at the same time to answer all of Israel's charges.

Begrich, in his edition of Gunkel's *Einleitung im die Psalmen,* outlined the structure of the *Gerichtsrede* ("lawsuit") as follows:

I. A description of the scene of judgment
II. The speech of the plaintiff
   A. Heaven and earth are appointed judges
   B. Summons to the defendant (or judges)
   C. Address in the second person to the defendant
      1. Accusation in question form
      2. Refutation of possible arguments
      3. Specific indictment.[21]

Examples from elsewhere are Isaiah 1:2–3; Micah 6:1–8; and Jeremiah 2:4–13. Those from Isaiah 40–55 are 41:1–5, 21–29; 43:8–13, 22–28; 44:6–8; 48:11; and 50:1–2a. Through even more detailed analysis Begrich concluded that a subcategory of the *Gerichtsrede* is the *Disputationswort,* the purpose of which is to convince an opponent of one's view. Apparently Begrich was the first to make this important distinction clearly.

Alternate views as to the sources of the polemic genres were submitted by von Waldow [22] and Harvey.[23] The former maintained a distinction between the cultic and secular types which he identified respectively in 41:1–5, 21–29; 43:8–13; 44:6–8; and 43:22–28; 50:1–3. But even the secular had cultic origins, as can be seen in the fact that Yahweh is both Prosecutor and Judge, something foreign to secular trials. Von Waldow later changed this stance by admitting that the lawsuit was modeled after secular prototypes in form but, in the hands of the prophets, derived its content from covenant traditions.

Harvey drew attention to the possibility of international law as the inspiration for the prophetic lawsuit genre. He cited only 42:18–25 and 48:12–19 as examples from Isaiah 40–55 and held that even these are incomplete.

Gemser, after surveying the phenomena in Israelite life and the vocabulary employed to describe them, turned to the prophets where he found that the "*rib*-metaphor" lawsuit received a thoroughly new content and application.[24] This is notably true of Isaiah, who, Gemser suggested, applied the pattern "in a most developed, perfected form"[25] both because of his unusual artistic skills and the subjects of his kerygma: the incomparability of Yahweh as opposed to other gods and the theodicy of Yahweh who treated His people righteously and redemptively. The prophetic use of the genre shows that Yahweh is personal. He is righteous and unpredictable, but one can make appeal to Him, to His heart, His compassion, His grace.

Schoors assigned to the lawsuit the term "trial speech,"[26] giving the following examples in Isaiah 40–55: 41:1–5, 21–29; 42:18–25; 43:8–13, 22–28; 44:6–8; 45:18–25; 50:1–3. Schoors agreed with von Waldow that the form comes from the administration of law in the city gate, but the content comes from the covenant tradition.[27] Schoors described 42:18–25; 43:22–28; and 50:1–3 as *rib*-speeches since they involved Yahweh with Israel. The remainder are secularized lawsuits whose direct historical background are the anticipated religious persecutions at the hands of the Babylonians.[28] Even the *rib*, however, undergoes modification by the prophet. Schoors pointed out that "instead of accusations we have challenges and arguments, instead of condemnation there is the conclusion that the claims of the adversary are false. All this makes the dt.-Isaian *rib* a reality *sui generis*."[29]

In his closely reasoned investigation of the rhetoric of Isaiah 40–55, Melugin assessed the polemic genres as constituting two aspects of a trial speech: that between Yahweh and the nations and that between Yahweh and Israel. And for each he identified a different form. The trial involving the nations consists of the following elements:

1. Yahweh's opponents (or witnesses) are summoned to trial.
2. Yahweh argues His case in a highly stereotyped disputation style containing a question(s) introduced by *mi* ("who"); the answer is the key to the resolution of the dispute.

3. There is a closing by the first person assertion by Yahweh in the self-praise hymn style or by a question in that style.[30]

The trial involving Israel, in which Yahweh is the accused, takes this form:

1. A reproving question concerning the accusation.
2. An assertion of innocence by the accused.
3. A counteraccusation by the accused.
4. A call for a decision.[31]

It is clear from this convincing analysis that the distinctions between Yahweh as Plaintiff and Yahweh as Defendant are valid, at least formally. That He succeeded in prevailing in each circumstance presupposes that there are certain common arguments and stylistic devices such as self-praise and predicative ascription.

Nielsen has made an in-depth scrutiny of the lawsuit genre of the prophets. She traced the history of the discussion and then made some refinements of old positions as well as proposals of her own.[32] Perhaps the best way to understand her position is to see examples of her analyses. The first is 41:1–5, which she agrees is in lawsuit form but should not be considered a criminal case since the Babylonian gods have committed no crime. It is, rather, a response by Yahweh to claims made by these gods or (more technically) by their devotees.[33] Nielsen notes the following structure:

v. 1a: Yahweh calls the peoples as witnesses.
v. 1b: Yahweh summons the foreign gods to the trial.
v. 2–4a: The issue is presented in the form of a question: Who stands behind Cyrus?
v. 4a–b: The judgment: It is Yahweh who leads Cyrus.
v. 5:   Yahweh's concluding statement about the people's acceptance of the judgment.[34]

As an example of disputation she cited 43:8–13, where Yahweh is said to have presented Himself as the only one who actively intervenes in history.[35] This predication is vindicated by the inability of the opponents to contravene His testimony. This is all the more devastating in that Israel is both witness and judge and so must witness against herself. Nielsen's structuring follows:

v. 8–9a: Israel is called as a witness.

v. 9b–c: Yahweh challenges His opponents (the pagan gods) to produce evidence in the form of predictions.

v. 10a: There is an appeal for Israel to bear witness for Yahweh.

v. 10b–c: An account is given of the case in which Israel is to witness, and what she must come to understand, namely, that Yahweh is the only God.

v. 11–13:   The description of Yahweh's position as the only God continues and is followed by an appeal to Israel to bear witness to this (hymnically composed).[36]

As Schoors has suggested, following earlier scholars, there is a formal difference between the trial speech and the disputation. He stressed characteristics of the latter such as question and answer, and statement and counterstatement, as being unique to disputation. It usually begins with a question about the point at issue or a parallel point and then seeks to convince the opponent of this matter. Often the conclusion is not stated but is left for the opponent to deduce.[37] Such speeches start from the basis of Yahweh's creative power,[38] or sovereignty over history,[39] or both.[40] The corollary of Yahweh's power is the weakness of the other gods and their adherents.[41] The conclusion is that He can help His own people and will do as He pleases.[42]

Of all the forms in Isaiah 40–55, this is most likely the prophet's own creation.[43] This does not mean that he abandoned customary conventions from his own literary heritage, but that he took unusual freedom in the disputations to recombine and recast many elements in order to provide a medium suitable to the special task to which he addressed himself in a polytheistic milieu.

The Salvation Speeches

Since the discussion by Begrich,[44] the form known to Gunkel and Gressmann as *Verheissung* ("promise") has come to be accepted as "salvation oracle." Originally in the view of some the salvation oracle had its setting in cultic lamentation as an expression of thanksgiving following the granting of petition. In this respect the usage corresponds to Assyro-Babylonian practice where an oracle of salvation was attached, not to a community lament, but to a prayer, usually that of a king.

Begrich isolated the following examples of the salvation oracle in Isaiah 40–55: 41:8–13, 14–16; 43:1–3a, 5; (44:2–5?); 48:17–19; 49:7, 14–15; 51:7–8; 54:4–8. These, he said, originally followed the complaint and petition part of a lament psalm and preceded the certainty of a hearing.[45] The usual elements of their form follow:

1. A "fear-not" injunction
2. Direct address
3. A substantiating clause, usually in a nominative sentence
4. An expression that Yahweh has heard, couched in the perfect tense with Yahweh as the subject
5. An announcement of the future in the imperfect tense with Yahweh or other subjects. [46]

In an important article on the salvation oracle,[47] Harner argued that the genre consists of at least four parts:

1. Direct address to the recipient
2. The reassurance "fear not"
3. Divine self-predication
4. Message of salvation.[48]

Examples from Isaiah 40–55 are 41:8–13; 41:14–16 (a modified form with individual lament elements); 43:1–7 (which consists of two oracles: vv. 1–4 and vv. 5–7); and 44:1–5. Less complete examples are 44:6–8; 51:7–8, 12–16; and 54:4–8.

Harner identified several points of contact between the salvation oracle as formulated and used by Isaiah and that from the Mesopotamian world. Though these cannot be considered here, it is worth noting that Isaiah's extensive use of the genre may well have been prompted by the need for a suitable channel through which to communicate hope to a people who would be languishing in Babylonian exile.[49]

Schoors accepted Westermann's analysis on the whole and identified the following as representatives of the genre in Isaiah 40–55: 41:8–13, 14–16; 43:1–4, 5–7; 44:1–5; 54:4–6. The basic structure, according to Schoors, is this:

1. Introduction—usually "fear not"
2. Address
3. Assurance of salvation—usually introduced by כִּי

4. Substantiation
   a. Nominal—God's turning
   b. Verbal—God's intervention (in the perfect tense)
5. Outcome—imperfect tense
6. Goal.[50]

In line with previous scholars who connected the oracle of praise with the *Sitz im Leben* of cultic lament, Schoors noted that sometimes at the end of psalms of lamentation are found reversals of mood whereby the supplication changes to thanksgiving or praise. This is in response to oracles of salvation in which the petition of the prayer is granted.[51] Schoors then cited parallels from the cuneiform texts, many identical to those mentioned by Harner.

As suggested earlier, the salvation speeches consist not only of the oracles just described but another subgenre, proclamation of salvation. This type, first clearly articulated by Westermann,[52] differs from the oracle of salvation in the following ways:

1. It lacks a direct address.
2. It lays emphasis on a future aspect.
3. It speaks more concretely of what is to happen.
4. It is related to communal (not individual) lament.
5. It does not reflect any liturgical form.
6. It is delivered by a prophet, not a priest.[53]

Westermann analyzes the form (which he sees only in 41:17–20; 42:14–17; 43:16–21; 45:14–17; and 49:17–20) as follows:

1. Allusion to the collective lament.
2. Proclamation of salvation.
   a. God's turning to help (imperfect tense).
   b. God's intervention (imperfect).
3. Purpose of intervention (imperfect).[54]

This same scholar suggested that at times (e.g., in 49:17–26) the proclamation could be combined with other genres such as the disputation. This is not surprising since, as Schoors affirmed,[55] the message of Isaiah is theocentric, and both the trial speeches (which are based on historical acts of Yahweh) and the proclamation of salvation oracles (which are based on the present and future acts of Yahweh) are designed to defend His uniqueness and absolute sovereignty.

Conclusion

The foregoing brief survey of the literature of Isaiah 40–55 has shown that contemporary scholarship recognizes five major genres in the corpus: hymns, lawsuits, disputations, salvation oracles, and proclamations of salvation. In addition, of course, there are at least remnants of other types. It is perhaps remarkable that the genre "prayer," which is so common elsewhere in the Old Testament and in other ancient Near Eastern literature, is completely lacking in Isaiah 40–55. Prayer "forms" have indeed been suggested and the salvation speeches may have actually come in response to lament, as has been seen, but still no prayer text is found in those chapters. The best explanation for this seems to lie in the fact that Isaiah 40–55 as a whole is a book of optimism, of consolation; in a sense it is one massive response to prayers to be voiced by the exilic community. All that remained was to see the Lord unfold this response historically.

The Old Testament Scriptures are more than mere literature, but they are literature nonetheless and must be studied by means of the best methods of literary criticism. The foregoing study has attempted to review the course of one hundred years of traditional literary criticism of Isaiah 40–55 and of later form criticism and rhetorical criticism. It is clear from this study that literary method, while essentially neutral as a tool, can be and has been used to the detriment of sound biblical scholarship. On the other hand because it is only what its users make of it, it has the potential to provide hermeneutical and theological insight into the text in ways little imagined by those who refuse to take advantage of it. The ground has been broken in this respect largely by critical scholars. It is now time for evangelicals to work the soil and bring forth the fruit which inevitably will come at the hand of reverent scholarship.

CHAPTER 12

Structure and Meaning in Lamentations

Homer Heater

T he Book of Lamentations is perhaps the best example in the Bible of a combination of divine inspiration and human artistic ability. The depth of pathos as the writer probed the suffering of Zion and his own suffering is unprecedented. Each chapter is an entity in itself, a complete poem.[1] The most obvious literary device utilized by the poet is the acrostic; that is, poems are built around the letters of the alphabet. As is well known, chapters 1 and 2 have three lines in each of their 22 verses, and the first line of each verse begins with a different letter of the Hebrew alphabet.[2] Chapter 3 also has 66 lines, with the first three lines each beginning with the first letter of the alphabet, the second three lines beginning with the second letter of the alphabet, and so forth. Chapter 4 has two lines per verse, with only the first line of each verse beginning with the successive letter of the alphabet. Chapter 5 is unique in that it has 22 lines (the number of the letters in the Hebrew alphabet), but the alphabetic structure is not used. Gottwald describes the tenor of this structure.

> It is the belief of the present writer that the author of the Book of Lamentations selected the external principle of the acrostic to correspond to the internal spirit and intention of the work. He wished to play upon the collective grief of the community in its every aspect, "from Aleph to Taw," so that the people might experience an emotional catharsis. He wanted to bring about a complete cleansing of the conscience through a total confession of sin. Even then his purpose was not spent. He was also determined to inculcate an attitude of submission and a prospect of hope. By intimately binding together the themes of sin, suffering, submission and hope, he intended to implant the conviction of trust and confidence in the goodness and imminent intervention of Yahweh. That this is the case is evident in the third poem where the acrostic form is intensified at precisely the point where hope becomes the strongest.[3]

150

This chapter examines the structure of the Book of Lamentations in relation to the book's content and message and discusses the possibility of a "mini-acrostic" in 5:19–20.

Scholars from all persuasions agree that the writer of Lamentations was a contemporary with the events of the fall of Jerusalem in 586 B.C. described in the book.[4] Most agree that the writer wrote of himself in chapter 3 (though even there he spoke as a representative of the people). Hillers represents many commentators when he suggests that five poems by that many authors were brought together as an acrostic.[5] However, Renkema, in the most detailed structural analysis to date, argues for a concentric design so intricate that the entire work must be attributed to one person.[6] Over the years scholars have debated the authorship of Lamentations. Though the biblical text does not ascribe the work to anyone, early tradition, including the Septuagint translation, assigned Lamentations to Jeremiah. The date of the events, the similarity of the suffering of the man in chapter 3 to that of Jeremiah, and the fact that Jeremiah wrote laments about Josiah (2 Chron. 35:25) lend credence to the tradition, though the question should be left open.

While some of the recent analyses of Lamentations may be overdrawn,[7] it is important to note that the level of sophistication for an Old Testament poet, whether Jeremiah or some other, was high.

> There can be no question about the literary excellence of these five poems. Among the collective laments of the ancient Near East they are without peer. Under the discipline of acrostic form and the chaste economy of the Qinah metre, the poet has created in clearly defined strophes a sincere and powerful vehicle of expression. His wealth of imagery is ceaseless; his turn of phrase generally felicitous.[8]

The Split Alphabet

Each of chapters 1–4 of Lamentations seems to include a pattern of splitting the alphabet: א (*aleph*) to כ (*kaph*) in the first half of the chapter and ל (*lamed*) to ת (*taw*) in the second half. This pattern is quite clear in chapter 1.[9] The first unit (*aleph* to *kaph*) discusses the pitiable state of Jerusalem, which is personified throughout. The form is third person except in two places where Zion breaks out in a cry to Yahweh: "See, O Lord, my affliction, for the enemy has magnified himself" (1:9) and "See, O Lord, and look, for I am despised" (v. 11).

The utter desolation of the city and the temple (v. 10) are set forth in graphic terms. All segments of society—princes, priests, and people—have been affected. Jerusalem suffered because of her many sins (vv. 5, 8), and there is no effort to claim unjust punishment, as some of the exiles claimed (Ezek. 18:2).[10] Even so, Zion raised her voice to her God and cried out for mercy.[11] Surely Yahweh could at least look on her in her hour of deep distress. This demand (introduced with "See" [רְאֵה] at both Lamentations 1:9 and 1:11) is a device that anticipates the second unit (vv. 12–22), in which the motif shifts to personified Jerusalem talking about herself. She demanded again that Yahweh look on her distress (v. 20) and that He hear her groaning (v. 22).

Renkema is correct in seeing the center of the poem at verses 11–12.[12] The poet cried out on behalf of Jerusalem for both God and man to look on the devastation Yahweh had wrought on His people. The point of the chapter, Renkema says, is "God/men! Look at our misery."[13] Jerusalem freely admitted her culpability (vv. 14, 18, 20). She also attributed the calamity to Yahweh as just punishment (vv. 12–15, 17–18, 21). But the same God can reverse Himself and bring judgment on the instruments of His wrath, and this is what the poet cried out for Him to do (vv. 21–22).

Through artistic creation of a poem with 22 strophes divided clearly into two equal parts, the poet expressed his despair. Simultaneously he affirmed God's sovereign control of events.

The same pattern is found in chapter 2, which has 22 strophes, each beginning with a different letter of the alphabet. One might expect the pattern of chapter 1 to be repeated in chapter 2. Both poems begin with the same word. Chapter 1 identifies the source of Judah's calamity as Yahweh Himself. In the first half (1:1–11) He is identified as such once (v. 5) and in the second half (vv. 12–22) some six times. In the first half of the second poem (2:1–11), however, there is hardly a verse that omits the attribution (only vv. 10–11). Vivid language is used to describe Yahweh's treatment of His people. He had hurled, swallowed, torn down, cut off, burned, strung His bow, poured out, destroyed, laid waste, rejected, handed over, stretched out a line over, and broken Jerusalem. The writer wanted everyone to understand that the calamitous events of 586 B.C. were not random. No matter how painful, the truth is that Yahweh did these terrible things to His own people. Edom, the archetypal enemy of Israel, is not mentioned until 4:21–22, and Babylon, the human perpetrator of the calamity, is not mentioned at all. Only general language is used to refer to Israel's enemies. All must understand that Yahweh had become the enemy of His people. The first unit closes at 2:10 with a statement summarizing the state of Jerusalem. Starting in verse 11, the writer explained to Judah in gentle but chiding language why the calamity had happened. The misleading message of the false prophets was a major reason for their deception (v. 14), and Yahweh carried out His predicted judgment without equivocation (v. 17).

Since the speech of the writer in the first person makes a logical break in the poem, one might have expected him to have begun speaking in 2:12, if the *aleph* to *kaph* pattern were being followed. A case could be made that the *kaph* and *lamed* strophes (vv. 12–13) form the kernel of the poem with the poignant description of the starving children. However, the delineation is not so clear as in chapter 1 and so cannot be used to support the division of the alphabet as a literary device.

Chapter 3 differs from chapters 1–2 in that the writer wrote in the first person and also was someone other than Jerusalem. The chapter is also different in that, as already stated, each member of each set of three of its 66 lines begins with the same letter of the Hebrew alphabet, with the 22 sets going successively through the alphabet.[14] In chapter 3 the writer presented classical wisdom teaching on retribution: punishment for sin, but a merciful God who gives relief (3:19–24). The response of the writer in chapter 3 is more like that urged by Job's friends than Job. There are also imprecatory elements in the last portion of the chapter.

The author placed himself in the Jobian mold as one who had suffered at the hands of God (cf. Lam. 3:14 with Job 30:9 and Lam. 3:12 with Job 16:12). Yet unlike Job he did not protest his innocence (Lam. 3:39–40). Echoes of Jeremiah also seem evident (cf. Lam. 3:14 with Jer. 20:7 and Job 12:4). This person is not Zion personified, so who is he? Surely he is the author of Lamentations and one who has personally suffered along with the people. His suffering has been more personal and intense, however. He became a laughing stock of his own people (Lam. 3:14); people tried to kill him by placing him in a pit (vv. 53–57), from which he prayed and God delivered him; people plotted against him (vv. 61–62).[15]

After reciting the acts of God against him (3:1–18), the writer argued that people should accept God's punishment with equanimity (vv. 19–30). Each line in the ט (*tet*) strophe (vv. 25–

27), beginning with the word "good," speaks of Yahweh's goodness and of the propriety of submitting to Him. The writer amplified this in the ' (*yod*) strophe (vv. 28–30) by explaining how the people should humble themselves. This brings the reader to the middle of the poem, in which the lines begin with *kaph* and *lamed*. As if expecting his message to be criticized, the poet wrote three lines each beginning with the word "Because." In these lines he defended the justice of God. They are followed in verses 34–36 by three intensive infinitives, each introduced with a *lamed*. These infinitives assert what Yahweh does not do. He does not crush underfoot, deny a man his rights, or deprive a man of justice. Only the *tet, kaph,* and *lamed* strophes use the same word three times.[16] The *kaph* and *lamed* strophes seem to be the center of the argument. How can Judah raise her head after the awful disaster? God is good, compassionate, and just. This theodicy is then discussed through verse 42. It is followed by a renewed complaint against Yahweh's inaccessibility. The chapter then concludes with an imprecatory statement and prayer (vv. 52–66). Chapter 3, like chapter 1, illustrates the writer's method of dividing the contents of his poems at the halfway point of the alphabet. In this way he artfully drew attention to his central argument that God is gracious.

Chapter 4 is constructed like chapters 1 and 2 except that each verse has two lines rather than three. In the first half of the poem—*aleph* to *kaph*—the writer delineated again the desolate condition of the people of Zion. The punishment of his people, he wrote, was even greater than that of Sodom (v. 6). He concluded the unit by mentioning for the first time in the chapter the name of Yahweh. He "has accomplished His wrath, He has poured out His fierce anger; and He has kindled a fire in Zion which has consumed its foundations" (v. 11). As the *kaph* strophe, this aptly ends the first half of the poem. The *lamed* strophe (v. 12) begins the second half with the statement that no one believed this could happen to Jerusalem. Again the writer stated the reason for the calamity (blaming the prophets and priests) and described the way the leaders were ostracized (vv. 13–16). He joined sympathetically with the people in describing their futile hope in other nations (v. 17) and in their own king (v. 20).[17] He ended the strophe with an imprecation on Edom and a breath of hope for Zion (vv. 21–22). The sense break in chapter 4 seems to coincide with the alphabetical break (vv. 1–11 and vv. 12–22). This further exemplifies the writer's tendency to divide the content of a poem in the middle of the alphabet.

Chapter 5 continues to puzzle commentators because it does not use the acrostic system, though it has 22 lines, the number of letters in the Hebrew alphabet. Renkema suggests that the phrase in 5:3 "there is no father" (אֵין אָב) is unusual as a singular (orphans, mothers, and widows are all plural) and may be a cryptic way of saying "no aleph, no beth."[18] This is a bit too esoteric to evaluate, and there may be another reason for the lack of an alphabetic acrostic in chapter 5, which will be discussed later. The question now is whether the poem is divided in half like the other chapters.

Chapter 5 emphasizes prayer, thus making an appropriate conclusion to the book. Verse 1 begins with a cry to Yahweh, asking Him to "remember us." It concludes in verse 21 with a prayer for restoration and renewal. In between is another catalog of disaster. The members of the community—orphans, mothers, fathers, slaves, women, virgins, princes, elders, young men, boys— have all been devastated. This leads to verse 18 in which Mount Zion (in destruction language) "lies desolate [and] foxes prowl in it." If there were a sense break in the middle of the chapter, it would occur between verses 11 and 12, but such a break does not seem to be there.

Chapters 1, 3, and 4 seem clearly to be divided in the middle of the alphabet. Possibly chapter 2 also follows this pattern, but it is not as clear. Therefore it may be assumed that the writer deliberately used the split alphabet as one of his devices.

A "Mini-acrostic" in 5:19–20

In 5:19–20 the writer carefully chose his words to summarize the teaching of the entire book, by using the split alphabet to convey it.[19] Verse 19 embraces the first half of the alphabet by using an *aleph* word (אַתָּה, "you") to start the first half of the verse, and a *kaph* word (כִּסֵּא, "throne") to start the second half. This verse reiterates the theology of God's sovereignty expressed throughout the book. He has the right to do as He chooses; humans have no right to carp at what He does. Wisdom teaching grappled with this concept, and God's speech at the end of the Book of Job, which does not really answer Job's many sometimes querulous questions, simply avers that the God of the whirlwind cannot be gainsaid (Job 38–41). Job must accept who God is without criticism. Then Job bowed to this very concept (42:1–6). Now the writer of Lamentations also bowed before the throne of God, accepting the implications of such sovereignty.

Such a theological concept, however, is small comfort in the midst of great distress. Quoting Scripture to a sick or hurting person is little help unless he has drawn personally from the well of biblical doctrine. The writer turned in 5:20 to ask the pragmatic question, "Why dost Thou forget us forever; why dost Thou forsake us so long?" This is the *lamed* ("Why," לָמָּה) to *taw* ("you forsake us," תַּעַזְבֵנוּ) part of the acrostic. Since God is sovereign, why does He not keep His covenant and show kindness? Zion suffers justly, but does her Lord dare let her suffer overmuch? Surely complete abandonment by Him is not in keeping with His sovereign work on behalf of Israel.

So there is an alphabetic device in chapter 5 in the very verses that combine two main themes running through the book: God is sovereign and just, but Zion's suffering is so great. The split alphabet is used here to make a point, as it is used in other chapters. One reason there is no full acrostic in chapter 5 may be that the writer wanted the emphasis to fall on these two verses near the conclusion of the book. In so doing, he has adroitly drawn attention to the only hope for people in despair.

Progression in the Structure

What can be learned from the general configuration of the five poems? Many have noted that chapter 3 with its 66 lines epitomizes the emphasis on hope in the book. One may go a step further and say that the writer was visually showing progression from chapter 1 through chapter 3. It seems that the emphasis of the book is somewhat "level" in chapters 1 and 2, since both chapters have 67 lines with every third line beginning with one of the 22 letters of the Hebrew alphabet.[20] This pattern, however, intensifies in chapter 3, for though it too has 66 lines, each line of the three-line sets carries out the acrostic pattern by beginning with the set's letter of the alphabet. After chapter 3 there is a diminution of emphasis, since chapter 4 has only 44 lines, with the first word of each two-line set beginning with a different Hebrew letter. The message then seems to drop to a whisper in chapter 5, in which there are only 22 lines and no acrostic is followed.[21] Since other compositions have 22 lines but not an acrostic, such a structure in chapter 5 is not unusual. However, it seems that the lack of an alphabetic structure (except for the "mini-acrostic" in 5:19–20) in the context of the Book of Lamentations is part of the diminution of chapters 4 and 5.

Chapter 3 reaches a crescendo of both despair and hope. The triple lines of the alphabet clang on the reader's ears, crying for him to see the agony of the writer and his people. At the same time strong emphasis is placed on the mercy and goodness of God and the good that will eventually come to those who trust in Him.

In chapter 4 the emphasis drops lower than that of chapters 1–2. The reduced emphasis is not in the content (see 4:10–11) but in the style, and the purpose of the stylistic reduction is itself designed to direct one's thinking in a quieter way to the magnitude of the injustice. Such injustice cries out for vengeance on Edom and for hope for Israel's future (vv. 21–22).

Chapter 5 follows the same reduction pattern. Since no acrostic is followed in that chapter, the tone of the book seems to drop to a whisper. The writer begins with a plea to the Lord to remember, he reiterated the suffering of the people, and then drew the message of the entire lament together in the "mini-acrostic" in verses 19–20. This provides a dramatic effect for the work and focuses attention on the very issue the writer wanted to emphasize.

The creedal statement of the "mini-acrostic" in 5:19–20 is amplified in 5:21–22. The five-poem lament closes on a strongly negative note, which commentators have struggled to explain. In Jewish liturgy verse 21 is read again after verse 22.

What is the meaning of verse 22? A summary of various answers is given by Hillers[22] and Gordis.[23] Hillers believes verse 22 is restating the facts as they were: God had abandoned His people. Gordis has a similar view as seen in his translation: "Even though you had despised us greatly and were angry with us." He rejects the common translation, "unless you have utterly rejected us," on two grounds: (a) the other uses of the words כי אם in the Hebrew Bible imply a negative response, and (b) the "unless" clause would be an inappropriate assumption at this point in the prayer. However, "unless" does expect a negative response. The sense may be this: "It may look as though You have abandoned us forever, but that contradicts everything we believe about You and so it cannot be true." It is also appropriate in its place as a "ploy" of the suppliant to cause Yahweh to face up to His covenant obligations.

The Reversal of ע (*'ayin*) and פ (*peh*)

An unusual feature of three of the acrostic poems is the reversal of the 16th and 17th letters (*peh* before *'ayin* in 2:16–17; 3:46–51; and 4:16–17.[24] This "sphinx" has not yielded its secret in spite of much effort by interpreters. Hillers, after disagreeing with Grotius's explanation that there was a fluctuating order of the alphabet, says that "no more reasonable hypothesis has been advanced."[25]

Wiesmann discusses seven suggestions as to why the order of these letters was inverted.[26] (1) Riegler suggested that the poet simply chose to invert the letters. But, as Wiesmann asks, why would one set out to write an acrostic poem and then not follow the alphabet? Further, why invert only these two letters? (2) Grotius argues that the order of these letters may not have been fixed at that time.[27] However, Wiesmann says, nothing is known of such a different order of the alphabet. Furthermore, as Hillers points out, the order seems to be already fixed in the alphabet of Ugaritic literature, written some seven hundred years earlier than Lamentations.[28]

(3) Houbigant, Kennicott, and Jahn attribute the rearrangement to a copyist's error. Wiesmann correctly asks why the same error occurs in three places. Chapter 3 would be especially difficult in that six lines would have to be rearranged. Also the textual evidence, as indicated above, points away from a copyist's error. In addition, a similar inversion occurs in Proverbs 31 and possibly in Psalms 9–10 and 34. (4) Bertholdt, says Wiesmann, argues that the original poet simply made a mistake. Wiesmann argues again that it is difficult to assume the same original mistake in three places. Furthermore, the visual nature of the acrostic makes it difficult for this kind of error to escape the eye. (5) Pareau and Keil see in the change the poet's right to deviate from a fixed form if the content of his material demands it. Wiesmann wonders why the author would not have the ability to fit the content to the alphabetic structure, and Wiesmann also argues again that this would deny the alphabetic pattern the author set out to create. (6) Some argue for a temporary or local fluctuation in the order of the alphabet. The responses to Grotius's position could also be given here. (7) After presenting Boehmer's view that the inversion signifies something about the magic of the alphabet, Wiesmann replies that there is no known significance to the words formed by the inverted order of the two Hebrew letters.[29] Wiesmann maintains that the question of the order of the two letters remains unanswered.[30]

If there was an existing poetic device of inverting the 16th and 17th letters, is there any internal evidence to explain why the writer of Lamentations used it in his work? Gottwald says that the "reversal motif" found in funeral laments is the most dominant theme in the Book of Lamentations. "From the literary viewpoint, it is *dramatic contrast,* and from the theological, it is *tragic reversal.*"[31] He then presents Jahnow's analysis of the funeral songs.[32] The praise element in funeral songs describes the person's past glory while the lament element bewails the sadness of the present loss.[33] This is where the theme of "tragic reversal" enters. Lamentations is complex with respect to all the *gattungen.* The same is true when the funeral lament is discussed, for both the past glory and the present sadness are emphasized. Lamentations advances the funeral song by adding (a) the element of humiliation of Judah in contrast to the exaltation of her enemies and (b) the future exaltation of Judah and the future humiliation of her enemies (cf. Lam. 1:9 and 2:17 with 4:21–22). Gottwald calls this the "reverse of the reversal."

A tentative suggestion about the use of the two reversed Hebrew letters in chapters 2–4 is that the *peh* lines in chapters 2 and 3 (2:16 and 3:46–48) are almost identical in speaking of the enemies opening wide their mouths against Zion. This is the reversal of fortunes spoken of above. The enemies of Judah are now in a superior position. Has the writer reversed the lines here to make that point? The *'ayin* line follows in 2:17 with an assertion that Yahweh caused this reversal and in 3:50 with a plea for Yahweh to take note of what has happened. The *peh* line in 4:16 differs in content from that of chapters 2 and 3, but there is a play on the word "face" (פנֵי). The priestly benediction on Israel included the words "May the Lord lift up His face to you and give you peace" (Num. 6:26). In the destruction of Jerusalem in 586, however, God's "face" destroyed His people; further reversal is seen in that the "face" of the priests will not be "lifted up," that is, respected (Lam. 4:16). No other verse in chapter 4 uses the same word twice.

Thus the reversal of *'ayin* and *peh* in Lamentations helps the reader see from the construction as well as the content that Judah's position of favored status with God and victor over her enemies has been reversed.[34]

The artistry of Lamentations has been pressed into the service of practical theology. The trauma of the loss of the temple coupled with the awful suffering of the people during and after the siege resulted in a serious reexamination of faith. The crucible of suffering brought forth both the fine gold of a recognition of God's justice in bringing judgment on Judah, and also a deeply felt lament urging Yahweh to act in accord with His ancient covenant with His people.

CHAPTER 13

The Archaeological Background of Daniel

Edwin M. Yamauchi

C onservative scholars are aware that some serious problems face the traditional view of Daniel as a prophetic work. An important attempt to confront some of these major issues has been contributed in a work by five distinguished British scholars—D. J. Wiseman, T. C. Mitchell, R. Joyce, W. J. Martin, and K. A. Kitchen.[1] This chapter is a discussion of some of these historical problems in the light of extra biblical data.

Historical Problems

NEBUCHADNEZZAR

The apparent contradiction between the third year of Jehoiakim (Dan. 1:1) and the fourth year of Jehoiakim (Jer. 46:2) for the date of Nebuchadnezzar's initial attack can readily be explained by the use of different calendars (Nisan and Tishri), and of different regnal systems.[2] Though Hartman and Di Lella list in their bibliography[3] the monograph by Wiseman and others which addresses this problem,[4] their commentary still asserts, "Whatever the case, Nebuchadnezzar did not besiege Jerusalem in 606 B.C., as Dan 1:1 would have us believe, for . . . he did not become king of Babylon till the following year."[5] Millard points out the possible solution:

> However, on the accession year system and with an autumnal New Year, his [Jehoiakim's] first year would run from September 608 to September 607, his second 607–6, his third September 606—October 605. This last would just accommodate the statement of Daniel 1:1 in chronological terms.[6]

As to the further question of whether there was indeed a Babylonian campaign against Jerusalem, McNamara asserts, "The siege of Jerusalem mentioned in 1,1 for the third year of his reign (i.e. 603 B.C.) is, however, an anachronism; the first siege of Jerusalem by Nebuchadnezzar known to history was in 597 B.C. (but compare 2 Kings 24:10–16 with 2 Chron. 36:6–10)."[7] In rebuttal Wiseman points out that the *Chaldean Chronicles*, which he published in 1956, indicate that Nebuchadnezzar claims to have conquered "all Hatti land," that is, Palestine, in 605.[8] In a recent work Wiseman has written, "In the following years (604–603 B.C.), the Babylonians marched unopposed through Palestine ('Hatti-land'). Heavy tribute was brought to them by all the kings and with it many prisoners (including Daniel) were sent back to Babylon."[9] Elsewhere Wiseman has suggested still another possible date for Daniel's deportation. In referring to a passage in the *Babylonian Chronicle* (BM 21946, rev. 4) he writes, "If this passage does refer to numerous persons it could well be that in this year 602 B.C., rather than in 605 B.C. (as CCK [*Chronicles of Chaldaean Kings*] 26), captives, possibly including Daniel and other Judeans, were taken to Babylon."[10] It should be noted that the biblical text in Daniel 1:1 does not explicitly state that Daniel and his companions were deported in the very first attack against Palestine, though many writers (including this writer) have assumed this conclusion.

The Babylonian names given to Daniel and his three companions in Daniel 1:7 have sometimes been regarded as artificial. But recently a distinguished Assyriologist has proposed satisfactory explanations of these names on the basis of Akkadian analogies as follows:[11]

Belteshazzar from *bēlet-šar-uṣur*, "Lady protect the king."
Shadrach from *šāndurāku*, "I am very fearful (of God)."
Meshach from *mēšāku*, "I am of little account."
Abed-nego, "Servant of the Shining One," using west Semitic *abed* instead of Akkadian *'arad* "servant," and assuming a play on the name of the god *Nebō*.

The restless nature of Nebuchadnezzar, who could not sleep at night because of his dreams (Dan. 2:1; cf. 6:18 and Esther 6:1), may be illustrated by a text published by Lambert in 1965, which he called "The King of Justice."[12] The unnamed king, who must be identified with Nebuchadnezzar, is so concerned with justice that it is claimed, "he did not rest night or day." Of course, one must reckon with the probability that both in the biblical texts and in the Babylonian text such a trait of restlessness brought on by responsibility is a general characteristic of royalty rather than the distinctive feature of a given monarch.

Scholars have frequently regarded the use of the term "Chaldean(s)" in Daniel 2:2 and elsewhere in its professional sense as "astrologer" in addition to its ethnic sense (Dan. 3:8; 9:1) as a clear case of anachronism.[13] The term "Chaldean" (*Kaldu*) is used originally in its ethnic sense, for example, in the texts of Shalmaneser III (9th century B.C.). In the Persian, Hellenistic, and Roman periods the name "Chaldean" became a designation for astrologers.

As Millard points out, during the Neo-Babylonian period there is as yet no known example of its use as either an ethnic or professional term.[14] Surely this is the result of the accidents of survival and/or publication.

Certainly the Babylonians were interested in astrology long before the Chaldean or Neo-Babylonian Empire. An interesting Greek text of Pseudo-Berossus asserts:

> From the time of Nabonassar (747–734 B.C.), the Chaldeans accurately recorded the times of the motion of the stars. The polymaths among the Greeks learned from the Chaldeans that—as Alexander (Polyhistor) and Berossus, men versed in Chaldean antiquities, say—Nabonassar gathered together (the accounts of) the deeds of the kings before him and did away with them so that the reckoning of the Chaldean kings would begin with him.[15]

Now this account is somewhat confused inasmuch as Nabonassar was the king of Babylon who fought against rebellious Chaldeans. But it does preserve an accurate tradition in that both the Babylonian Chronicle and the Ptolemaic Canon commence their accounts in 747 with the reign of Nabonassar. As Brinkman notes, "From this point on, chronologically precise records of historical events were kept systematically."[16]

The Chaldeans, who fought against the Assyrians under Merodach-baladan II (at the end of the 8th century B.C.) and established their own kingdom under Nabopolassar and his great son, Nebuchadnezzar, must have inherited the established traditions of astronomical observation from Babylonian scholars. Although quite different in origins, the word "Chaldean" underwent an evolution similar to the word "Magi," which originally meant the priestly tribe of the Medes and gradually came to mean "astrologer" or "magician."[17]

The ceremony in which Nebuchadnezzar ordered his subjects

to do homage to his statue (Dan. 3:2–6) is rather different from the usual rites which were conducted by the priests in private. This practice may possibly be illustrated by the discoveries of Leonard Woolley in the Neo-Babylonian stratum at Ur. Woolley presents an interesting theory in describing the E-NUN-MAH sanctuary originally dedicated to the moon god Nannar and his wife Ningal.

> Nothing could be more unlike the conditions of the old temple than this spacious building in which there was room for a multitude of people and everything was so arranged as to focus attention on the rites in progress: the change in the temple plan must correspond to a change in religious practice. The explanation which was given when the discovery was made has been generally accepted; it is drawn from the story of "the Three Children" in the book of Daniel. . . . what was novel here was not the setting up of the image but the order that all were to share in the adoration of it. Nebuchadnezzar was substituting a form of congregational worship for the mysteries of an esoteric priesthood.[18]

NABONIDUS AND BELSHAZZAR

Clear cuneiform evidence now demonstrates why the Book of Daniel names Belshazzar, rather than his father, Nabonidus, as king of Babylon. Nabonidus, who venerated especially the moon god Sin of his native city Harran, became alienated from the people of Babylon. He took the unprecedented step of moving to the Arabian city of Tema, leaving "kingship" in the hands of his son.[19]

A recent reexamination of all the relevant cuneiform data has helped clarify the chronology of the coregency. Hasel has argued that the third year in the Persian Verse Account should not be equated with the third regnal year but with the sixth. As a result the coregency of Nabonidus and Belshazzar should be dated as early as 550 and not just before the fall of Babylon in 539. Hence Daniel's vision in the first year of Belshazzar (Dan. 7:1) should be dated 550, and his vision in the third year (Dan. 8:1) should be dated 547.[20]

NEBUCHADNEZZAR'S DERANGEMENT AND NABONIDUS'S EXILE

In view of the lack of any cuneiform attestation for Nebuchadnezzar's derangement (Dan. 4),[21] liberal scholars have accepted the view that this episode is a garbled version inspired by Nabonidus's "madness" in withdrawing to the desert.

After the publication of the *Nabonidus Chronicle* in 1882, F. Hommel and P. Riessler in 1902 first proposed such a transference.[22] This view has gained wide currency among commentators who discuss the passage (Dan. 4).[23] This position has now been reinforced by the publication in 1956 of the celebrated "Prayer of Nabonidus" (4QOrNab) from Qumran.[24] There are indeed some broad parallels between this text and the text of Daniel 4:

1. In both accounts a Babylonian king is afflicted by God.
2. As Nebuchadnezzar was afflicted for "seven times," Nabonidus is smitten for "seven years."
3. Daniel helped secure Nebuchadnezzar's sanity; an unnamed Jewish exorcist (GZR) urged Nabonidus to repent from his worship of "the gods of silver and gold . . . wood, stone and clay."[25]

Scholars have disagreed about the possible relationships between the Qumran Nabonidus text and Daniel. (1) Dupont-Sommer and Geveryahu assume the priority of Daniel. (2) Others such as Milik, Dommershausen, and Hartman affirm the priority of the Nabonidus text, taking the late date of Daniel for granted. Typical is the comment by Jongeling: "It is fairly safe to assume that the original Nabonidus tradition . . . was transferred in Daniel to the well-known Nebuchadnezzar II . . . and that the seer, a Jewish man, was not yet identified with Daniel in 4QOrNab."[26] (3) Freedman and others argue that the differences preclude any direct literary dependence.[27]

Despite the ready assumption of a common tradition between the historical Nabonidus, the Qumran Nabonidus, and Daniel's Nebuchadnezzar, there are far more dissimilarities than resemblances in these three sources.[28]

1. The names of the two kings are, of course, different. Moreover, Nebuchadnezzar is afflicted in Babylon, whereas Nabonidus was in Tema in Arabia.
2. According to Daniel 4:13, 20, 22, Nebuchadnezzar was to be banished for a period of seven "times," which may or may not mean seven years as in the case of the Qumran Nabonidus text. The Aramaic word עִדָּן (עִדָּנִין, plural) is the general word for "time" or "season," as can be seen from other biblical passages and from the Aramaic papyri.[29] The related Akkadian word *adannu* is used in

the Harran text to designate the entire period of Nabonidus's sojourn in Arabia, which was *ten* years and not seven as previously surmised.

3. Nebuchadnezzar was afflicted with lycanthropic insanity.[30] But the Qumran Nabonidus was smitten with שְׁחִין (literally "inflammation"), a skin ailment (cf. Ex. 9:9; Job 2:7), and not with madness.

4. The phrase in the Persian Verse Account (*ANET*, p. 134a) "the king is mad" does not depict Nabonidus as insane but as angry (Akkadian *a-gu-ug šarru*).[31] Though some of his contemporaries may have thought the king's behavior strange, the Harran texts show that Nabonidus went to Arabia for a justifiable reason—he felt that the people of Babylon had offended his god, Sin.

5. As pointed out by van der Woude and by Grelot,[32] Jongeling's restoration of line 3 in the Qumran Nabonidus text, שׁוי [לחיותא] וכן "and so I came to be li[ke the animals]," is quite gratuitous, resting on the assumption that the Qumran text conformed to Daniel 4.[33]

6. The literary contexts of the Qumran text and Daniel 4 are quite different. The former is a descriptive narrative, whereas Daniel 4 is a public proclamation by the king himself. Hartman concedes, "There is no sign of literary dependence of one story on the other; the relatively few words and expressions which they have in common are standard terms that could occur anywhere."[34]

In the face of these rather important discrepancies critics, including Hartman, have still chosen to derive Daniel's story of Nebuchadnezzar's madness from a garbled tradition about Nabonidus's illness.

DARIUS THE MEDE

The identification of Daniel's "Darius the Mede" remains as contested as ever.[35] There have been two major attempts to resolve the problem: (a) the proposal by Whitcomb that Darius the Mede is to be identified with Gubaru/Gobryas, the provincial governor of Babylon,[36] and (b) the proposal by Wiseman that Daniel 6:28 be translated, "Daniel prospered in the reign of Darius even the reign of Cyrus the Persian," that is, taking the former name as a throne name.[37]

A recent attempt has been made by Bulman to add further support to Wiseman's thesis. Bulman notes the use of dual names, points to the Septuagint and Theodotion which render Daniel 11:1 the " first year of Cyrus" rather than the "first year of Darius," and cites other passages in which statements attributed to Darius the Mede may be compared to the career of Cyrus. He explains the use of the byname "Darius the Mede" for Cyrus in Daniel as follows: "Unlike the authors of Chronicles and Ezra, however, he does not represent Cyrus as the agent of fulfillment of prophecy. But since Jeremiah, who mentioned no name, emphasized the Medes as conquerors of Babylon, Daniel was led . . . to use the name which was associated with them."[38]

Schedl has identified Darius the Mede with Darius I, the great Persian king.[39] He argues that the title comes from the fact that Darius I marched into Media to quell the revolt of Fravartis. This, however, is hardly a convincing theory.

In conclusion, none of the proposed solutions to the identity of Darius the Mede is entirely convincing. Yet one need not despair of an ultimate resolution, if one recalls the history of attempts to identify Daniel's Belshazzar. As Dougherty recounts, before the discovery and publication of cuneiform documents demonstrating that Belshazzar was Nabonidus's son, scholars proposed that Belshazzar was (a) a pure invention, (b) a brother or son of Evil-Merodach, or Evil-Merodach himself, (c) Neriglissar, (d) a grandson of Nebuchadnezzar, or (e) another name for Nabonidus.[40]

The failure to appreciate the fragmentary nature of available evidence leads to the false assumption that a figure in literary sources must be unhistorical if contemporary epigraphical documentation for his existence is unavailable. It was not until 1961 that the first epigraphical text for Pontius Pilate was discovered, and it was not until 1966 that similar documentation for Felix, the governor of Judea, was found.[41]

After surveying all the historical problems involving Nebuchadnezzar, Nabonidus, Belshazzar, and Darius the Mede, Baldwin affirms, "In concluding this section on the historical assumptions of the writer of the book of Daniel I strongly assert that there is no reason to question his historical knowledge."[42]

Linguistic and Archaeological Data

AN EGYPTIAN LOANWORD

In discussing the interpretation of Nebuchadnezzar's dream by Daniel, Hartman with other critics has concluded that here is a clear case of literary dependence on the similar story of the interpretation of pharaoh's dreams by Joseph: "The borrowing in Dn is evident from the fact that, with all the other words used here for various kinds of soothsayers, Dn (1,20; 2,2.10.27; 4,4.6) also uses the same word for 'magicians' (Heb. ḥarṭummim) that occurs in Gn 41,8.24. . . ."[43] Hartman argues, "this is a loanword from Egyptian and should, strictly speaking, be used only in regard to Egyptian magicians (who would hardly be at the Babylonian court of Nobuchodonosor!)."[44]

Though the Egyptian loanword may be used in these passages without any reference to Egyptian nationals, the idea that there were Egyptian magicians and soothsayers in Mesopotamia is not so farfetched as Hartman believes. The Jehoiachin ration tablets indicate that, among other nationals, Egyptians were given provisions by the royal court.[45] Moreover, a recent study by Eph'al indicates that among the Egyptians who resided in Mesopotamia in the fifth and sixth centuries B.C. were the following professionals: ᴸᵘbārê "diviners," ᴸᵘḥarṭibi "dream interpreters," and ᴸᵘmušlaḫḫê "snake charmers."[46] *Harṭōm* and *ḥarṭibi* are cognate.[47]

ARAMAIC

Rowley, in his meticulous study published in 1929, has argued that the Aramaic of Daniel is compatible with a 2d century B.C. date despite certain affinities with earlier Official Aramaic.[48] He stressed what he regarded as parallels with the later Targums.

From a recent examination of seven pairs of words which Rowley has used, Coxon, on the basis of new evidence, concludes, "In the lexical field Biblical Aramaic contains unmistakable traits of Official Aramaic. In his attempt to reaffirm the second century (date) of *Daniel* ROWLEY fails to do them justice."[49]

Fitzmyer, who extends the classification of Official Aramaic from 700 to 200 B.C. and who dates the final redaction of Daniel to 165 B.C., is willing to concede with Albright that the Aramaic portions of Daniel may well be older than the second century.[50]

In a review of Kitchen's important study on "The Aramaic of Daniel,"[51] which had refuted many of his own arguments, Rowley reaffirmed that he still regarded the spelling of the Aramaic of Daniel as a key to its late date.[52] In a very important survey of the recent developments in the study of Aramaic, the eminent Israeli scholar, Kutscher, sided with Kitchen against Rowley.[53] Kutscher cited the new evidence from the Hermopolis papyri, which were contemporary with the 5th century B.C. Elephantine papyri, but which employed different spelling conventions. On the basis of spelling alone one might mistakenly date the Hermopolis papyri a thousand years too late.[54]

THE GREEK WORDS FOR MUSICAL INSTRUMENTS

As expressed long ago in S. R. Driver's classic statement, the Greek loanwords in the Aramaic of Daniel have been regarded as objective proof for the late date of Daniel. As restated by Coxon, "Of all the linguistic arguments which have been used in the debate concerning the age of the Aramaic sections of *Daniel* and the date of the composition of the book, the Greek loans seem to provide the strongest evidence in favor of the second century B.C."[55] Though Hartman and Di Lella list Kitchen's study which demonstrates otherwise, they reiterate the standard critical position: "The Greek names for the musical instruments in 3:5 probably do not antedate the reign of Alexander the Great (336–323 B.C.)."[56]

The three Greek words in Daniel 3:5 are all musical terms[57] (variant spellings are found in other verses):

Aramaic:		Greek:	
קַיתְרֹס	qaytᵉrōs	κίθαρις	kitharis
פְּסַנְתֵּרִין	pᵉsantērîn	ψαλτήριον	psaltērion
סוּמְפֹּנְיָה	sumpōnᵉyâ	συμφωνία	symphōnia

The first instrument was a kind of lyre. As to the specific Greek word which was borrowed, Coxon observes that its spelling indicates that the loan was adopted in the pre-Hellenistic period:

> The fact that the Ionic form *kitharis* found its way into the list in Dan. 3 and not the Attic *kithara* is a striking one, especially in view of the consistent use of *kithara* in Greek material of the post-Alexander period. Heirs of Attic literary tradition, the Septuagint, the New Testament and patristic sources alike know only *kithara*. One might suppose that the *kitharis*-form stems from Asia Minor and/or the Greek islands and that it was absorbed by Official Aramaic as a result of cultural and linguistic contacts at a period much earlier than the second century B.C.[58]

Though the Greek ψαλτήριον was a harplike instrument, Sendry suggests that Daniel's *pᵉsantērîn* was more akin to a dulcimer. He further suggests that it had been one of a number of musical instruments originally imported from the east, improved by the Greeks, and reexported to the east.[59]

It is altogether surprising that the Anchor Bible commentary reverts to the discredited view of *sumpon^eyâ* as a "bagpipe" in the light of clear evidence that this was a very late sense of the word.[60] The earliest meaning of the Greek word συμφωνία was "sounding together," that is, the simultaneous playing of instruments or voices producing a concord. Jerome, commenting on Luke 15:25 where the word occurs, noted: "The *symphōnia* is not a kind of instrument, as some Latin writers think, but it means concordant harmony. It is expressed in Latin by *cosonantia*."[61] Coxon concludes as follows:

> We have tried to show that the use of *sumphōnia* in Dan. 3 accords with its older meaning and not, as in the later classical sources, with an individual musical instrument. But since the traditional meaning of "harmony, concord of sound" is also found late (Polybius, Athenaeus, etc.) the classical evidence in so far as it affects Dan. 3 must be pronounced neutral.[62]

Rowley in his review of Kitchen's work still maintained that the evidence of these particular Greek words was proof of the late date of Daniel's Aramaic.[63] Kutscher's appraisal of this argument is worth quoting at length.

> Rowley's argument that the Greek loans ψαλτήριον and συμφωνία as names for musical instruments occur in Greek several hundred years after the suggested date of Daniel also does not sound convincing. After all, if we assume Greek influence prior to Alexander, it is not the Attic dialect, or other dialects of Greece, that must be taken into consideration as the place of origin of these loans, but rather dialects of Asia Minor and/or those of the Greek isles. What do we know about the Greek of Asia Minor and of the Greek isles during the period in question? To the best of my knowledge, very little. . . .
> The fact that the field of music is the only one where Greek influence has come to light, calls to mind Otto Jespersen's words . . . : "If all other sources of information were closed to us except such loan-words in our . . . North-European languages as *piano, soprano, opera, libretto, tempo, adagio*, etc., we should still have no hesitation in drawing the conclusion that Italian music has played a great role all over Europe." . . . Greek musicians might have been dominant enough to make their impact felt in those (Near Eastern) languages, as the Italian musicians did in English.[64]

As this writer has shown elsewhere, the exchange of musicians and their musical instruments played a prominent role at royal courts from time immemorial.[65] To these examples the following may be added.

Speaking of 15th-century B.C. Egypt, Drower notes: "The influence of Asiatic on Egyptian music was profound: new instruments included the long-necked lute, the lyre (*kinnōr*), the angled harp and the double flute, and the Syrian musicians who introduced them must have popularized new melodies and new dances."[66]

Texts from the Kassite period of Mesopotamia (12th century B.C.) indicate that there were Elamite singers who entertained the royal household of Marduk-apal-iddina I at Dur Kurigalzu."[67]

Referring to 8th-century Nimrud, Mallowan reports, "It is also of interest that a tablet, ND 6219, discovered in Fort Shalmaneser, referred to the king's male choir which included Kassite, north Syrian and Assyrian singers, a further testimony to the Assyrians' delight in music."[68]

Ellermeier has made a detailed study of the distribution of the Near Eastern double flute (or oboe), which has been found in Mesopotamia, Syria, Palestine, Egypt, Cyprus, Crete, and Greece. He notes that the Syrian *embūbu* passed into Latin as *ambubaiae*, a word which designated both the instrument and the Syrian girls who played them.[69]

Conclusion

It is clear that liberal commentators do not acknowledge that there are possible solutions to the historical problems in the Book of Daniel. Nor do many liberal scholars seem to be aware of the mass of linguistic and archaeological data that demonstrates the ample contacts between the Aegean and the Near East before Alexander's conquests. The Greek words for musical instruments in the Aramaic are therefore no obstacle for a pre-Hellenistic date for Daniel's composition.

Conservative scholars welcome the increasing mass of linguistic and archaeological data which helps support an early date or at least helps undermine arguments for a late date for Daniel. They are convinced that Daniel indeed was a true prophet with a message both for his generation and for today.

CHAPTER 14

Daniel's Seventy Weeks and New Testament Chronology

Harold W. Hoehner

While Daniel was in the Babylonian captivity (605–538/ 37 B.C.), he was given the prophecy of the 70 weeks (Dan. 9:24–27), which has become the subject of many discussions and interpretations. The purpose of this is to determine how this prophecy relates to the chronology of Christ's life.

The Context of the 70 Weeks

In the first year of Darius, 538–537 B.C. (Dan. 9:1; 2 Chron. 36:21–23; Ezra 1; 6:3–5), Daniel observed that the 70-year captivity prophesied by Jeremiah (Jer. 25:11–12; 29:10) was nearing its completion. The reason for Israel's captivity was their refusal to obey the Word of the Lord from the prophets (Jer. 29:17–19) and to give their land sabbatical rests (2 Chron. 36:21). God had stated that Israel, because of her disobedience, would be removed from her land and scattered among the Gentiles until the land had enjoyed its sabbaths (Lev. 26:33–35).

According to 2 Chronicles 36:21 the land would be desolate for 70 years. One may therefore conclude that in the eight-hundred year history of Israel in the land, 70 sabbatical years were not kept. Now Daniel, seeing that the 70 years of captivity were nearing their completion, realized that before the exiles could return to their homeland they needed to confess and repent of their sin of disobedience before God (Lev. 26:40–46). Hence, Daniel confessed on behalf of his people the disobedient course they had followed and pleaded that God's anger would be turned away so that Israel would return to her land. While Daniel was making his petition, the angel Gabriel came to give him understanding of the prophetic message of the 70 weeks. Daniel had asked about Israel's imminent return to their land, but instead God gave him the revelation of the 70 weeks which was to assure Daniel that

God will fulfill His covenant promises to the nation. Gabriel informed Daniel that God would bring Israel back into their land and set up the messianic kingdom. However, Gabriel added that this would not be ultimately fulfilled at the end of the 70-year captivity in Babylon but at the end of the 70-week period stated in 9:24–27.

The Terminology of the 70 Weeks

INTRODUCTION

Over the centuries the meaning of the 70 weeks has been a *crux interpretum*. Some writers see the 70 weeks already fulfilled in some way during the Maccabean times.[1] Others view the weeks as merely symbolic. According to Young, "Since these numbers represent periods of time, the length of which is not stated, and since they are thus symbolical, it is not warrantable to seek to discover the precise lengths of the sevens."[2]

However, in the light of Daniel's inquiry about the consummation of a literal 70-year captivity in Babylon, it seems most reasonable that the 70 weeks are not symbolic but are to be interpreted literally. As Wood observes, the fact of Daniel's use of definite numbers—7, 62, and 1—makes it difficult to think of symbolic indefinite periods of time.[3] Hence in the light of the context the literal interpretation makes the most sense.

INTERPRETATION

The term שָׁבֻעִים *in the Old Testament.* The term שָׁבֻעִים is the plural form of שָׁבוּע, a unit or period of seven, heptad, or week.[4] It is used 20 times in the Old Testament. Three times it means a unit of seven and is followed by יָמִים "days" (Ezek. 45:21; Dan. 10:2–3); six times it means "week(s)," a normal seven-day week (Gen. 29:27, 28; Deut. 16:9 [twice]; Lev. 12:5; Deut. 16:10, 16; 2 Chron. 8:13); and six times it is used as a "unit of seven" without reference to days (Dan. 9:24–25 [twice], 26–27 [twice]). Therefore, the context determines its meaning. This can also be illustrated by עָשׂוֹר which is normally translated "ten days" because the context demands this rendering 13 out of 16 occurrences in the Old Testament. However, three times (Pss. 33:2; 92:43; 144:9) it has reference to a musical instrument and would have to be translated "ten strings."[5] Thus עָשׂוֹר has the idea of a "unit of ten" as determined by the context.

The term שָׁבוּעַ, then, means "a unit of seven" and its particular meaning must be determined by the particular context.

The term שָׁבֻעִים in Daniel 9:24–27. In this passage the term refers to units of seven years and thus Daniel was speaking of 70 of these units of seven years or a total of 490 years. The reasons for this conclusion are as follows.

First, in the context Daniel had been thinking in terms of years as well as multiples (ten times seven) of years (Dan. 9:1–2).

Second, Daniel had been considering Jeremiah 25:11 and 29:10 regarding the 70-year captivity. The captivity was a result of violating the sabbatical year, which was to have been observed after every six years (2 Chron. 36:21; cf. Lev. 26:34–35, 43). Each year of captivity represented one seven-year cycle in which the seventh or Sabbath year had not been observed. Thus it is clear that the context refers to years, not days. Daniel then saw another 490 years into Israel's future. This can be diagrammed in the following way:

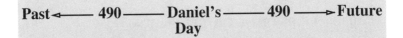

Past◄—— 490 —— Daniel's —— 490 ——►Future
Day

Third, the only other usage of שָׁבֻעִים by Daniel is in 10:2–3 where the phrase שְׁלֹשָׁה שָׁבֻעִים יָמִים is literally "three units of seven days" or 21 days. This has reference to Daniel's mourning for three weeks since the word יָמִים is included. The very fact that Daniel adds יָמִים indicates that he did not want his readers to think of the unit of seven the same way it was used in chapter 9. Everyone would have realized that Daniel would not have fasted 21 years, but the fact that he inserted יָמִים "days" in 10:2, 3 when it was not necessary would seem to indicate that he *would* have used יָמִים in 9:24–27 if there he meant 490 "days." Therefore in 9:24–27 Daniel was referring to years and not days.

Fourth, it is impossible to fit the events described in 9:24–27, regardless of the terminus a quo, into 490 days or weeks. Only that number of years is viable.

Fifth, in 9:27 the covenant that will be confirmed for one "unit of seven" (שָׁבוּעַ) will be broken in the middle of that unit of seven. If one accepts the שָׁבוּעַ as a unit of seven years, this would mean that the covenant will be broken at the three and one-half year point and the last three-and-one-half years will be a time of trouble and desolation. This fits well with the trouble described by the temporal note "time, times, and half a time" in Daniel 7:25 and 12:7 as well as in Revelation 12:14.

Sixth, although the term שָׁבוּעַ does not refer to years elsewhere in the Bible, it has this meaning in the Mishnah.[6]

In conclusion the term שָׁבֻעִים in Daniel 9 most reasonably refers to a unit of seven years. To make it anything else does not make good sense. However, for the sake of clarity this unit of seven years will be called "week(s)" in this chapter, for it is simpler to refer to 70 "weeks" than to 70 "units of seven years." Therefore Daniel's reference to 70 weeks means a period of 490 years.

The Terminus a Quo of the 70 Weeks

Daniel 9:25 states that the starting point of the 70 weeks is the issuance of a command to restore and rebuild Jerusalem where a plaza (or square) and a moat (or trench) will be built during distressing times.

THE DESCRIPTION OF THE REBUILDING

Three things are to be noted in the description of the rebuilding of Jerusalem. First, the words לְהָשִׁיב וְלִבְנוֹת ("to restore and to rebuild") suggest that the city was raised to its former state. It is not a partial rebuilding but a complete restoration.[7]

Second, the words רְחוֹב וְחָרוּץ ("plaza and moat") give weight to the position for a complete restoration of the city. The first of these words means a plaza, street, or square, "the broad spaces, generally just inside the city gates, the center of city life."[8] It is a wide and free unoccupied place in the city (cf. Ezra 10:9; Esther 4:6; 2 Chron. 32:6; Neh. 8:1, 3). The second word, חָרוּץ, is more difficult to define. It is a passive participle of חָרַץ meaning "to cut, to sharpen, to decide."[9] In the Old Testament it is used fourteen times: four times it refers to a sharpened threshing instrument, a threshing sledge (Isa. 28:27; 41:15; Amos 1:3);[10] one time it suggests the idea of being maimed, cut, or mutilated (Lev. 22:22); six times it is used poetically of gold from the idea of the sharp bright color or from the idea that it is eagerly desired by men (חָרַץ can have the idea "to be eager, to covet") (Ps. 68:13 [Heb. 14]; Prov. 3:14; 8:10, 19; 16:16; Zech. 9:3); two times it refers to "something decided," a strict decision as in the phrase "valley of decision" (Joel 3:14); and once it is used in Daniel 9:25. Outside the Bible this term is used in Aramaic of a "trench";[11] in Akkadian it has the idea of a "city moat";[12] in the Qumran writings it is used of a "moat of the rampart or bulwark";[13] and in mishnaic and targumic literature it has the idea of an incision, furrow, or trench.[14] Thus its basic idea is to make an incision or cut or dig a trench.

Commentators are divided on how to apply the two words, רחוב וחרוץ, to Daniel 9:25, but it is best to take the first word *plaza* as referring to the interior of the city and the second word *trench* as referring to a moat going around the outside of the city. Part of Jerusalem's natural defenses consisted of a great cutting in the rock along the northern wall, which is still visible, for the purpose of building a defense wall.[15] Montgomery states that these "two items present a graphic picture of the complete restoration."[16]

Third, it should be noted that the rebuilding of Jerusalem would be done in times of distress or oppression.

In conclusion, then, Daniel described the rebuilding of Jerusalem as being a complete restoration during troublous times.

THE TIME OF THE REBUILDING

Having discussed the description of the rebuilding of Jerusalem, one needs to determine when this occurred.

The decree of Cyrus. The first decree is the one of Cyrus to rebuild the temple, probably given on October 29, 539 B.C.[17] (2 Chron. 36:22–23; Ezra 1:1–4; 6:3–5). This decree concerned the return of the captives and the rebuilding of the temple but not a complete restoration of the city. However, Keil,[18] Leupold,[19] and Young[20] feel this decree marks the starting point of the 70 weeks. Young states:

> This edict [Cyrus's], furthermore, was issued in fulfillment of the prophecy of Jer., and it speaks expressly of going to Jerusalem and building there the temple—the first and most important step in rebuilding of the city. In this connection also one should consider the prophecies of Isa. 44:28 in which Cyrus is described as "saying to Jerusalem, Thou shalt be built; and to the temple, Thy foundation shall be laid." Likewise Isa. 45:13 declares of Cyrus, "he shall build my city, and he shall let go my captives." Lastly, it should be noted that the book of Ezra pictures Jerusalem as an existing city (cf. Ezra 4:12, 9:9).
>
> It cannot be denied that this was the year in which the effects of the going forth of a word began to appear in history. Cyrus issued the decree which brought an end to the exile and again turned the Jews toward Jerusalem. It is not justifiable to distinguish too sharply between the

building of the city and the building of the temple. Certainly, if the people had received permission to return to Jerusalem to rebuild the temple, there was also implied in this permission to build for themselves homes in which to dwell. There is no doubt whatever but that the people thus understood the decree (cf. Haggai 1:2–4). The edict of Cyrus mentions the temple specifically, because that was the religious center of the city, that which distinguished it as the holy city of the Jews. If, therefore, we are to discover in history the effects of the going forth of a Divine word we discover them first appearing during the first year of Cyrus the king, and this year is thus to be regarded as the *terminus a quo* of the 70 sevens.[21]

While at first sight this all seems quite convincing, there are several problems with this view. First, Cyrus's edict refers to the rebuilding of the temple and not to the city. Although it is granted there were inhabitants and a city was built in Cyrus's time as predicted by Isaiah, certainly it was not a city that could defend itself as described in Daniel 9:25. Young cites two Scripture verses from Ezra to substantiate his view. The first passage—Ezra 4:12 (see also vv. 13 and 16)—is not applicable for it is referring not to Cyrus's time but to Artaxerxes' reign (465/464–423 B.C.) as even Young argues vigorously in another work of his.[22] The second passage—Ezra 9:9—also refers to Artaxerxes' reign and not Cyrus's reign. Also the word for "wall," גָּדֵר, is a fence used to surround a vineyard and not a military defensive wall.[23] It is never used in Nehemiah in relation to building a defensive wall. Most likely it is metaphorically speaking of security brought about by the protection of the Persian kings.[24] The only other references to the walls in Ezra are the walls of the temple (Ezra 5:3, 8–9). Therefore, neither of these Scripture passages is in the context of Cyrus's decree and has no reference to a defensive wall.

Second, a distinction should be made between the rebuilding of a city and the restoration of a city to its former state. Japan rebuilt itself after World War 11, but that is quite different from restoring it to its pre-World War II military state. The commencement of the rebuilding began with Cyrus's decree but the city's complete restoration was not at that time.

Third, if one accepts the 70 weeks as beginning with Cyrus's decree, how does one reckon the 490 years? Young states:

> The 7 sevens apparently has [*sic*] reference to the time which should elapse between the issuance of the word and the completion of the city and temple; roughly, to the end of the period of Ezra and Neh. The 62 sevens follows [*sic*] this period. In vs. 25 these 62 sevens are not

characterized, but in vs. 26 we are told what will happen after the expiry of the 62 sevens. The 62 sevens therefore have reference to the period which follows the age of Ezra and Neh. to the time of Christ.[25]

Though Young is not specific regarding the final week, it seems that he would make the first half of that week include all of Christ's incarnation and the destruction of the temple in A.D. 70, but with no indication of the terminus ad quem of the 70th week.[26]

Young's formulation, according to the first seven weeks, would cover a period of about one hundred years (each week thus representing about 14 years); the second period of 62 weeks would cover from Nehemiah to the time of Christ, a period of about 450 years (each week representing about seven years); and the final week would be divided into two parts, the first half covering the life of Christ and going even until the destruction of the temple in A.D. 70, a period of 35 to 70 years (about 10 to 20 years for each week), and the second half of the 70th week would have no terminus ad quem. Of course other scholars who begin the decree with Cyrus do not all calculate the 70th week as Young does. However, it seems that this system makes havoc of Gabriel's sayings, which were rather specific. Also Young's lengthy explanation leads one to be suspicious of this interpretation. It seems highly subjective, as is evident when one reads the various commentators who hold to a symbolic interpretation.

In conclusion, then, it is most unlikely that Cyrus's decree marks the terminus a quo of the 70 weeks described in Daniel.

The decree of Darius. The next decree in the restoration of the temple in Jerusalem was made by Tattenai, governor of Judah, who questioned the Jews' right to rebuild the temple (Ezra 5:3–17). Darius had a search made of Cyrus's decree and then issued a decree himself about 519/518 B.C. to confirm Cyrus's original decree (Ezra 6:1–12). This decree will not serve as the beginning date for the 70 weeks because it has specific reference to the temple and not to the city, and because it really was not a new decree but only confirmed a former one.

The decree of Artaxerxes to Ezra. The third decree was the decree to Ezra in 457 B.C. It encouraged the return of more exiles with Ezra, the further enhancement of the temple and its accompanying worship, and the appointment of civil leaders (Ezra 7:11–26). It is thought by men such as Pusey,[27] Boutflower,[28]

Payne,[29] and Goss[30] that this decree marked the terminus a quo of
the 70 weeks and that the end of the 69th week brings one to A.D.
26 or 27 (depending on whether one dates the decree 458 or 457
B.C.), which marks the commencement of Christ's ministry. The
proponents of this view (with the exception of Goss) would see at
the middle of the 70th week the crucifixion of Christ in A.D. 30
and the terminus ad quem of the 70th week would be in A.D. 33,
the probable date of Stephen's death and Paul's conversion.

There are several problems with this view. First, and foremost,
is that this decree has not a word about the rebuilding of the city of
Jerusalem but rather the temple in Jerusalem.[31] This is even admitted
by Payne.[32]

The proponents of this theory say that a wall was permitted to
be built because Artaxerxes gave unlimited freedom to use the
leftover silver and gold (Ezra 7:18) and because Ezra was to
appoint civil authorities (7:25) who would want to build a wall.
But the leftover silver and gold was to be used for the temple
worship and the civil authorities were appointed for the purpose
of judging and not for building defense walls.[33]

Second, to have the 69 weeks terminate at the commencement
of Christ's ministry in A.D. 26 or 27 is untenable for two reasons:
(a) The cutting off of the Messiah (Dan. 9:26) is a very inappropriate
way to refer to the descent of the Holy Spirit on Jesus at the
commencement of His ministry. (b) The date for the beginning of
Jesus' ministry is not A.D. 26 or 27 but A.D. 29.[34]

Third, to what did Daniel refer in 9:27 when he spoke of
confirming a covenant? If it refers to Christ, then what covenant
was it and how did He break it?

Fourth, to say that the middle of the 70th week refers to
Christ's crucifixion in A.D. 30 is untenable on two grounds: (a) the
sacrifices did not cease at Christ's crucifixion, and (b) though the
date of A.D. 30 is possible, the A.D. 33 date is far more plausible.[35]

Fifth, to say that the end of the 70th week refers to Stephen's
death and Paul's conversion in A.D. 33 is pure speculation. There
is no hint of this in Daniel 9:27 and Acts 7 and 9 to denote the
fulfillment of the 70th week. Also the date of Paul's conversion as
well as Stephen's martyrdom was more likely in A.D. 35.[36]

In conclusion the decree of Artaxerxes to Ezra in 457 B.C.
serving as the starting point of the 70 weeks is highly unlikely.

The decree of Artaxerxes to Nehemiah. Another decree is that
of Artaxerxes to Nehemiah in 444 B.C. to rebuild the city of

Jerusalem (Neh. 2:1–8). Several factors commend this decree as the one prophesied by Daniel (9:25) for the commencement of the 70 weeks. First, there is a direct reference to the restoration of the city (2:3, 5) and of the city gates and walls (2:3, 8). Second, Artaxerxes wrote a letter to Asaph to give materials to be used specifically for the walls (2:8). Third, the Book of Nehemiah and Ezra 4:7–23 indicate that certainly the restoration of the walls was done in the most distressing circumstances, as predicted by Daniel (Dan. 9:25).

Fourth, no later decrees were given by the Persian kings pertaining to the rebuilding of Jerusalem.[37]

Keil objects to calling this a decree. He thinks it would more appropriately be seen as a "royal favor."[38] However, Daniel 9:25, though not requiring a decree,[39] does require a command (דבר) and certainly this was the case with Artaxerxes as seen in the letters he wrote to the governors of the provinces beyond the river and to Asaph (Neh. 2:7–9).

In conclusion this is the only decree that adequately fits the strictures given in Daniel 9:25. Hence this decree of Artaxerxes is considered the terminus a quo of the 70 weeks.

The date of this decree is given in the biblical record. Nehemiah 1:1 states that Nehemiah heard of Jerusalem's desolate conditions in the month of Chislev (November/December) in Artaxerxes' 20th year. Then later in Artaxerxes' 20th year in the month of Nisan (March/April) Nehemiah reported that he was granted permission to restore the city and build its walls (2:1). To have Nisan later than Chislev (in the same year) may seem strange until one realizes that Nehemiah was using a Tishri-to-Tishri (September/October) dating method rather than the Persian Nisan-to-Nisan method. Nehemiah was following what was used by the kings of Judah earlier in their history.[40] This method used by Nehemiah is confirmed by Jews in Elephantine who also used this method during the same time period as Nehemiah.[41]

Next, one needs to establish the beginning of Artaxerxes' rule. His father Xerxes died shortly after December 17, 465 B.C.[42] and Artaxerxes immediately succeeded him. Since the accession-year system was used[43] the first year of Artaxerxes' reign according to the Persian Nisan-to-Nisan reckoning would be Nisan 464 to Nisan 463 and according to the Jewish Tishri-to-Tishri reckoning would be Tishri 464 to Tishri 463. This could be charted in the following way:

The Report to Nehemiah

Julian (January New Year)	465		464	463
Persian (Nisan New Year)	21st Year of Xerxes	Accession Year of Artaxerxes	1st Year of Artaxerxes' Reign	2nd Year
Jewish (Tishri New Year)		21st Year of Xerxes	Accession Year of Artaxerxes	1st Year of Artaxerxes' Reign	2nd Year

XERXES' DEATH, ARTAXERXES' ACCESSION, DECEMBER 465

Thus the 20th year of Artaxerxes' reign, mentioned in Nehemiah 1:1 and 2:1, would be illustrated as follows:

The Decree of Artaxerxes

NISAN (Date of Decree, cf. Neh. 2:1)

Julian (January New Year)	445		444	
Persian (Nisan New Year)	19th Year	20th Year		21st Year
Jewish (Tishri New Year)	19th Year		20th Year	21st Year

CHISLEV (Date of Report, cf. Neh. 1:1)

In conclusion the report to Nehemiah (1:1) occurred in Chislev (November/December) of 445 B.C. and the decree of Artaxerxes (2: 1) occurred in Nisan (March/April) of 444 B.C.[44] Therefore, Nisan 444 B.C. marks the terminus a quo of the 70 weeks of Daniel 9:24–27.

The Terminus Ad Quem of the 69 Weeks

THE SEPARATION OF THE 69TH FROM THE 70TH WEEK

Keil, Leupold, Payne, Young, and others say that the 70th week follows immediately after the 69th week. However, it is far more plausible to see the 69 weeks fulfilled historically and the 70th week as yet unfulfilled. The reasons are as follows: First, to view the six things in Daniel 9:24—to finish the transgression, to make an end of sin, to make atonement for iniquity, to bring in everlasting righteousness, to seal up vision and prophecy, and to anoint the most holy place—as having been fulfilled in Christ's death at His first advent is impossible. All these have reference to the nation of Israel and none of these has been fulfilled to that nation. Israel has not yet finished her transgression, nor been purged of her iniquity. Nor has she experienced the everlasting righteousness promised her. Paul sees this still in the future for Israel (Rom. 11:25–27).[45] The anointing of the most holy is not a reference to Christ's anointing, as Young would have it;[46] instead the "most holy" (קֹדֶשׁ קָדָשִׁים) are technical words that are always translated in the Old Testament as the "holy of holies."

Second, the Messiah was cut off "after" the 69th week and not "during" the 70th. Gundry stated this point well.

> If the cutting off of the Messiah occurred in the middle of the seventieth week, it is very strange that the cutting off is said to be "after" the sixty-nine weeks (figuring the sum of the seven and the sixty-two weeks). Much more naturally the text would have read "during" or "in the midst of" the seventieth week, as it does in verse twenty-seven concerning the stoppage of the sacrifices. The only adequate explanation for this unusual turn of expression is that the seventieth week did not follow on the heels of the sixty-ninth, but that an interval separates the two. The crucifixion then comes shortly "after" the sixty-ninth but not within the seventieth because of an intervening gap. The possibility of a gap between the sixty-ninth and the seventieth weeks is established by the well accepted OT phenomenon of prophetic perspective, in which gaps such as that between the first and second advents were not perceived.[47]

An example of a gap between the two advents of Christ is seen in

Luke 4:18–19 when Christ quoted Isaiah 61:1–2, leaving in the words referring to His first advent but omitting the words referring to His second advent.

Third, the person who confirms the covenant in Daniel 9:27 cannot refer to Christ. (a) The nearest antecedent is "the prince who is to come," in verse 26.[48] (b) At no time in Christ's ministry did he confirm an already-existing covenant. Certainly Payne's attempt to say that Christ "cause[d] to prevail" an existing covenant rather than making a new covenant on the basis of the absence of the word "new" in some Greek manuscripts in Matthew 26:28[49] is tenuous, to say the least, for, as Gundry points out, the adjective "new" is in Luke 22:20 and 1 Corinthians 11:25 and the New Covenant is twice quoted in Hebrews.[50] (c) If Christ did confirm a covenant in His first advent, when did He break it? Would Christ break a covenant He had made? Thus the covenant-confirmer does not refer to Christ but to a prince who is yet to come.

Fourth, Christ's death did render inoperative the animal sacrifices but did *not* cause them to cease immediately. In fact the Jews sacrificed animals until Jerusalem's destruction in A.D. 70.

Fifth, the abomination of desolation has not yet been fulfilled. In Matthew 24:15 Jesus said that it would occur after His ministry on earth. He spoke of the appearance of the abomination of desolation in the Jerusalem temple as a signal of the great tribulation which is immediately followed by Christ's second advent. It is true that Jerusalem suffered destruction in A.D. 66–70 but Christ did not return in A.D. 70. In fact the Book of Revelation speaks of Jerusalem's desolation as yet future and not as having been fulfilled nearly a quarter century before its composition.[51]

Sixth, the person in view in Daniel 9:27 correlates very well with the wicked person in 7:25 and in Revelation 12 and 13, who has not yet appeared and been judged as described in Revelation 19.

Seventh, the events of the last half of the 70th week, described in Daniel 9:27b, fit well into the second three and one half years of the tribulation described in the Book of Revelation, which is yet future.

In conclusion it is far better to see an intervening gap between the 69th and 70th weeks than to view the 70th as following the 69th. The 70th week is yet to be fulfilled. The 69 weeks have been fulfilled.

THE COMPLETION OF THE 69 WEEKS

Thus far it has been concluded that the terminus a quo of the 70 weeks is Nisan 444 B.C. After the 62 weeks the Messiah will be cut off and have nothing (Dan. 9:26).[52] This has reference to Christ's death and indicates that in His first advent He would not acquire the messianic kingdom envisioned in the Old Testament. Thus the 69 weeks were to expire shortly before Christ's death. Hence the terminus ad quem for the 69th week is shortly before Christ's death. This writer holds that Christ's death occurred on Friday, Nisan 14 in A.D. 33.

Calculation with the solar year. If one multiplies the 69 weeks by seven solar years, the total is 483 years. Subtracting this from 444 B.C. gives the date of A.D. 38, five years after Christ's crucifixion. So it is obvious that a calculation using the solar year does not work.

Calculation with the sabbatical year. A new attempt has been made by Newman, who calculates 69 sabbatical years between the termini a quo and ad quem of the 69 years. His conclusion is that the 69th sabbatical year was A.D. 27–34.[53] However, there are some problems with this view. First, the first sabbatical period would be from 452 to 445 B.C., which is one year before the decree of Artaxerxes to Nehemiah. Thus one would have only 68 sabbatical years between the decree and Christ's death. Second, Daniel wrote that the Messiah would be cut off after the 69 weeks, and thus according to Newman's view Christ would have to be cut off after A.D. 34, a year after His crucifixion. Third, the figures in Daniel seem to be more specific than sabbatical years. If sabbatical years were used, one would expect the decree to have been given in a sabbatical year and Christ's death to have occurred in a sabbatical year. Fourth, although the 70-year captivity was for Israel's disobedience of not observing the sabbatical years, there is no specific reference to sabbatical years mentioned in the immediate context. Fifth, there is no direct biblical evidence as to which year the sabbatical year occurred. All the evidence Newman gives is from secondary sources. Therefore this system of calculation does not solve the problem.

Calculation with the prophetical year. The most plausible solution is the one introduced by Anderson. He proposed that the length of the year should be calculated as 360 days. He called these 360-day years "prophetic years."[54]

This makes good sense for several reasons. First, with modern astronomy one can reckon a year very precisely as being "365.24219879 days, or 365 days, 5 hours, 48 minutes, 45.975 seconds."[55] However, in ancient times various systems were used. It was common during at least some parts of the histories of Egypt,[56] India,[57] Assyria and Babylon,[58] and Greece[59] to have 12 30-day months making a total of 360 days for the year and then to have some system of intercalating the other five days so that the year would come out correctly. Although it may be strange to present-day thinking, it was common in those days to think of a 360-day year.

Second, in conjunction with the prophetic literature of the Bible, the 360-day year is used. Daniel's 70th week is a good illustration of this fact. A covenant will be confirmed for the seven years of the 70th week (Dan. 9:27) but it will be broken in the middle of the week. In the last half of the week, or for three and one-half years, there will be terrible persecution. This matches with the persecution mentioned in 7:24–25, which will last for "a time, times, and half a time," or three and one-half years. This phrase is also mentioned in 12:7. However, not until one comes to the New Testament is the duration of the year known. John used the same terminology of time, times, and half a time in Revelation 12:14. Speaking of the same situation within the same chapter, John wrote that the persecution will be for 1,260 days (12:6). John again used this figure of 1,260 days in 11:3 and that period is listed as being 42 months in the previous verse (11:2). Also the 42 month period is mentioned in 13:5, which speaks of the same period of persecution. Thus the 42 months equals the 1,260 days, and that equals the time, times, and half a time or three and one-half years, which in turn equals the half week in Daniel 9:27. Hence the month is 30 days in length and the year is 360 days.

Third, outside the prophetic literature the 360-day year is used one other time in the Bible. Genesis 7:11 states that the Flood began on the 17th day of the second month. According to Genesis 8:4 the Flood ended on the 17th day of the seventh month, exactly five months later. Genesis 7:24 and 8:3 state that the duration of the flood was 150 days. Hence five months equals 150 days or each month equals 30 days.

Therefore in the light of these observations the prophetic year of 360 days should not be too surprising.

Does the 360-day year correlate with the date of the cutting off of the Messiah? Anderson multiplies the 69 weeks by seven years for each week by 360 days and comes to the total of 173,880 days. His terminus a quo for the 69 weeks is Nisan 1 in Artaxerxes' 20th year or March 14, 445 B.C., and his terminus ad quem is the Triumphal Entry on Nisan 10, April 6, A.D. 32. He shows that this works out perfectly. The time between 445 B.C. and A.D. 32 is 476 years; multiplying 476 by 365 days totals 173,740 days. He adds 116 days for leap years and 24 days for the difference between March 14 (of 445 B.C.) and April 6 (of A.D. 32) and thus arrives at a total of 173,880 days.[60]

Anderson's calculations include some problems. First, in the light of new evidence since Anderson's day, the 445 B.C. date is not acceptable for Artaxerxes' 20th year; instead the decree was given in Nisan, 444 B.C. Second, the A.D. 32 date for the crucifixion is untenable. It would mean that Christ was crucified on either a Sunday or Monday.[61] In fact Anderson realizes the dilemma and he has to do mathematical gymnastics to arrive at a Friday crucifixion. This makes one immediately suspect. Actually there is no good evidence for an A.D. 32 crucifixion date.

Reckoning Jesus' death according to the Julian calendar, Christ died on Friday, April 3, A.D. 33.[62] As already discussed, the terminus a quo occurred in Nisan, 444 B.C. Thus Nisan 1 in 444 B.C. was March 4, or more likely March 5 since the crescent of the new moon would have been first visible so late at night (ca. 10 P.M.) on March 4 and could easily have been missed.[63]

Using the prophetic year the calculation would be as follows. Multiplying the 69 weeks by seven years for each week by 360 days gives a total of 173,880 days. The difference between 444 B.C. and A.D. 33 then is 476 solar years. By multiplying 476 by 365.24219879 or by 365 days, 5 hours, 48 minutes, 45.975 seconds, gives the total of 173,855 days, 6 hours, 52 minutes, 44 seconds, or 173,855 days. This leaves only 25 days to be accounted for between 444 B.C. and A.D. 33. By adding the 25 days to March 5 (of 444 B.C.), one comes to March 30 which was Nisan 10 in A.D. 33. This is the date of Jesus' Triumphal Entry into Jerusalem.

Conclusion

Daniel inquired about the termination of the 70-year captivity. Gabriel said that Israel would not come to its messianic rest until 70 weeks were completed. It was concluded that the 70 weeks refer to 490 years, which are to be calculated according to the prophetic year of 360 days. The terminus a quo of this 70-week period was reckoned as being March 4 or 5 (more probably the latter). It was decided that there is a gap between the 69th and the 70th week. The terminus ad quem of the 69th week was on the day of Christ's Triumphal Entry on March 30, A.D. 33.

As predicted in Zechariah 9:9, Christ presented Himself to Israel as Messiah the King for the last time and the multitude of the disciples shouted loudly by quoting from a messianic psalm: "Blessed is the king who comes in the name of the Lord" (Ps. 118:26; Matt. 21:9; Mark II: 10; Luke 19:38; John 12:13). This occurred on Monday, Nisan 10 (March 30) and only four days later on Friday, Nisan 14, April 3, A.D. 33 Jesus was cut off or crucified.

The 70th week of Daniel's prophecy is yet to be fulfilled. When that is accomplished, Daniel's inquiry will be fully realized, for Israel will be back in her homeland with her Messiah.

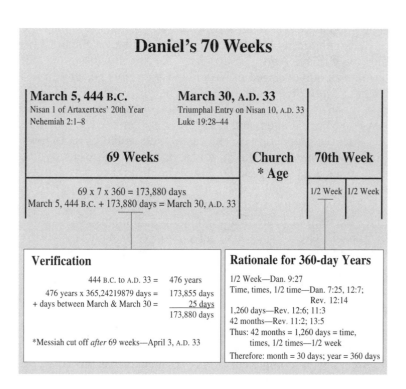

Daniel's 70 Weeks

March 5, 444 B.C.
Nisan 1 of Artaxertxes' 20th Year
Nehemiah 2:1–8

March 30, A.D. 33
Triumphal Entry on Nisan 10, A.D. 33
Luke 19:28–44

69 Weeks

69 x 7 x 360 = 173,880 days
March 5, 444 B.C. + 173,880 days = March 30, A.D. 33

Church * Age

70th Week

1/2 Week | 1/2 Week

Verification

444 B.C. to A.D. 33 =	476 years
476 years x 365,24219879 days =	173,855 days
+ days between March & March 30 =	25 days
	173,880 days

*Messiah cut off *after* 69 weeks—April 3, A.D. 33

Rationale for 360-day Years

1/2 Week—Dan. 9:27
Time, times, 1/2 time—Dan. 7:25, 12:7; Rev. 12:14
1,260 days—Rev. 12:6; 11:3
42 months—Rev. 11:2; 13:5
Thus: 42 months = 1,260 days = time, times, 1/2 times—1/2 week
Therefore: month = 30 days; year = 360 days

CHAPTER 15

"For Three Sins . . . Even for Four": The Numerical Sayings in Amos

Robert B. Chisholm, Jr.

The Old Testament prophets were adept at luring hostile audiences into listening to their judgment speeches. First Kings 20:35–43 records how a prophet resorted to bizarre tactics just to trick Ahab into unwittingly decreeing his own guilt and punishment. Recalling Nathan's artful use of a parable in his accusation against David (2 Sam. 12:1–14), Alter observes that "prophetic poetry is thus very often constructed as *a rhetoric of entrapment.*"[1]

Amos 1–2 contains one of the clearest examples of this "entrapment" technique in the writing prophets. In a series of seven judgment speeches against Israel's neighbors, Amos moved from foreigners (Aram, Philistia, Tyre) to blood relatives (Edom, Ammon, Moab) to Judah, Israel's sister kingdom to the south (1:3–2:5).[2] The prophet's Israelite audience, anticipating a day of divine deliverance from their enemies (5:18), must have listened with delight to this series of messages, especially when their longtime rival Judah appeared, like a capstone, as the seventh nation in the list. As Shalom Paul notes, Amos's "captive northern audience, who must have been enjoying every minute of it, would psychologically be in a state of mind which would lead them to believe that he had reached his climax with his fulmination against Judah."[3] The sevenfold list would have suggested completeness and finality. However, to the shock of his listeners, Amos was finished. Expanding his list from seven members to eight, he delivered a scathing accusation and announcement of judgment against Israel (2:6–16).[4]

At this point the preceding seven oracles come into focus. Rather than being self-contained pronouncements of judgment, the earlier messages set up the climactic denunciation of the prophet's primary target group, the sinful Northern Kingdom. As

Paul explains, "The minute he continued his eighth and unexpected oracle, for him the sole purpose of his extended prolegomenon, they would have been taken completely unawares, and Amos, who delighted over and over again in making use of surprise endings, would have forcefully and compellingly made his final indictment."[5]

When compared to the preceding seven oracles, the structure and content of this final oracle draw attention, in at least three ways, to Israel's guilt that surpassed that of its neighbors. First, the prophet expanded the accusation proper (2:6–8) by adding a lengthy recital of the Lord's benefits to His people (2:9–11), with which he then contrasted their ingratitude (2:12). Second, the specific punishment ("I will crush you," 2:13)[6] differs from that of the preceding oracles, in which the Lord invariably threatened to judge the various nations with fire. Third, the description of the effects of judgment, with its sevenfold statement of the Israelite army's demise (2:14–16), is more extensive than the corresponding descriptions in the other oracles. The point of this variation from the earlier pattern seems clear: Israel's unique degree of guilt (heightened by its ingratitude) demanded a unique punishment.

A clear rhetorical pattern thus emerges in Amos 1–2. In the preliminary oracles the prophet gained his audience's attention and approval, leading them to believe that the Lord would soon intervene on their behalf and destroy the surrounding nations. When the prophet finally sprang his trap, he made it clear that Israel would be the primary object of the Lord's judgment because its guilt surpassed that of its neighbors.

Amos's use of the saying, "for three sins . . . even for four," which appears in the introduction to each of the eight oracles, contributes to this rhetorical pattern. Amos creatively altered the $x/x + 1$ (in this case 3/4) numerical pattern so as to arouse his audience's curiosity and highlight their guilt. Before developing this proposal more fully, the functions of the $x/x + 1$ numerical pattern in general will be discussed and the structure of Amos's oracles will be examined especially with respect to the number of crimes specified in each case.

The Functions of the x/x + 1 Numerical Pattern

The $x/x + 1$ pattern has two basic functions.[7] Sometimes this device indicates an indefinite number, in which case no itemized list follows. When so used the numerical saying can point to a relatively small number (Deut. 32:30; Job 40:5; Isa. 17:6; Hos. 6:2) or communicate the idea of abundance or completeness, the pattern 7/8 being a logical choice in the latter case because of the symbolic significance of the number seven (Eccl. 11:2; Mic. 5:5).[8] At other times the x/x + 1 pattern indicates a definite number of items, in which case a list corresponding to one of the numbers, almost always the second, is attached. Examples include 1/2 (Ps. 62:11–12), 3/4 (Prov. 30:15–16, 18–19, 21–23, 29–31), and 6/7 (Job 5:19–22; Prov. 6:16–19).[9]

The Structure of Amos's Oracles

Each of the eight oracles in Amos 1–2 begins with the same formula, the parallelism of which may be outlined as follows:

For three	sins of PN [proper name]	
Even for four	(sins of PN)	I will not take him back.[10]

For the sake of balancing the lines, the element "sins of PN" is omitted by ellipsis in the second line. "I will not take him back" completes the thought left suspended in the first line.

In each oracle the construction עַל (in a causal sense; "because") + infinitive construct + pronominal suffix (used as subject) follows the formula, stating a specific accusation or introducing a list of charges against the nation. The accusations vary considerably in both form and length. In most cases (the Aram and Moab oracles are exceptions) it is difficult to know how many crimes are enumerated. Does one proceed in a strictly formal fashion and count each verbal statement (with the possible exception of those in subordinate clauses) as a distinct crime? Or does one take into account poetic parallelism and determine the number of crimes on a conceptual basis? Since it might appear arbitrary to choose one method over the other, both are employed in the following analysis of the oracles' structure.

As already noted, the oracles against Aram and Moab present no problem. Both specify only one crime. Aram was guilty "because she [lit. "they"] *threshed* Gilead with sledges having iron teeth" (1:3b), while judgment would fall on Moab "because he *burned*, as if to lime, the bones of Edom's king" (2:1b).

Unfortunately the other oracles are not so easily analyzed. The accusations against Philistia and Ammon contain a statement of a crime followed by a purpose clause:

Philistia (1:6b)   "Because she [lit. 'they'] *took captive* whole
                      communities and *sold* [lit. '*in order to sell*,'
                      Heb. לְהַסְגִּיר] them to Edom."

Ammon (1:13b)   "Because he [lit. 'they'] *ripped open* the
                      pregnant women of Gilead *in order to
                      extend* his [lit. 'their'] borders."

One could count each verbal statement as a separate crime, in
which case two sins are enumerated. However, viewed conceptually
only one basic crime is denounced in each case. Philistia was
guilty of large scale slave trade and Ammon of cruel imperialistic
expansion.

The accusation against Tyre includes two statements: "Because
she [lit. 'they'] *sold* whole communities of captives to Edom,
disregarding a treaty of brotherhood" (1:9b). Proceeding along
strictly formal lines, one may delineate two separate crimes (slave
trade and breach of treaty), but the point seems to be that slave
trade was the act whereby the covenant was broken. The second
line does not actually present a distinct sin, but rather emphasizes
the shocking ramifications of the crime described in the first line.
Viewed conceptually then, the oracle denounces only one crime
(slave trade of allies).

The accusation against Edom (1:11) is the longest of those
directed against foreign nations. Four separate statements appear:

> Because he *pursued* his brother with a sword,
> and *destroyed* his allies,[11]
> because his anger *raged* continually
> and his fury *flamed* unchecked.

When allowance is made for parallelism (note the two basic
units, each of which contains two synonymously parallel lines),
two crimes are discernible. Since the second unit appears to
emphasize the attitude with which Edom perpetrated the violence
referred to in the first unit, one might argue that the oracle
denounces only one crime (intense hostility against allies). Even
so, the repetition produced through parallelism highlights Edom's
sin in a unique way.

The accusation against Judah (2:4b) contains three separate
statements:

> Because they have *rejected* the law of the LORD

and have *not kept* his decrees,
because they have been *led astray* by false gods,
the gods their ancestors followed.

If one takes into account the synonymous parallelism of the first two lines, then no more than two crimes are enumerated. If the second unit is then viewed as giving a specific example of how the people rejected the Lord's Law (viz., by following in the idolatrous footsteps of their ancestors; cf. 2 Kings 17:15), only one crime (breach of covenant through idolatry) is in view.

The oracle against Israel is the most difficult to analyze. The accusation (2:6b–8, 12) is arranged in five units, each of which contains two corresponding lines:

2:6b	They *sell* the righteous for silver, and [they *sell*] the needy for a pair of sandals.
2:7a	They *trample* on the heads of the poor as upon the dust of the ground *and* deny *justice to the oppressed.*
2:7b	Father and son *use* [lit. "go to"] the same girl and so *profane* my holy name.
2:8	They *lie down* beside every altar on garments taken in pledge. In the house of their god they *drink wine* taken as fines.
2:12	But you *made* the Nazarites *drink* wine and *commanded* the prophets not to prophesy.

In a strictly formal sense 10 crimes are enumerated. If one understands verse 7b (note the infinitival construction ["and so profane," Heb. לְמַעַן חַלֵּל] which subordinates the statement to the preceding line) as denouncing just one crime, the number can be reduced to nine (seven in vv. 6–8 and two more in v. 12).[12] However, if allowance is made for the virtually synonymous parallelism throughout and the sins are viewed conceptually, only four crimes appear: (1) oppressing the innocent/poor (2:6b–7a),[13] (2) engaging in pagan religious practices (2:7b; cf. v. 8),[14] (3) abusing the system of pledges and fines (2:8), and (4) showing lack of respect for God's special servants (2:12).[15]

The following chart lists the number of crimes according to both the formal and the conceptual methods of enumeration:

Number of Crimes

Oracle	Formal		Conceptual	
Aram (1:3–5)	1		1	
Philistia (1:6–8)	2	(1?)	1	
Tyre (1:9–10)	2		1	(2?)
Edom (1:11–12)	4		1	(2?)
Ammon (1:13–15)	2	(1?)	1	
Moab (2:1–3)	1		1	
Judah (2:4–5)	3		1	(2?)
Israel (2:6–16)	10	(9?)	4	

When compared with the normal patterns of the $x/x + 1$ saying observed above, the structure of Amos's oracles is puzzling. If Amos were using the 3/4 pattern to indicate an indefinite number of sins, then one would not expect to find specific crimes listed after the formula. At the same time, Amos's oracles do not correspond to the enumerative pattern of the $x/x + 1$ saying, for in only one case (whether the formal or conceptual method is employed) does the expected fourfold list of specific crimes appear. If one follows the formal method, only the Edom oracle lists four crimes, while the Israel oracle contains more than twice that many. Viewed conceptually, only the accusation against Israel has the expected number of crimes.

Interpretations of Amos's Numerical Saying

What is one to make of Amos's use of the introductory statement, "For three sins . . . even for four"? Scholars have various suggestions, the most attractive of which are now considered.

Wolff proposes that the lists are purposely shortened with only the fourth crime, "the one which tips, indeed overloads, the scales," being specifically mentioned.[16] He points out that the final item of a numerical saying is often highlighted and suggests that Amos chose to include only this emphatic concluding element, bypassing the preliminary items in the list.

This interpretation fails to explain adequately the prophet's inconsistent application of the technique, especially if one uses the formal method to count the crimes. Even if one uses a conceptual method in enumerating the crimes, the Israel oracle differs from the others. Wolff's proposal fails to explain why the first seven oracles mention only the "last straw," while the Israel oracle follows the normal pattern by enumerating four crimes. To see in this some sort of emphasis on Israel's sin puts one on the right track, but a more precise explanation for the variation is desirable and possible.

Others prefer to dissociate Amos's introductory formula from the numerical saying pattern. For example B. K. Soper states that "the clause cannot be understood as a 'numerical saying . . . because of structural differences between the two."[17] He then appeals to the Babylonian Talmud, which observes that three sins may be forgiven, but not a fourth. He suggests that this fourth crime, the one that exhausts God's patience and necessitates divine judgment, is the one included in the oracles. Recently Barré has followed this line of argument as well. He translates Amos's statement as follows: "Because of three rebellious acts of GN—and now a fourth!"[18] This line of approach is subject to the same criticism as Wolff's. Barre suggests that the variation in the final oracle may signal "the conclusion of the series." This may indeed be true, but the variation has a much more significant rhetorical purpose as well.

Weiss, like Soper, contends that Amos's introductory formula is not really a numerical saying at all. He points to structural differences between Amos's sentence and numerical sayings used elsewhere, namely, Amos's placement of the predicate in the second line only and the absence of genuine parallelism.[19] According to Weiss, the numbers are to be added with the resulting sum (seven) symbolizing completeness. In support of this proposal Weiss delineates seven sins in the final oracle (in the case of the other nations, only their "complete and greatest" sin is included). To arrive at this number he follows a formal method of enumeration, though he says the subordinate clause of verse 7b ("and so profane my holy name") is not referring to a separate sin.[20]

There are at least two problems with Weiss's solution. First, it does not count the crimes denounced in verse 12. Following Weiss's formal method of enumeration, one would arrive at a total of nine sins if verse 12 were included.[21] Second, Weiss acknowledges, "There are no other examples, either in the Bible or outside of it, of a usage of two numbers such as we have assumed for this case."[22]

Amos's Rhetorical Adaptation of the x/x + 1 Numerical Pattern

Rather than understanding Amos's accusations as an elliptical form of the x/x + I pattern (Wolff) or rejecting any connection with the numerical saying (Soper, Weiss), it is proposed that Amos purposely altered the normal enumerative form of the x/x + 1 pattern for rhetorical purposes. His adaptation of the pattern contributed to the overall theme of chapters 1–2, namely, that Israel would be the focal point of divine judgment because its sins surpassed those of its neighbors. This is the case no matter which of the enumerative systems (formal or conceptual) is employed. Though the details of Amos's rhetorical scheme differ according to each system, the basic point is the same.

As noted earlier, if one follows the formal method of enumeration, then only the Edom oracle exhibits the expected fourfold list of crimes, while the Israel oracle contains more than twice that many. However, if one proceeds through the series oracle by oracle, a rhetorical purpose for this lack of uniformity is apparent. As Amos delivered his first three sayings (against Aram, Philistia, and Tyre), the audience must have puzzled over their structural oddities (the truncated lists and the syntactical peculiarities noted by Weiss). When he finally provided a list of four crimes in the fourth oracle, they would have thought (correctly) that the prophet was emphasizing the degree of hated Edom's sin. When one fills out lists of crimes for the surrounding nations, Edom's list fills up faster than the others. Some may have expected the speech to conclude here, perhaps reasoning that the 3/4 pattern of the introductory saying would be mirrored in the structure of the speech as a whole (the oracles against three nations concluding with a special denunciation of a fourth). However, the series continues. Two more truncated sayings (against Ammon and Moab) follow, and then Judah appears as the seventh nation. As discussed, Amos's Israelite audience would have delighted in this and would have expected the speech to conclude here, probably with another fourfold list of crimes like that of Edom. Their expectations were almost realized, but instead of capping off the list of Judah's sins with a fourth charge (the list includes only three formal accusatory statements), Amos delivered a brief announcement of judgment (2:5) and then surprisingly turned to Israel. Israel was the worst rebel of all, for she fills up two lists of crimes and part of a third before other nations complete one such list or despised Edom can start on a second! If divine judgment was coming, then it meant certain doom, not deliverance, for Israel, the chief of sinners.

If the conceptual method of enumeration is followed, the main point is the same. In this case only one or two crimes are listed in the first seven oracles, with the sins of Edom and Judah being seemingly highlighted through repetitive parallelism (perhaps, as indicated, to make the audience think that the speech was about to end, first with Edom and then with Judah). As Amos's audience rejoiced over the news of their enemies' demise, they should have, at the same time, puzzled over the structural oddity of the oracles. Suddenly Amos confronted them with a full list of crimes— their own! When filling out lists of four sins, one could complete Israel's before the second or third sin of its neighbors could be identified. In this case, the structure of the Israel oracle mirrors the 3/4 pattern of the introductory saying in that the recital of the Lord's benefits (2:9–11) separates the first three crimes (2:6–8) from the fourth (2:12).[23]

Conclusion

In his oracles against the nations Amos purposely altered the normal x/x + 1 enumerative pattern to emphasize that Israel's guilt surpassed that of its neighbors. Contrary to its expectations, Israel, not the surrounding nations, would be the focal point of the approaching divine judgment because its crimes far outnumbered those of others.[24]

CHAPTER 16

The Day of the Lord in Zephaniah

Greg A. King

R ecent scholarship has suggested that the time is ripe for a reassessment of the day of the Lord, a concept that is prominent in the prophetic books. Several factors invite this reassessment. First, to this writer's knowledge no major systematic study of the day of the Lord texts has been made in recent years.[1] Second, some previous attempts to elucidate what the prophets wrote about this significant concept incorrectly restricted their investigation to the precise phrase, "the day of the Lord."[2] Scholars now recognize that many similar phrases, especially the phrase "on that day," also refer to the day of the Lord and must be considered if this concept is to be understood fully.[3] Third, some past studies have tended to minimize the blessing or salvific aspect of the day of the Lord and have understood the day simply as the Lord's holy war against His enemies. This is unfortunate because many occurrences of "the day of the Lord" and related expressions refer to a future time of blessing and salvation.[4]

This study on Zephaniah's proclamation of the day of the Lord is one contribution toward a reassessment of this concept. Zephaniah is a worthwhile book on which to focus because this frequently ignored book makes an important contribution to this topic in Old Testament theology. As von Rad states, "Zephaniah's prophecy concerning the day of Yahweh is certainly one of the most important sources of material at our disposal for the various concepts connected with this subject."[5]

This delineation is based on the exegesis and theological assessment of the entire Book of Zephaniah. This methodology is in harmony with what was mentioned above about the recent recognition of the importance of considering the full range of what could be called day of the Lord terminology. Though the exact expression "the day of the Lord" (יוֹם יְהוָה) appears only three times in Zephaniah (once in 1:7 and twice in 1:14), a careful

analysis of the context of the many other verses where the word
"day" is used leaves little doubt that they refer to the same
concept. For example in chapter 1 phrases like "the day of
Yahweh's sacrifice" (1:8), "on that day" (1:9–10), and "the day of
Yahweh's fury" (1:18), are clearly used as synonyms for the
phrase "the day of Yahweh."[6] In fact the Hebrew word "day" (יוֹם)
appears in the singular 20 times in the three chapters of Zephaniah,
and every appearance is connected with Zephaniah's proclamation
of the day of the Lord. Also the prophet used other temporal
references, such as "at that time" (1:12), to refer to this concept. In
summary every major section of the book and even every unit
should be linked to Zephaniah's teaching on the day of the Lord.[7]
Therefore it is appropriate to consider the entire book in order to
discern what the prophet said about the day of the Lord. Also this
is in keeping with current trends in studies on Zephaniah, for most
recent scholars from both evangelical and critical camps tend to
approach the Book of Zephaniah wholistically.[8]

The Day of Yahweh's Intervention

Zephaniah's teaching on the day of the Lord features a number
of aspects. One aspect that is strongly emphasized is that the day
of the Lord brings Yahweh's intervention into human affairs. In
other words God will intrude into the human realm. There will be
a divine-human "collision."

Zephaniah expressed this divine intervention and the divine-
human encounter in a variety of ways. First, the command, "Be
silent before Lord Yahweh" (1:7), is clear evidence of the nearness
of deity. Humans are called to be mute in light of the approaching
encounter with Yahweh on His day. In fact the word הַס ("Be
silent") itself seems to denote the presence of Yahweh in this
instance.[9] As one writer observes, "This solemn summons to
silence by the prophet implies the imminence of the Lord himself.
Standing before his awesome majesty on his great day inspires the
most humble and reverent demeanor."[10]

A second way Zephaniah portrayed divine intervention into
human affairs is through the repeated use of the verb פָּקַד; by
Yahweh in the first person singular. Three times in chapter 1
Yahweh declared פָּקַדְתִּי; (vv. 8–9, 12). This word is usually
translated "I will punish" in these three instances, and "punish"
probably conveys the sense of what is intended here as well as any
other single word.[11] However, this translation may mask the

personal intrusion of Yahweh connoted by this Hebrew verb. The meaning of the root word is "to visit or inspect in order to take appropriate action."[12] Keller captures something of the personal involvement by Yahweh implied by this word, when he states that פָּקַד; "signifies simply to inspect, to control and if need be, to intervene in one manner or another in order to reestablish the order."[13] In other words the personal intervention of Yahweh is accentuated by the use of this particular verb.

In light of this broader meaning, Yahweh announced that He will pay a personal visit to inspect the government officials (v. 8), those wearing foreign garments (v. 8), those participating in pagan rituals (v. 9), and other miscreants. Indeed, all who are spiritually stagnant in Jerusalem are scheduled for an encounter with Yahweh (v. 12).

A third way Zephaniah highlighted this divine intrusion is with Yahweh's avowal in 1:12, "I will search Jerusalem with lamps." This portrayal, one of the best known from Zephaniah, is a stunning picture of Yahweh. The Lord is not described as directing executioners to conduct the investigation as in Ezekiel 9:1–6, nor as allowing His living word to seek out the wrongdoers as in Zechariah 5:1–4. No, Yahweh Himself will handle the matter. Yahweh declared His intention to probe the dark corners of Jerusalem Himself. These two clauses, "I will punish" (1:8–9, 12) and "I will search" (1:12), combine to trumpet the message, "Get ready for a personal encounter with Yahweh on His day."

Zephaniah expressed this divine intervention in several other places. Repeatedly Yahweh is quoted as using first-person verbs in declaring His plans to intrude into human affairs. Zephaniah contains a host of such announcements: "I will destroy" (1:2–3), "I will cut off" (v. 3), "I will stretch out My hand" (v. 4), "I will gather" (3:18), "I will give them praise and renown" (vv. 19–20), and "I will bring you in" (v. 20). Moreover, some third-person verbs, such as "He will stretch out His hand" (2:13), "He will destroy" (2:13), and "He will rejoice" (3:17), also signify Yahweh's intervention in human affairs. He is the actor in the drama that will occur on His day, and the arena of His activity is the human realm.

This divine involvement in human affairs is probably the most salient feature of Zephaniah's proclamation of the day of the Lord. This is not surprising in light of a careful examination of the phrase "the day of Yahweh." As many scholars have noted, the emphasis in this phrase is not on a specific time period.[14] On the contrary, the emphasis in the phrase יוֹם יְהֹוָה is on the proper noun, Yahweh, the one who intervenes in human affairs to initiate and bring to pass certain events. As Koch noted, "This is rather a day which actually *is* Yahweh, in which his Godhead will take fully visible form."[15] VanGemeren notes similarly, "The day of the Lord signifies first and foremost Yahweh's intrusion into human affairs. His coming (theophany) is portrayed in the conceptual imagery of Warrior, Judge, and the great King."[16]

Perhaps the reason Zephaniah articulated this aspect of the day of the Lord so forcefully is to contradict the belief of some Jerusalemites that Yahweh is uninvolved in human affairs. Their heartfelt sentiment was, "Yahweh will not do good, nor will He do evil" (1:12).[17] Achtemeier calls this verse the central indictment of the entire book.[18] Evidently a significant group of people in Jerusalem could be called deists or even practical atheists, because their sentiment was tantamount to believing that Yahweh will do nothing at all.

What a surprise is in store for these practical atheists! Yahweh, whom they held to be dormant and passively detached from the earth, will intervene in a decisive way. Far from being inactive and static, Yahweh is depicted "as being personally involved in his judgment, which will be devastating in its totality."[19] His actions on the day of the Lord will give the lie to those who accuse Him of passivity and detachment. According to Zephaniah, the day of the Lord is a time of divine intervention.

The Day of Yahweh's Universal Sovereignty and Superiority

Another aspect of the day of the Lord expressed by Zephaniah is that this day demonstrates Yahweh's universal sovereignty and unrivaled superiority. Though Yahweh is the King of Israel (3:15), He is much more than that. His dominion knows no boundaries. His hegemony extends to all nations. Moreover, He can brook no rivals and will tolerate no pretenders or other claimants to the throne, since He is superior to all of them. On the day of the Lord He is shown to be without peer.

Emphasis on Yahweh's universal sovereignty comes to the fore quickly in the Book of Zephaniah. Immediately after the superscription, Yahweh announced, "I will completely destroy everything upon the face of the earth" (1:2). This macrocosmic judgment, which will overwhelm all animate life, implies the extent of Yahweh's dominion and sovereignty. He is Lord over all the world. Universal judgment indicating Yahweh's worldwide sovereignty is proclaimed again in 1:18, which reiterates the warning that Yahweh will suddenly and completely destroy all the inhabitants of the earth.

Chapter 2 proclaims this same aspect of the day of the Lord but expresses it differently. The Philistines, Moabites, Ammonites, Cushites, and Assyrians are all slated for punishment. Of interest here is the fact that these nations represent the four points of the compass. Yahweh's dominion is not limited to Judah, nor does it extend from there in only one direction. Rather, it stretches westward (to Philistia), eastward (to Moab and Ammon), southward (to Cush), and northward (to Assyria). On His day Yahweh is shown to be no localized deity, restricted or hampered by political or geographic boundaries.

The third chapter of Zephaniah also heralds Yahweh's universal sovereignty. Yahweh announced His purpose to assemble the nations on the day of the Lord and then to execute judgment on all the earth (3:8). In fact this is probably the clearest statement in Zephaniah of the universal dominion of Yahweh. A few commentators say 1:2 and 18 may refer to a localized destruction of Judah instead of a universal destruction.[20] While it is true that אֲדָמָה (v. 2) and אֶרֶץ (v. 18) can both mean land (i.e., of Judah) and not necessarily the entire earth, Zephaniah clarified the extent of the judgment on the day of the Lord in chapter 3. As a prelude to destroying the earth (אֶרֶץ), Yahweh will assemble "nations" (גּוֹיִם) and "kingdoms" (מַמְלָכוֹת, 3:8). These words in the plural elucidate the meaning of earth (אֶרֶץ), clarify the extent of the coming judgment, and point up the universal sovereignty of Yahweh.

Happily, Yahweh's worldwide hegemony is revealed not only through His acts of judgment. His redemptive acts also serve to demonstrate His sovereignty. More will be said about these redemptive acts later, but suffice it to state here that peoples from the most distant places the mind can conceive (2:11; 3:9–10) will experience salvation and will worship Yahweh on His day. He is the redemptive King not only of the Judahites, but also of people from many nations.

Zephaniah developed this concept of the Lord's universal sovereignty by proclaiming that the day of the Lord will also reveal His unrivaled superiority. Yahweh has no equals. He shares His throne with no one. This fact is especially prominent in chapter 2, in which Yahweh is portrayed as eliminating two types of false claimants to deity.

First, 2:11 states that Yahweh will "starve" or "weaken" the other gods. If Yahweh has the ability to starve or weaken these other gods, then He is unquestionably superior to them. Also He is peerless around the globe, for "all the gods of the earth" will meet their demise at His hands.

Yahweh's superiority over the second pretender to deity is expressed in 2:13–15. Whereas in verse 11 Yahweh is said to deal with the false gods of the nations, here He will deal with a nation that thinks itself to be god. Nineveh, capital of the most powerful nation on the earth at that time, thought it dwelt "securely" (v. 15). The Hebrew root word here is בטח, the verbal form of which is often translated "to trust." Nineveh was simply trusting in itself, apparently unaware that trust reposed in any object other than God will end in shame (Pss. 115:3–11; 118:5–9; 146:3–5).[21]

But this was not Nineveh's worst sin. Personified, Nineveh said in its heart, "I am, and there is none besides me" (Zeph. 2:15). It posited itself as the ultimate reality. This blasphemous claim was equivalent to saying, "I am the lord, and there is no other" (Isa. 45:5, 14, 18, 21). As Achtemeier notes, "No God who is really God can let such a claim go unchallenged."[22] And indeed He did not. Nineveh, with its overweening attitude, inflated by its own greatness, thinking itself to be without equal, was destined for a collision on the day of the Lord with the only One who is truly without peer. Nineveh, the flower of civilization, would become a heap of ruins and an object of derision.

Evidently Nineveh did not realize what the day of the Lord would clearly reveal. There is only one Sovereign and His dominion has no boundaries. His preeminence is without question.

The Day of Yahweh's Judgment

Yet another aspect of the day of the Lord, related to the previous one, is that it brings the outpouring of Yahweh's judgment. This is both a universal judgment and a localized or specific judgment. In other words it has both macrocosmic and microcosmic elements.

The phrase "from the face of the earth," which is strategically placed as an inclusio in 1:2–3, underscores the theme of universal judgment at the outset of the book. Ball has observed that this "exact phrase is found thirteen times in the MT, all but one involving punishment."[23] Twice it is used in the Flood narrative when Yahweh declared His intentions to blot out humans and animals "from the face of the earth" (Gen. 6:7; 7:4). By using this phrase in the context of judgment, Zephaniah raised the specter of a destruction along the lines of the Flood, but he added that judgment on the day of the Lord will surpass even the Flood in its totality. According to Zephaniah 1:3, no living creature will be spared punishment, whether human, animal, fish, or fowl. This presents a contrast with the Flood for in that event fish were not destroyed (Gen. 7:21–23). Thus the judgment on the day of the Lord will be the most complete ever experienced.

The full extent of this judgment is understood only when it is realized that it is the undoing or "reversal of creation."[24] The original order of creation was fish, birds, animals, and humans (Gen. 1:20–24, 27). This order is almost completely reversed in Zephaniah. Zephaniah was stressing that just as Yahweh was active in the creation of animate life, so on His day He will be active in its "decreation," its removal from the earth. Yahweh's destruction "will be just as bleak as his creating was abundant."[25]

Though Zephaniah declared that the day of the Lord will bring about destruction on all animate life, he emphasized in several ways its judgment on people, who are the primary recipients of Yahweh's punishment. First, in Zephaniah 1:3 humans are twice specified as the object of God's punishment, while the other creatures are referred to only once. Moreover, in verse 3 the verb "to cut off" (כָּרַת), which denotes the judgment on human beings, is a strong term "used at times in the technical sense of carrying out the death penalty (cf. Ex. 31:14; Lev. 20:3–6)."[26] Also the succeeding verses and chapters elaborate on the judgment on humans, applying it to specific groups of people.

The microcosmic dimensions of judgment are demonstrated with the singling out of the nation of Judah in Zephaniah 1:4–13 and some of the surrounding nations in chapter 2.

But why this judgment on the day of the Lord? The statement, "because they have sinned against Yahweh" (1:17), does double duty, supplying the general reason for the coming judgment and also indicating that Yahweh is not capricious or arbitrary in sending it. Rather, this punishment is a result of and in response to human choices.

Zephaniah mentioned several sins that invite judgment on the day of the Lord. One such sin is the lack of social justice. This mistreatment of others, a prominent theme in the prophetic books, is mentioned several times by Zephaniah. Some people were said to "fill the house of their lord with violence and treachery" (1:9). It is uncertain whether this "house" is the temple of Yahweh, a pagan temple, or the king's palace. But wherever it is, some heinous conduct was transpiring there for, as Haag notes, "violence" (חָמָס) signifies primarily the oppression of the poor and humble. More specifically, it connotes "cold-blooded and unscrupulous infringement of the personal rights of others, motivated by greed and hate and often making use of violence and brutality."[27]

In 3:1 Jerusalem is labeled as a "defiled" and "oppressing" city. "Defiled" (נִגְאָלָה) is used in Isaiah 59:3 of hands stained with blood because of social injustice. Oppressing (יוֹנָה) is a participle implying mistreatment of the poor and needy (Ezek. 18:12). When these words are used in tandem to describe Jerusalem, they suggest that tyrannical and unjust abuses of power were being practiced. The citizens of Jerusalem were defiant of Yahweh (Zeph. 3:2) and despotic to humanity.

That the poor were being mistreated comes as no surprise because the judges, who should have been defending the rights of the oppressed, were instead joining in the despotism. The judges were like "evening wolves, who have no strength in the morning" (3:3). Writers disagree on the meaning of this metaphor. A plausible explanation is that these judges were exhausting all their energies by preying on those whose rights they were supposed to protect, and they were doing it so thoroughly that they had no strength left for the morning, when justice should have been dispensed (3:5; Jer. 21:12).

Not surprisingly, these actions garnered the censure of Yahweh, for He does no injustice at all (Zeph. 3:5). In fact He works to counter the actions of wicked judges by bringing His justice to light every morning (v. 5). Perhaps these corrupt judges had forgotten that Yahweh is the Defender of the rights of the poor and needy (Ps. 109:31). Such a dearth of social justice prompts a severe judgment on the day of the Lord.

Another sin inviting Yahweh's judgments on His day is self-aggrandizement, attempting to magnify oneself at the expense of Yahweh or His people. The Moabites and Ammonites reproached Judah and made boasts against it (Zeph. 2:8). Unfortunately for Moab and Ammon, the people whom they taunted and boasted over in an attempt to shame and disgrace them are no ordinary people.

They are Yahweh's people who enjoy a special relationship with Him. Interestingly, before 2:8, the prophet did not use a possessive pronoun or divine title to indicate any special relationship between Yahweh and His people, but now he did so with relish. Five times in three verses Zephaniah underscored this special relationship ("My people," vv. 8–9; "Yahweh of hosts, the God of Israel," v. 9; "my nation," v. 9; "the people of Yahweh of hosts," v. 10).

This special relationship makes Moab and Ammon's taunting remarks and boastful attitude particularly abhorrent. They reviled the people of Yahweh, and by extension, Yahweh Himself. Zephaniah so closely identified Israel with Yahweh that a sin against the former was an offense against the latter. As Szeles observes, "Since Yahweh entitles himself 'God of Israel,' he reveals that when hurt touches his people, it touches him too."[28] Because Moab and Ammon attempted to disgrace Yahweh's people, the Lord in turn will disgrace them on His day.

Nineveh's self-aggrandizement was discussed in the preceding section. Its claim to lordship incited the punishment of Yahweh. Its pompous, blasphemous pronouncement, "I am, and there is none besides me" (2:15), will result in its becoming a spectacular ruin on Yahweh's day.

This judgmental aspect of the day of the Lord emphasizes that it is a time of universal accountability. As 3:8 indicates, Yahweh will summon all the nations of the world to a grand assize where He will sit as the arbiter. Everyone will be held accountable for his or her actions. On His day Yahweh will execute judgment on those who have violated His principles of justice and those who have magnified themselves against Him.

Zephaniah stressed that this judgment will expose the inadequacy of any earthly protection or security on the day of the Lord. The powerful warrior (1:14) will not be able to withstand the judgment of that day. The mighty soldier may have shown exemplary courage in the past. Perhaps he has never been frightened in his life. But on that day he will cry out bitterly in view of his impotence and his imminent defeat.

The fortified cities are perhaps thought invincible by their inhabitants, and the corner towers are the most impregnable parts of these fortresses (1:16). Yet these two objects are singled out as targets for judgment on the day of the Lord. What is most defensible from a human point of view is rendered defenseless before the onslaught of Yahweh's wrath.

People might think their silver and gold (1:18) will render them immune from misfortune. Even if they face an enemy army, their wealth could be used to pay tribute, thus buying off the enemy. But Zephaniah wrote that silver and gold will be totally powerless to bring about deliverance on that day. Human strength, human structures, and human resources will all prove futile to shield anyone from Yahweh's judgment on His day. This fact suggests that if anyone is to be delivered or saved, it will be by divine intervention, an act of Yahweh's mercy and grace.

No one will be able to avoid the judgment bar of Yahweh on His day. If some might think they can hide from the judgment, Yahweh announced, "I will search" (1:12). And if any think the darkness will enshroud them, thereby enabling them to avoid the search, Yahweh expressed His intention to use lamps. Indeed the day of Yahweh is a day of inescapable, universal judgment.

The Day of Covenant Implementation

An additional aspect of the day of the Lord proclaimed in Zephaniah is that it will implement the terms of the covenant between Yahweh and Israel. In other words the events that await Israel on the day of the Lord comport closely to curses and blessings delineated in the Mosaic Covenant, and the sins that prompted the onset of these curses parallel sins condemned therein. This is especially evident when some of the terminology and concepts contained in Zephaniah are compared with the terminology and concepts of Deuteronomy, a book that some scholars consider the quintessential covenant document. According to Zephaniah, Yahweh, who has viewed the violation of His covenant, will implement its terms, first for woe and then for weal.

This linkage between the day of the Lord and the covenant is not unique to Zephaniah. In fact Fensham has posited that the whole concept of the day of the Lord in the Old Testament should be understood against the background of covenant curses. He holds that the day of the Lord is the time when Yahweh comes to invoke the treaty curses against the violation of His covenant.[29]

Robertson adds in a related vein:

> The day of Yahweh therefore may be seen as the day of his Covenant. On this day, he establishes his sovereign lordship over men. Either by instituting the covenant or by enforcing the provisions of the covenant, Yahweh manifests his lordship on that day. No other day may be so

fittingly designated as belonging to him than the day of covenant establishment and enforcement.[30]

While it may be an overstatement to equate the day of Yahweh with the day of Yahweh's covenant as the preceding quotation seems to do, several of the prophetic books do imply a strong connection between the day of the Lord and the covenant,[31] and certainly the Book of Zephaniah does.[32]

This linkage between the covenant and the day of the Lord is apparent in several places in Zephaniah. First, in 1:15 the wording, "a day of darkness and gloom, a day of clouds and thick darkness," resembles that of Deuteronomy's description of Yahweh's appearance at Sinai when He made covenant with Israel. Three of the words in 1:15 come from Hebrew roots (חשׁך, ענן, and ערפל) that appear together twice in Deuteronomy's portrayal of the Sinai theophany (Deut. 4:11; 5:22–23). Besides these three references in Zephaniah and Deuteronomy, these three words are used together in only one other place in the entire Old Testament.[33] Yahweh, whose appearance when He instituted the covenant was marked by supernatural phenomena in the skies, will appear again on His day, accompanied by the same phenomena. However, there is a different purpose for this second appearance. On the day of the Lord "the curses of the covenant will be inflicted, not merely inscribed. Now covenant enforcement replaces covenant inauguration."[34]

Second, the covenant aspect of the day of the Lord is demonstrated by the nature of the indictment against the covenant people. Though certainly not their only sin, perhaps the sin that most readily provoked the covenant curses was their idolatrous worship practices. These deviant worship practices are especially prominent in Zephaniah 1:4–6 (cf. vv. 8–9). According to these verses, some of the people were devoted to Baal, the god whose worship held allurement for many in Israel over several centuries. Evidently also a group of non-Yahwistic priests were plying their trade. Moreover, some were incorporating obeisance to the astral bodies in their worship, a practice explicitly forbidden in the covenant (Deut. 17:3). Additionally, some were invoking another name in addition to that of Yahweh in their oaths. Commanded in the covenant to swear by Yahweh's name and to worship Him alone (Deut. 6:13–14), these people were invoking the name of another deity as well.

The people of Israel were engaging in a wide range of idolatrous worship practices. This is ominous in light of the strong emphasis in the covenant on worshiping Yahweh and Him alone (Deut. 6:4–9). In fact it is possible that the main theme of Deuteronomy is that of opposition to idolatry.[35] According to Zephaniah, such a blatant violation of the covenant invites Yahweh's judgments on His day.

Third, the nature of the judgment on the day of the Lord indicates that it is a time of covenant implementation. As predicted in Zephaniah 1:13, "Their property will become booty, and their houses a waste. They will build houses, but not inhabit them; they will plant vineyards, but not drink the wine from them." God also said, "I will bring distress on the human race, so that they shall walk about like the blind" (1:17). These verses have close parallels in the catalog of covenant curses in Deuteronomy (cf. Deut. 28:30, 39 for the former and 28:28–29 for the latter). According to Zephaniah there will be tragic consequences for the people's violations of the covenant. Their wealth will be pillaged, they will enjoy neither the comforts of the homes they built nor the wine from the vineyards they planted, and they will grope about blindly, unable to rectify the situation. The day of the Lord is clearly a day of execution of covenant curses.

Interestingly, Israel is not the only recipient of judgments that correspond to covenant curses. Moab and Ammon are headed for judgment as devastating as that which overwhelmed Sodom and Gomorrah (2:9), those two perennial archetypes of wickedness. This warning is reminiscent of Deuteronomy 29:23, which describes punishment for violating the covenant, punishment along the lines of what engulfed Sodom and Gomorrah.

But the execution of the covenant curses is not the final word on the matter. The fact that Zephaniah announced a restoration beyond punishment, a new life after judgment, is a fourth indication that the day of the Lord is a time of covenant implementation. After the smoke of punishment from the covenant curses has cleared away, Zephaniah promised, "Yahweh their God will visit them and restore their fortune" (Zeph. 2:7; cf. 3:20). This closely resembles the terminology and message of Deuteronomy 30:3, which pledges that after the fulfillment of the covenant curses, "Then the Lord your God will restore your fortune."

With this promise Zephaniah was signaling the onset of covenant restoration blessings on the day of the Lord. Several features of this restoration agree closely with the covenant restoration blessings

in Deuteronomy. Yahweh promised to gather the banished and
return them to their own land (Zeph. 3:19–20), a promise that
resembles that of Deuteronomy 30:4. Moreover, the assurance
that Yahweh will rejoice over His people with a joyful cheer
(Zeph. 3:17) is reminiscent of the promise found in Deuteronomy
30:9. Also Yahweh's pledge to grant His people praise and renown
among all the peoples of the earth (Zeph. 3:19–20) compares
closely with the same pledge in Deuteronomy 26:19. Besides
Zephaniah 3:19–20 only one other verse in the Old Testament—
Jeremiah 13:11—includes these words "praise" (תְּהִלָּה) and
"renown" (שֵׁם).

The theophanic imagery of the day of the Lord, the rationale
and description of the judgment to be meted out at that time, and
the portrayal of the restoration to be granted, combine in Zephaniah
to indicate that the day of the Lord is a day of covenant
implementation.

The Day of Salvation

Another aspect of the day of the Lord expressed in Zephaniah
is that it results in salvation for some groups of people. In other
words it is not only a time of cataclysmic, destructive,
overwhelming judgment as already described. It is also a time of
salvation so thrilling and wonderful that Yahweh Himself will
burst into songs of rejoicing (3:17).

At first glance this salvific aspect of the day of the Lord may
seem incongruous with Zephaniah's emphasis on judgment in that
day. However, analysis reveals the close nexus between these two
aspects and that neither is complete without the other. As Patterson
states, "Judgment and hope, then, rather than being irreconcilable
themes, are two aspects of one divine perspective. Both are
designed and intertwined to accomplish God's purposes."[36]
According to Zephaniah there is a cause-and-effect relationship
between these two aspects, because it is only through the judgment
of evil that the salvation of God's people can be accomplished.

This salvific aspect of the day of the Lord is expressed in
several ways in Zephaniah. One of the most important ways is
through Zephaniah's delineation of the remnant concept.
Zephaniah's development of the remnant concept is important in
its own right.[37] The word "remnant" denotes survivors, specifically
those Israelites who survive the judgments sent by Yahweh on His
day. The term in itself underscores the salvific aspect of the day of

the Lord because it stresses the fact that some people remain alive. Though the judgment threatens to wipe out all living creatures on the earth (1:2, 18), especially God's covenant people (v. 4), Zephaniah promised that Yahweh will deliver a remnant (3:12). In 3:11–13, Zephaniah developed this concept of the remnant, describing their ethics and the future reward to be granted to them. In brief, since their ethics are like those of Yahweh (cf. v. 13 with v. 5) and since they find their security in trusting Yahweh (v. 12), He will provide lasting security for them. The description of this remnant, delivered and restored and blessed by Yahweh, demonstrates that the day of the Lord is a day of salvation.

Zephaniah also expressed the salvific aspect of the day of the Lord through his portrayal of the universal worship of Yahweh. On two occasions (2:11; 3:9–10) Zephaniah depicted worship of Yahweh taking place on a worldwide basis by those who are delivered from the judgment. Neither the judgment on the false gods (2:11) nor the judgment on the nations (3:8) is an end in itself. Rather, both of these judgments are immediately followed by their intended result, namely, the people of the world declaring their allegiance to Yahweh. And this is not worship by only a few isolated people. On the contrary there will be so many that they will stand shoulder to shoulder, serving Yahweh unitedly (3:9). The fact that Yahweh will deliver these people from the midst of the conflagration that will consume the earth testifies that this is a day of salvation.

Perhaps the foremost indicator of the salvific aspect of the day of the Lord is the structure of the Book of Zephaniah. The book is arranged so that the climax, the concluding note, trumpets the message of salvation. The book builds to a crescendo with the proclamation of salvation in the final verses. Moreover, the phrases "on that day" (3:16) and "at that time" (3:19–20) certify that these verses announcing salvation speak of the same epoch earlier portrayed as a time of devastating judgment (cf. 1:9–10 in which "on that day" appears in the context of judgment).

The joyful cheers of Yahweh (3:17) and His people (v. 14) replace the bitter cry of the warrior (1:14). Yahweh promised to deal with the enemies of His people, to gather His people home, and to exalt them in an international setting. With their judgments past and their enemies eliminated, the covenant people will celebrate the Lord's presence in their midst and He will reign over them (3:15, 17). The last image of the book is that of the covenant people, saved, restored, and exalted.

In light of this climax in the book it is difficult to overstate the importance of the salvific aspect of the day of the Lord. Yahweh clearly relishes His work of salvation. This is apparent when He sings elatedly on restoring His people. This is the only place in the entire Old Testament that refers to a jubilant Yahweh singing over the people He loves. Zephaniah's implication seems to be that Yahweh's ultimate purpose in all the events that will occur on His day is to bring salvation to as many as possible. This is only fitting, for the day of the Lord is a day of salvation.

Is the Day of Yahweh Historical or Eschatological?

When will or did the day of the Lord occur? According to Zephaniah, is it a historical event, that is, one which happens within history, or is it eschatological, the event that will bring down the curtain on this age and usher in the next one? Since evidence supports both positions in Zephaniah, it is best to see it as both historical and eschatological, as occurring in history and also as part of the final drama of history.

> Though the Lord's acts of judgment take place throughout the history of redemption, each act foreshadows the final judgment when all the doers of evil, corruption, and sin will be absolutely and radically judged and removed from the earth (1:3). Each judgment in history is an intrusion of the eschatological judgment, whether on Israel, Judah, or the nations.[38]

Though this interpenetration of the historical and the eschatological in Zephaniah's presentation of the day of the Lord may seem confusing, it should not be surprising. As Merrill notes, "The line between historical and eschatological fulfillment is often a very fine one and difficult to discern. Here in Zephaniah, as in all the prophets, that demarcation is blurry."[39]

Perhaps this historical and eschatological interpenetration aids in understanding Zephaniah's insistence on the imminence of the day of the Lord. The fact that Yahweh might intervene at any time in history (and has already done so on many occasions) warns that His final intrusion might take place soon. Three times Zephaniah used the adverb "near" to describe the closeness of that day (1:7, 14). Though he did not proclaim an exact time frame, his insistence on the nearness of the day suggests that it loomed so large on the horizon that little else was visible. Under such menacing circumstances, what else could the prophet proclaim but that the day is near?

Goals of the Day of the Lord

Zephaniah had both present goals and future goals in mind in writing of the day of the Lord. The present goal was simply to motivate the people of Israel to engage in wholehearted worship of Yahweh and to carry out righteous ethical practices. Regarding the worship of Yahweh, Zephaniah 1:4–6 implies that only exclusive, devoted, wholehearted worship of Yahweh is acceptable. Nothing else will suffice. Those totally given over to idolatry along with the syncretists are heading for severe judgment. Yahweh wants His people to seek Him and Him alone. Regarding ethical practices, the exhortation of 2:3 to seek righteousness and the descriptions of the wicked in 3:1–4 and the righteous remnant in 3:12–13 point up the importance of righteous conduct in treatment of others. Only those who act in the same manner as Yahweh (3:5) can aspire to be part of the remnant.

Regarding the future goal of the day of the Lord, Zephaniah pointed toward the establishment of Yahweh's kingdom on the earth. This day signifies the time of "vindication, glorification, and full redemption of the godly (3:14–20)."[40] This will occur when Yahweh is exalted as King in the midst of His people and will reign over them forever. This is the final goal for which the day of the Lord still awaits.

Chapter Notes

Chapter 1

1. For discussion of creation myths in different ancient civilizations see Samuel Noah Kramer, *Mythologies of the Ancient World* (Garden City, NY: Doubleday, 1961), pp. 36, 95, 120–21, 281–89, 382–85, 415–21, 449–54.
2. Bruce K. Waltke, *Creation and Chaos* (Portland, OR: Western Conservative Baptist Seminary, 1974), p. 18.
3. Ibid., p. 19.
4. See especially Allen P. Ross, *Creation and Blessing* (Grand Rapids: Baker, 1988), pp. 106–7, 723; and Victor P. Hamilton, *The Book of Genesis, Chapters 1–17*, New International Commentary on the Old Testament (Grand Rapids: Eerdmans, 1990), p. 117.
5. *The New Scofield Reference Bible* (New York: Oxford University Press, 1967), 1, n. 5, and 752–53, n. 2. For an extensive defense of the gap theory see Arthur C. Custance, *Without Form and Void* (Brockville, Ontario: n.p., 1970).
6. Isaiah 14 and Ezekiel 28 are often cited as biblical support for this teaching.
7. Waltke, *Creation and Chaos*, 19. Also see Gordon J. Wenham, *Genesis 1–15*, Word Biblical Commentary (Waco, TX: Word, 1987), p. 15.
8. Waltke, *Creation and Chaos,* p. 24.
9. For a comprehensive refutation of the gap theory see Weston W. Fields, *Unformed and Unfilled: A Critique of the Gap Theory of Genesis 1:1, 2* (Winona Lake, IN: Light and Life Press, 1973).
10. Waltke, *Creation and Chaos*, p. 25. This traditional view is also reflected in A. S. Hartom and M. D. Cassuto, "Genesis," in *Torah, Prophets, and Writings* (Jerusalem: Yavneh, 1977), p. 14 (in Hebrew).
11. Westermann offers the same objection to this position (Claus Westermann, *Genesis. 1–11: A Commentary*, trans. John J. Scullion [London: SPCK, 1984], p. 95).
12. It is generally accepted that the phrase constitutes a merism and thus refers to all things, that is, the universe (Westermann,

Genesis. 1–11: A Commentary, p. 101; Nahum M. Sarna, *Genesis*, JPS Torah Commentary [Philadelphia: Jewish Publication Society, 1989], p. 5; Ross, *Creation and Blessing*, p. 106; John H. Sailhamer, "Genesis," in *The Expositor's Bible Commentary* [Grand Rapids: Zondervan, 1990], p. 23; Harry M. Orlinsky, "The Plain Meaning of Genesis 1:1–3," *Biblical Archaeologist* [1983]: 208; and Waltke, *Creation and Cosmos*, p. 26). Similar expressions to denote the universe occur in Egyptian, Akkadian, and Ugaritic literature (Wenham, *Genesis 1–15*, p. 15).

13. Waltke, *Creation and Chaos,* pp. 25–26. Similarly, see John Skinner, *A Critical and Exegetical Commentary on Genesis*, International Critical Commentary (Edinburgh: T. & T. Clark, 1910), p. 14; and Hamilton, *The Book of Genesis, Chapters 1–17*, p. 105.

14. Waltke, *Creation and Chaos*, p. 24. Waltke and others maintain that Genesis 1:2 refers to something negative.

15. Ibid., p. 26. Similarly, Skinner wrote, "A created chaos is perhaps a contradiction" (Skinner, *A Critical and Exegetical Commentary on Genesis*, p. 13).

16. Second Esdras 6:38 and *b. Ḥag.* 12a. Sailhamer also maintains that Genesis 1:1 was part of the first day of creation. This is the reason the author referred to יוֹם אֶחָד, "day one" (Gen. 1:5) instead of the expected יוֹם רִאשׁוֹן, "first day" ("Genesis," pp. 26, 28).

17. Wenham, *Genesis 1–15*, pp. 12–13, 15. Also see Eduard König, *Die Genesis* (Gütersloh: C. Bertelsmann, 1925), p. 136.

18. Martin Luther, *The Creation: A Commentary on the First Five Chapters of the Book of Genesis*, trans. Henry Cole (Edinburgh: T. & T. Clark, 1858), p. 27. See also C. F. Keil and F. Delitzsch, *Pentateuch*, 3 vols., Biblical Commentary on the Old Testament (Grand Rapids: Eerdmans, 1973), 1:48; Henry M. Morris, *The Genesis Record* (San Diego: Creation-Life, 1976), pp. 40–41; Sailhamer, "Genesis," p. 26. This was also the view of Origen, Philo, and Gregory of Nyssa. See Custance, *Without Form and Void*, p. 18; and J. C. M. van Winden, "The Early Christian Exegesis of 'Heaven and Earth' in Genesis 1,1," in *Romanitas et Christianitas*, ed. W. den Boer, P. G. van der Nat, C. M. J. Sicking, and J. C. M. van Winden (Amsterdam: North-Holland, 1973), pp. 373–74.

19. David Toshio Tsumura, *The Earth and the Waters in Genesis 1 and 2: A Linguistic Investigation*, JSOT Supplement Series 83 (Sheffield: JSOT Press, 1989), pp. 155–56. See also "תֹהוּ וָבֹהוּ," in *Encyclopedia Miqrait*, 8:436 (in Hebrew); and Johann

Fischer, *Das Buch Isaias. II. Teil: Kapitel 40–66,* Die Heilige Schrift des Alten Testamentes (Bonn: Peter Hanstein, 1939), p. 83. The understanding of בֹּהוּ as "empty" is reinforced by the Aramaic Targum rendering of the word as רוֹקְנִיא. The New International Version renders the phrase "formless and empty."

20. Waltke, *Creation and Chaos,* 27. Also see Ross, *Creation and Blessing,* pp. 106, 722.

21. John Peter Lange, "Genesis," in *Lange's Commentary on the Holy Scriptures* (Grand Rapids: Zondervan, 1978), p. 499; Edward J. Young, "The Interpretation of Genesis 1:2," *Westminster Theological Journal* 23 (1960–61): 154; R. N. Whybray, *Isaiah 40–66,* New Century Bible (Greenwood, SC: Attic, 1975), pp. 110–11; Fields, *Unformed and Unfilled: A Critique of the Gap Theory of Genesis 1:1, 2,* pp. 123–24. This text thus corresponds to the account in Genesis 1, which indicates that God did not leave the earth in this state. Thus John Calvin, *Commentary on the Book of the Prophet Isaiah,* 4 vols., trans. William Pringle (Grand Rapids: Eerdmans, 1947), 3:418; Keil and Delitzsch, *Pentateuch,* 1:227; and John L. McKenzie, *Second Isaiah,* Anchor Bible (Garden City, NY: Doubleday, 1968), p. 83. Waltke's contention that Isaiah 45:18 refers to the completed creation at the end of the six days does not undermine this view that Isaiah 45:18 is concerned with the purpose of creation. For Waltke's view, see "The Creation Account in Genesis 1:1–3. Part II: The Restitution Theory," *Bibliotheca Sacra* 132 (1975): 144.

22. J. Skinner, *The Book of the Prophet Isaiah, Chapters XL–LXVI* (Cambridge: Cambridge University Press, 1898), p. 65; and Sailhamer, "Genesis," pp. 24–25.

23. For discussion of the use of antonyms or binary opposites in delimiting and clarifying the meaning of terms in context see John Lyons, *Introduction to Theoretical Linguistics* (Cambridge: Cambridge University Press, 1968), pp. 460–70; and John Barton, *Reading the Old Testament* (Philadelphia: Westminster, 1984), pp. 109–12.

24. Young, "The Interpretation of Genesis 1:2," p. 170; s.v. "וָבֹהוּ תֹהוּ," *Encyclopedia Miqrait,* 8:436.

25. Tsumura, *The Earth and the Waters in Genesis 1 and 2,* pp. 33–34. This would also pertain to the phrase in Isaiah 34:11. The threat would be that the land would become a desolation and waste and thus unfit for inhabitants (E. J. Young, *The Book of Isaiah II,* New International Commentary on the Old Testament [Grand Rapids: Eerdmans, 1969], p. 438).

26. See Sailhamer, "Genesis," p. 27.
27. Tsumura, *The Earth and the Waters in Genesis 1 and 2*, p. 156. For a similar understanding in postbiblical Jewish literature, see Jacob Newman, *The Commentary of Nahmanides on Genesis Chapters 1–6* (Leiden: Brill, 1960), p. 33.
28. Tsumura, *The Earth and the Waters in Genesis 1 and 2*, pp. 42–43. Also see Sailhamer, "Genesis," pp. 24–25.
29. Many commentators have observed this general structure (e.g., U. Cassuto, *A Commentary on the Book of Genesis*, trans. Israel Abrahams [Jerusalem: Magnes, 1961], p. 17; Ross, *Creation and Blessing*, p. 104; and Wenham, *Genesis 1–15*). The present chart most closely resembles Sarna, *Genesis*, p. 4.
30. Sarna, *Genesis*, p. 6. Also see Franz Delitzsch, *A New Commentary on Genesis*, 2 vols. (Minneapolis: Klock & Klock, 1978), 1:80; and Fields, *Unformed and Unfilled: A Critique of the Gap Theory of Genesis 1:1, 2*, pp. 123–24.
31. Waltke, *Creation and Chaos*.
32. The word בְּרֵאשִׁית is thus used in the absolute sense, "in *the* beginning." See Westermann, *Genesis 1–11*, pp. 94–98; Carl Herbert Leupold, *Exposition of Genesis*, 2 vols. (Grand Rapids, Baker, 1942), 1:42; Keil and Delitzsch, *Pentateuch*, 1:46–47; Walter Eichrodt, "In the Beginning," in *Israel's Prophetic Heritage: Essays in Honor of James Muilenburg*, ed. Bernhard W. Anderson and Walter Harrelson (New York: Harper & Brothers, 1962), pp. 3–4, 6; and Sailhamer, "Genesis," pp. 20–21. This has been the traditional understanding since the Hebrew Bible was translated into Greek by the Jews of Alexandria (Harry M. Orlinsky, *Notes on the New Translation of the Torah* [Philadelphia: Jewish Publication Society, 1969], p. 49). The Greek phrase Ἐν ἀρχῇ at the beginning of the Gospel of John reflects the Septuagint's translation of בְּרֵאשִׁית from Genesis 1:1. This usage also reinforces the idea that the absolute beginning is what is in view (Walter Wifall, "God's Accession Year according to P," *Biblica* 62 [1981]: 527; and Marc Girard, "La structure heptaparite du quatrième évangile," *Recherches de Sciences religieuses* 5/4 [1975–76]: 351).
33. See Bruce K. Waltke, "The Creation Account in Genesis 1:1–3, Part III: The Initial Chaos Theory and the Precreation Chaos Theory," *Bibliotheca Sacra* 132 (1975): 221; affirmed more recently by Waltke in "The Literary Genre of Genesis, Chapter One," *Crux* 27 (1991): 3. Similarly see Skinner, *A Critical and Exegetical Commentary on Genesis*, p. 14; S. R. Driver, *The Book of Genesis* (London: Methuen, 1904), 3; Henri Blocher, *In*

the Beginning, trans. David G. Preston (Downers Grove, IL: InterVarsity, 1984), 63.

Brongers, Cassuto, Eichrodt, Gunkel, Procksch, Schmidt, Strack, von Rad, Westermann, and Zimmerli also hold to the summary view according to Hasel (Gerhard F. Hasel, "Recent Translations of Genesis 1:1: A Critical Look," *Bible Translator* 22 [1971]: 164).

34. Waltke also cites the narrative that begins in Genesis 3:1 as having an analogous grammatical structure, though it lacks the initial summary statement (Waltke, *Creation and Chaos*, pp. 32–33).

35. Ibid., pp. 32–34. Wenham holds a similar view (Gordon J. Wenham, *Genesis 1–15*, Word Biblical Commentary [Waco, TX: Word, 1987], pp. 3, 15).

36. Waltke, *Creation and Chaos*, p. 33.

37. Ibid., p. 49.

38. Ibid., p. 50.

39. Waltke, "The Creation Account in Genesis 1:1–3, Part III," p. 221.

40. Waltke, *Creation and Chaos*, 58. Darkness is understood to represent evil and death (ibid., 52; and Allen P. Ross, *Creation and Blessing* [Grand Rapids: Baker, 1988], 106, 722). Also see P. W. Heward, "And the Earth Was without Form and Void," *Journal of the Transactions of the Victoria Institute* 78 (1946): 16; and John C. L. Gibson, *Genesis* (Philadelphia: Westminster Press, 1981), 29.

41. Waltke, "The Creation Account in Genesis 1:1–3, Part III," p. 221.

42. Bruce K. Waltke, "The Creation Account in Genesis 1:1–3, Part IV: The Theology of Genesis 1," *Bibliotheca Sacra* 132 (1975): 339.

43. Waltke, "The Creation Account in Genesis 1:1–3, Part III," pp. 220–21.

44. Ibid., p. 221.

45. Waltke, *Creation and Chaos*, p. 44.

46. Ibid., p. 51.

47. Ibid., p. 49.

48. Ibid., p. 43.

49. Westermann, *Genesis 1–11*, p. 97; Hasel, "Recent Translations of Genesis 1:1: A Critical Look," p. 161; and Sailhamer, "Genesis," p. 21.

50. Barr's caveat against formulating conclusions about thought patterns based on language structure may be in order here. See James Barr, *The Semantics of Biblical Language* (Oxford: Oxford University Press, 1961).

51. Anton Pearson, "An Exegetical Study of Genesis 1:1–3," *Bethel Seminary Quarterly* 2 (1953): 20–21. Hasel argues that the *waw* conjunction that begins Genesis 1:2 is an argument against understanding verse 1 as a summary statement. The importance of the copulative *waw* of verse 2a is given its full due by linking verse 1 and verse 2 closer together than is possible with the position which considers verse 1 as merely a summary introduction expressing the fact that God is Creator of heaven and earth (Hasel, "Recent Translations of Genesis 1:1: A Critical Look," 165). Also see Derek Kidner, *Genesis: An Introduction and Commentary*, Tyndale Old Testament Commentaries (Downers Grove, IL: InterVarsity, 1967), p. 44.

52. Waltke, *Creation and Chaos*, 33. In this reference and in "The Creation Account in Genesis 1:1–3, Part III," p. 227, Waltke erroneously states that the list of examples of this grammatical phenomenon is in E. J. Young, *Studies in Genesis One* (Philadelphia: Presbyterian and Reformed, 1964), p. 15. The references are actually found on page 9, n. 15.

53. The passages Young lists are Genesis 38:25; Numbers 12:14; Joshua 2:18; 1 Samuel 9:11; 1 Kings 14:17; 2 Kings 2:23; 6:5, 26; 9:25; Job 1:16; and Isaiah 37:38 (ibid., 9).

54. It may be that the lack of cognates with this root in other Semitic languages confirms the term's uniqueness. Other Hebrew words for "create" have broader cognate evidence.

55. Thomas J. Finley, "Dimensions of the Hebrew Word for 'Create' (בָּרָא)," *Bibliotheca Sacra* 148 (October–December 1991): 409–23.

56. Ibid., pp. 411–12. See also Ross, *Creation and Blessing*, pp. 725–28, and Wenham, *Genesis 1–15*, p. 14.

57. As Ross states, "Humans may make [*'asa*], form [*yaṣar*], or build [*bana*]; to the Hebrew, however, God creates" (*Creation and Blessing*, pp. 105–6).

58. Finley, "Dimensions of the Hebrew Word for 'Create' (בָּרָא)," p. 409.

59. Sarna, *Genesis*, p. 5. See also Julian Morgenstern, "The Sources of the Creation Story in Genesis 1:1–2:4," *American Journal of Semitic Languages* 36 (1920): 201; Finley, "Dimensions of the Hebrew Word for 'Create' (בָּרָא)," p. 409; Fields, *Unformed and Unfilled*, pp. 54–55; Keil and Delitzsch, "Pentateuch," 1:47; Edward J. Young, "The Relation of the First Verse of Genesis One to Verses Two and Three," *Westminster Theological Journal* 21 (1959): 138–39.

60. Thomas E. McComiskey, "בָּרָא," in *Theological Wordbook of*

the Old Testament, p. 127. Hasel lists Aalders, Childs, Henton Davies, Heidel, Kidner, König, Maly, Ridderbos, Wellhausen, and Young as those who maintain that Genesis 1:1 refers to *creatio ex nihilo* (Hasel, "Recent Translations of Genesis 1:1: A Critical Look," p. 163). See also Walter Eichrodt, "In the Beginning," p. 10; and Blocher, *In the Beginning,* p. 63. Ross acknowledges that the verb may have this connotation (*Creation and Blessing,* p. 724). For evidence of early Jewish scholars who subscribed to *creatio ex nihilo,* see Emil G. Hirsch, "Creation," in *The Jewish Encyclopedia,* 12 vols., 4:336; and Frances Young, "'Creatio ex Nihilo': A Context for the Emergence of the Christian Doctrine of Creation," *Scottish Journal of Theology* 44 (1991): 141 for Gamaliel II's comment in Midrash Genesis Rabbah.

61. Passages such as Genesis 1:27 and Isaiah 45:7 would be examples of the usage not meaning *creatio ex nihilo.* These were noted by the medieval Hebrew exegete Ibn Ezra. See Pearson, "An Exegetical Study of Genesis 1:1–3," p. 17.

62. Both Kidner and Ross specifically mention the importance of context for determining the meaning of בָּרָא for an individual passage (Kidner, *Genesis: An Introduction and Commentary,* p. 44; Ross, *Creation and Blessing,* p. 728).

63. Finley, "Dimensions of the Hebrew Word for 'Create' (בְּרָא)," p. 410. This would be true even if one agreed with Waltke and understood verse 1 to be a summary statement. If the verse functions in this manner, it would be logically separated from its context in that it referred in a general way to the entire process of Genesis 1. In addition in Waltke's view Genesis 1:2 is subordinated to verse 3, leaving verse 1 as an independent clause, which does not contain any reference to materials being used with a בְּרָא creation.

64. Leupold, *Exposition of Genesis,* pp. 40–41.

65. Calvin, *Commentaries on the First Book of Moses Called Genesis,* trans. John King (Grand Rapids: Baker, 1979), p. 70. Also see Luther, *The Creation: A Commentary on the First Five Chapters of the Book of Genesis,* p. 31.

66. Newman, *The Commentary of Nahmanides on Genesis Chapters 1–6,* p. 33. Similarly, Young, "The Relation of the First Verse of Genesis One to Verses Two and Three," p. 139. Winden argues that understanding Genesis 1:1 as referring to *creatio ex nihilo* was considered the orthodox understanding of the verse by the early church fathers (J. van Winden, "The Early Christian Exegesis of 'Heaven and Earth' in Genesis 1,1," pp. 372–73).

67. See George Bush, *Notes on Genesis,* 2 vols. (Minneapolis: James & Klock, 1976), 1:26–27. Hence Waltke's objection that the ancient versions did not understand the verb in this way is undermined. Furthermore Waltke's statement that other Hebrew verbs may describe *creatio ex nihilo* does not diminish the fact that בָּרָא as *the* distinctive verb for creation, having God as its only subject, also may clearly have this nuance (Waltke, "The Creation Account in Genesis 1:1–3, Part IV," pp. 336–37).

68. Sarna, *Genesis,* p. 5. *Creatio ex nihilo* was also distinct from Greek philosophy. See especially Plutarch's denial of *creatio ex nihilo* (John Dillon, *The Middle Platonists* [London: Duckworth, 1977], p. 207, cited by Young, "'Creatio Ex Nihilo': A Context for the Emergence of the Christian Doctrine of Creation," pp. 139–40). See also Winden, "The Early Christian Exegesis of 'Heaven and Earth' in Genesis 1,1," pp. 372–73.

69. Young, *In the Beginning,* pp. 24–25.

70. Waltke, *Creation and Chaos,* p. 50.

71. Westermann's caveat that "we should be careful of reading too much into the word; nor is it correct to read *creatio ex nihilo* out of the word" may be appropriate here (Westermann, *Genesis 1–11,* p. 100).

72. Hasel, "Recent Translations of Genesis 1:1: A Critical Look," p. 165. The occurrence of the verb following the phrase "in the beginning" gave rise to the Jewish and Christian traditions of *creatio ex nihilo* (Wifall, "God's Accession Year according to P," p. 527).

73. Waltke, *Creation and Chaos,* 19. Shanks holds the same view (Hershel Shanks, "How the Bible Begins," *Judaism* 21 (1972): 58, n. 2. In reference to this assumption Waltke states that chaos occurred before the original creation. What does he mean by "original" here? If matter is already in existence, then subsequent creation should not be viewed as original. The same applies to his use of the term "creation." He speaks of preexisting matter in existence before God began to work in Genesis 1 and yet he calls the work that of creation. Similarly, in discussing Isaiah 45:18 Waltke states, "The Creator did not leave His job half-finished. He perfected the creation, and then He established it. He did not end up with chaos as Isaiah noted" (*Creation and Chaos,* p. 60). When Waltke says that God "did not leave His job unfinished," he seems to be arguing that God was involved in bringing the state described in Genesis 1:2 into existence. On the other hand, elsewhere he indicates that the presence of the state described in verse 2 is a mystery, as the Bible never says

that God brought the unformed state, the darkness, and the deep into existence by His word (*Creation and Chaos*, p. 52).

74. John C. Whitcomb, *The Early Earth* (Grand Rapids: Baker, 1972), pp. 123–24.

75. David Toshio Tsumura, *The Earth and the Waters in Genesis 1 and 2: A Linguistic Investigation*, JSOT Supplement Series 83 (Sheffield: JSOT, 1989), pp. 33–34.

76. Merril F. Unger, "Rethinking the Genesis Account of Creation," *Bibliotheca Sacra* 115 (1958): 30. Payne suggests that if the author had desired to make a statement about the darkness expressing evil, the stronger word for darkness would have been used. The darkness is חֹשֶׁךְ, not the stronger synonym עֲרָפֶל (D. F. Payne, "Approaches to Genesis i 2," *Transactions* 23 [1969–70]: 67.

77. Waltke, *Creation and Chaos*, p. 52.

78. Wiseman, as quoted by Bruce, suggests that this position leads to an inevitable comparison with pagan views (F. F. Bruce, "And the Earth Was without Form and Void," *Journal of the Transactions of the Victoria Institute* 78 [1946]: 26). Westermann notes that the opposition between darkness and creation is widespread in the cosmogonies and creation stories of the world (Westermann, *Genesis 1–11*, p. 104). The connection between the *Enuma Elish* account of creation because of the similarity between the Hebrew word תְּהוֹם ("deep") and the name of the goddess Tiamat is not etymologically defensible (see Westermann, *Genesis 1–11*, p. 105; and Ross, *Creation and Blessing*, p. 107).

79. Young, "The Interpretation of Genesis 1:2," p. 157, n. 114.

80. Ibid., pp. 170–71, n. 33. Waltke does acknowledge that the darkness from this context must later be viewed as good. "Though not called 'good' at first, the darkness and deep were called 'good' later when they became part of the cosmos" (Waltke, "The Creation Account in Genesis 1:1–3, Part IV," pp. 338–39). The explanatory phrase, "became part of the cosmos," is difficult to understand, and it should be admitted there is no explicit support to this effect from the context.

81. Wiseman, "And the Earth Was without Form and Void," p. 26.

82. Fields, *Unformed and Unfilled*, pp. 132–33.

83. Whitcomb, *The Early Earth*, pp. 125–27.

84. Keil and Delitzsch, *Pentateuch*, 1:49. Also see Westermann, *Genesis 1–11*, pp. 102, 106, and Fields, *Unformed and Unfilled*, pp. 83–84. Since the three clauses are coordinate, Westermann and Schmidt would argue that they should be viewed in the same light, either positively or negatively. See Wenham, *Genesis 1–15*, p. 17, and Payne, "Approaches to Genesis i. 2," p. 66.

85. Young, "The Interpretation of Genesis 1:2," p. 170.
86. Waltke, *Creation and Chaos,* pp. 27–28.
87. Wiseman, cited in Bruce, "And the Earth Was without Form and Void," p. 26.
88. Westermann, *Genesis 1–11,* pp. 94, 102; Young, "The Interpretation of Genesis 1:2," 170; Sailhamer, "Genesis," p. 24; and Augustine who along with other ancient scholars understood the darkness in Genesis 1:1 as a reference to heaven (Winden, "The Early Christian Exegesis of 'Heaven and Earth' in Genesis 1,1," p. 378).
89. Young, "The Interpretation of Genesis 1:2," p. 174. Childs and Hasel suggest that the verse must be viewed in a negative light if one argues that Genesis 1:1 is merely a summary statement (Brevard S. Childs, *Myth and Reality in the Old Testament* [Naperville, IL: Allenson, 1960], p. 39, and Hasel, "Recent Translations of Genesis 1:1: A Critical Look," p. 165). Childs also hints at the need to play down the significance of בָּרָא if one views Genesis 1:2 as indicating something negative (ibid., p. 40).
90. Young, "The Relation of the First Verse of Genesis One to Verses Two and Three," p. 144 and n. 20.
91. Waltke, *Creation and Chaos*, p. 43.
92. Ibid.
93. Ibid., p. 31. Also see Hasel, "Recent Translations of Genesis 1:1: A Critical Look," pp. 162–63, and Westermann, *Genesis 1–11*, p. 97.
94. Waltke, however, does speak of the Creator bringing the universe into existence by His command in Genesis 1 (Waltke, "The Creation Account in Genesis 1:1–3, Part IV," p. 338). It is unclear what Waltke means by existence here, since the precreation chaos theory of Genesis 1 describes God's transforming activity of the already existing physical state described in Genesis 1:2. Similarly in contrasting the purpose of Psalm 104 with Genesis 1, he states that Genesis refers to "the origin of the creation" ("The Creation Account in Genesis 1:1–3, Part V," p. 35). Yet Genesis 1 does not refer to the original creation in the same sense as Psalm 33 and Hebrews 11, according to Waltke's interpretation.
95. Gabrini has well noted the inevitable conclusions that must be drawn, particularly in regard to the existence of matter, by those who adhere to the translation "in the beginning." He writes, "At this point, the current interpretation of the first sentence of Genesis requires some consideration. When we translate 'In the beginning God created the heaven and the earth,' we meet two

difficulties. First of all, we lend the Jewish writer the Christian conception of creation *ex nihilo:* such conception is totally missing among the peoples of the ancient Orient, where creation by gods always displays itself in a shapeless but existing world, so that creation *ex nihilo* in Genesis would appear truly baffling. In the second place, if we admit that God created the world *ex nihilo* (heaven and earth are two complementary parts to indicate the whole), then we are obliged to admit also that the creation took place in two different moments. Firstly, God created the world in the darkness; secondly, he began to create forms" (Giovanni Gabrini, "The Creation of Light in the First Chapter of Genesis," in *Proceedings of the Fifth World Congress of Jewish Studies,* ed. Pinchas Peli [Jerusalem: World Union of Jewish Studies, 1969], 1:2).

    The existence of matter at the beginning of creation could easily be understood as the principle of evil coexisting with God from eternity, hence denying the Judeo-Christian concept of God (Winden, The Early Christian Exegesis of 'Heaven and Earth' in Genesis 1,1," pp. 372–73).

96. Waltke, *Creation and Chaos,* p. 58. Waltke does maintain that one of the purposes of the Mosaic account is a polemic against the myths of Israel's environment (Waltke, "The Creation Account in Genesis 1:1–3, Part IV," p. 328).

97. Waltke, *Creation and Chaos,* p. 45.

98. Ibid., p. 49.

99. Furthermore, Fields observes that Waltke had not considered the impact of passages such as Exodus 20:11; 31:17; and Nehemiah 9:6, which fit all that exists in the universe within the six days of creation (*Unformed and Unfilled,* p. 128, n. 43).

100. Waltke, *Creation and Chaos,* p. 19.

101. Benno Jacob, *The First Book of the Bible: Genesis, Interpreted by B. Jacob* (New York: KTAV, 1974), p. 1.

102. Waltke labeled the view the initial chaos view, but because of the uncertainty of what is meant by chaos this title is not so useful as referring to the position simply as the traditional one. See Young, "The Relation of the First Verse of Genesis One to Verses Two and Three," p. 145. Indeed, Waltke's recent assertion that Genesis 1:2 depicts an earth that was uninhabitable and uninhabited may indicate a shift in his own thinking about the meaning of the chaos. See "The Literary Genre of Genesis, Chapter One," p. 4.

103. Leupold, *Exposition of Genesis,* 1:40–41; Sarna, *Genesis,* p. 6; and Kidner, *Genesis: An Introduction and Commentary,* p. 43.

104. For references in apocryphal literature as well as early Jewish interpreters and church fathers, see Wifall, "God's Accession Year according to P," p. 527; Young, "'Creatio Ex Nihilo': A Context for the Emergence of the Christian Doctrine of Creation," p. 145; Pearson, "An Exegetical Study of Genesis 1:1–3," pp. 24–26; and Fields, *Unformed and Unfilled*, p. 26.

105. John 1:1–5; 8:12; 2 Corinthians 5:17; Matthew 28:1. Jesus in this sense inaugurated a "new Genesis." See Girard, "La structure heptaparite du quatrième évangile," p. 357. For the necessary theological juxtaposition of creation and redemption, see Willem A. VanGemeren, *Interpreting the Prophetic Word* (Grand Rapids: Zondervan, 1990), pp. 86, 226–27, and Young, "'Creatio Ex Nihilo': A Context for the Emergence of the Christian Doctrine of Creation," p. 140.

Chapter 2

1. In the vast amount of literature on the subject of the divine name, numerous renderings are used including YHWH (the original four-letter transliteration), Yahweh, the popular pronunciation Jehovah, Jahweh, Yahwe', Jahve, and "the tetragrammaton." Though the divine name will remain as written in the quotations, this writer uses the designation "YHWH" or "divine name."

2. Raymond Bowman, "Yahweh the Speaker," *Journal of Near Eastern Studies* 3 (January 1944): 100.

3. No attempts are made in this study to evaluate the various etymological derivations posited nor to evaluate the various alleged prebiblical precursors. For a survey of some of these see L. Blau, "Tetragrammaton," in *Jewish Encyclopedia*, 1906 ed., 12:118–20, and Walther Zimmerli, *Old Testament Theology in Outline* (Atlanta: Knox, 1978), pp. 19–21.

4. J. A. Motyer, *The Revelation of the Divine Name* (Leicester: Theological Students Fellowship, 1959), pp. 12–13 (italics added).

5. Ibid., pp. 15–16. Exodus 33:12–17; 1 Samuel 2:12; Jeremiah 16:21; and Ezekiel 6:7 support this view.

6. Sigmund Mowinckel, "The Name of the God of Moses," *Hebrew Union College Annual* 32 (1961): 126.

7. Motyer, *The Revelation of the Divine Name*, p. 20.

8. Raymond Abba, "The Divine Name Yahweh," *Journal of Biblical Literature* 80 (1961): 323. Martin Buber, the Jewish theologian, also concurs that the question seeks to find the expression in or behind that name (Pamela Vermes, "Buber's Understanding of the Divine Name," *Journal of Jewish Studies* 24 [Autumn

1973]: 147).

9. Dennis J. McCarthy, "Exod. 3:14," *Catholic Biblical Quarterly* 40 (July 1978): 316.

10. E. Schild, "On Exodus iii 14—'I Am That I Am,'" *Vetus Testamentum* 4 (July 1954): 301; cf. Zimmerli, *Old Testament Theology in Outline*, p. 21.

11. McCarthy, "Exod. 3:14," p. 316.

12. Blau, "Tetragrammaton," 12:118–20.

13. Mowinckel, "The Name of the God of Moses," p. 124.

14. Charles D. Isbell, "The Divine Name אהיה as a Symbol of Presence in Israelite Tradition," *Hebrew Annual Review* 2 (1978): 102–5. Isbell points out that in each case (Ps. 50:21 and Hos. 1:9) the context makes the tense clear and that therefore the term אֶהְיֶה is probably not needed unless understood as a name.

15. Motyer, *The Revelation of the Divine Name*, p. 23.

16. K.-H. Bernhardt, "הָיָה," in *Theological Dictionary of the Old Testament*, 3:373.

17. Ibid.

18. Zimmerli, *Old Testament Theology in Outline*, p. 20. Unfortunately Zimmerli does not provide good support for his view.

19. Ibid., p. 21.

20. Robert Lockyer, *All the Divine Names and Titles in the Bible* (Grand Rapids: Zondervan, 1975), p. 18. This seems to be typical of popular works on the subject of the divine name with very little support for the "ontological" view.

21. Merrill Unger, *Unger's Bible Dictionary* (Chicago: Moody, 1957), p. 56; Nathan J. Stone, *Names of God in the Old Testament* (Chicago: Moody, 1944), p. 20; Andrew Jukes, *The Names of God in the Holy Scripture* (New York: Whittaker, 1888), p. 40; J. A. Montgomery, "Hebrew Divine Name and Personal Pronoun HU," *Journal of Biblical Literature* (June 1944): 161–63.

22. Moses Maimonides, quoted in Stone, *Names of God in the Old Testament*, p. 21.

23. McCarthy, "Exod. 3:14," p. 318.

24. Schild, "On Exodus iii 14," p. 302.

25. Ibid., p. 298.

26. Bruce K. Waltke, quoted in Allen P Ross, "The Use of the Versions" (unpublished class notes in 103 Introduction to Hebrew Exegesis, Dallas Theological Seminary, Fall 1981), p. 3. See also Ernst Wurthwein, *The Text of the Old Testament* (Grand Rapids: Eerdmans, 1979), pp. 51–53.

27. Bernhardt, "הָיָה," 3:381.

28. A. B. Davidson, *The Theology of the Old Testament* (New York:

Scribner's Sons, 1906), p. 155; cf. Zimmerli, *Old Testament Theology in Outline*, p. 20; U. Simon, *A Theology of Salvation* (London: S.P.C.K., 1961), p. 89; J. H. Bernard, *A Critical and Exegetical Commentary on the Gospel according to St. John*, 2 vols. (Edinburgh: Clark), 1:cxxi.

29. Francis Brown, S. R. Driver, and Charles A. Briggs, *A Hebrew and English Lexicon of the Old Testament* (Oxford: Clarendon, 1972), p. 224.
30. Davidson, *The Theology of the Old Testament*, p. 55.
31. Mowinckel, "The Name of the God of Moses," p. 127.
32. Abba, "The Divine Name Yahweh," pp. 324–25; cf. Bernhardt, "הָיָה," 3:380. Bernhardt admits to a possibility of the present tense rendering in Ruth 2:13, but agrees that otherwise the meaning is always future.
33. McCarthy, "Exod. 3:14," p. 316.
34. Wurthwein, *The Text of the Old Testament*, p. 53.
35. Bernhardt, "הָיָה," 3:381.
36. Ibid., p. 380. Cf. Julian Obermann, "The Divine Name YHWH in Light of Recent Discoveries, " *Journal of Biblical Literature* 68 (1949): 303.
37. Bertil Albrektson, "On the Syntax of 'ehyeh 'asher 'ehyeh in Exodus 3:14," in *Words and Meanings*, ed. Peter R. Ackroyd and Barnabas Lindars (Cambridge: Cambridge University Press, 1968), pp. 27–28.
38. E. C. B. Maclaurin, "Yhwh: The Origin of the Tetragrammaton," *Vetus Testamentum* 12 (1962): 440.
39. W. F. Albright, *From the Stone Age to Christianity* (Garden City, NY: Doubleday, 1957), p. 259.
40. D. N. Freedman, "The Name of the God of Moses," *Journal of Biblical Literature* 79 (1960): 152–53. Also see Samuel S. Cohon, *Jewish Theology* (Assen: Royal Vangorcum, 1971), p. 197.
41. Obermann, "The Divine Name YHWH in Light of Recent Discoveries," p. 323. Obermann points out that this is also the view held by the eminent medieval authority Ibn Ezra.
42. Ibid.
43. Cf. Albright, *From the Stone Age to Christianity*, p. 16.
44. Freedman, "The Name of the God of Moses," p. 152.
45. Bernhardt, "הָיָה," 3:381; cf. Abba, "The Divine Name Yahweh," p. 325.
46. Motyer, *The Revelation of the Divine Name*, p. 24.
47. Georg Fohrer, *History of Israelite Religion*, trans. David E. Green (Nashville: Abingdon, 1972), p. 72.

48. Charles D. Isbell, "The Divine Name אהיה as a Symbol of Presence in Israelite Tradition," *Hebrew Annual Review* 2 (1978):101–18.
49. Abba, "The Divine Name," p. 328.
50. Mowinckel, "The Name of the God of Moses," p. 127.
51. Davidson, *The Theology of the Old Testament*, pp. 54–57, 70–71. Motyer sees הָיָה with a similar connotation of γινέσθαι instead of εἶναι (*The Revelation of the Divine Name*, p. 21).
52. It should be noted that most translations render the tense of אֶהְיֶה in Exodus 3:12 as future: "I will be with you."
53. Fohrer, *History of Israelite Religion*, p. 79. But Fohrer goes too far in his view of attributing a "becoming-ness" to YHWH.
54. Cf. Herbert F. Stevenson, *Titles of the Triune God* (Westwood, NJ: Revell, 1956), p. 21.
55. See Walther Zimmerli, *I Am Yahweh* (Atlanta: Knox, 1982), p. 5. In reference to the inclusion of the phrase "I Am Yahweh" Zimmerli asks "why all this could not be expressed much more simply with the statement, 'they will know Me.'" The reason is, as Zimmerli states further, "The entire historical task of leadership to which Moses is commissioned draws its God-willed significance not only from subsequent events, but also from the impact of precisely this fundamental, revelatory truth: the knowledge of Yahweh's name as an event of Yahweh's self-introduction" (p.10).
56. Robert Davidson, *The Old Testament* (Philadelphia: Lippincott, 1964), p. 27.
57. Sheldon H. Blank, "Studies in Deutero-Isaiah," *Hebrew Union College Annual* 15 (1940): 32–33. "I am YHWH" occurs in Leviticus 18:5–6, 21; 19:13, 16, 28, 30, 32, 37; 22:2–3, 8, 30–31, 33; 26:2, 45; 31:12. "I am YHWH who. . ." occurs in Leviticus 18:2, 4, 30; 19:3–4, 10, 25, 31, 34; 23:22, 43; 25:55; Numbers 10:10; 15:4. "For because I am YHWH . . . " occurs in Exodus 31:13; Leviticus 11:44; 21:15, 23; 24:22; 25:17; 26:1, 44. Of course this list is not exhaustive
58. W. Eichrodt, quoted in G. H. Parke-Taylor, *Yahweh: The Divine Name in the Bible* (Waterloo: Wildfrid Laurier University Press, 1975), p. 64.

Chapter 3

1. Hermann Gunkel, *Genesis* (Göttingen: Vandenhoeck & Ruprecht, 1917), p. 361. Gunkel understands these features to be characteristic of a certain type of religious story in which the hero fights a god (e.g., Hercules). His observation of the antiquity of the story must be seen in this connection.

2. Nathaniel Schmidt points out that the passage was intended to answer certain questions about customs and traditions; yet on a closer reading many other questions surface ("The Numen of Penuel," *Journal of Biblical Literature* 45 [1926]: 265).

3. Gerhard von Rad, *Genesis: A Commentary*, trans. John Marks (London: SCM, 1972), p. 319.

4. Josephus *Antiquities* 1. 331.

5. W. H. Roscher, "Ephialtes," *Abh. d. phil.-hist. Classe d. k. sachsischen Ges. d. Wissenschaften* 20 (1906), cited by Schmidt, "The Numen of Penuel," p. 263.

6. Philo *Legum allegoriarum* 3. 190.

7. Philo *De mutatione nominum* 87.

8. Clement of Alexandria *Paedagogus* 1. 7. 57.

9. Schmidt, "The Numen of Penuel," p. 263.

10. *Midrash Genesis* 77. 3.

11. Schmidt, "The Numen of Penuel," p. 267.

12. On the other hand such tensions can be plausibly harmonized: verse 25b may be the natural effect of verse 25a, the giving of the name is the token of the blessing, and the victory involves the crippling of human devices.

13. Schmidt, "The Numen of Penuel," p. 269.

14. John L. McKenzie, "Jacob at Peniel: Gen. 32:24–32," *Catholic Biblical Quarterly* 25 (1963): 73.

15. S. Gevirtz, "Of Patriarchs and Puns: Joseph at the Fountain, Jacob at the Ford," *Hebrew Union College Annual* 46 (1975): 50. While Gevirtz's reaction to these suggestions is helpful, his own interpretation is rather fanciful, as will be mentioned later.

16. J. Fokkelman, *Narrative Art in Genesis* (Assen: Van Gorcum, 1975), p. 210.

17. Herbert E. Ryle, *The Book of Genesis* (Cambridge: University Press, 1914), p. 323.

18. R. Barthes, "La Lutte avec L'Ange," in *Analyse structurale et Exégèse Biblique*, by R. Barthes, F. Bovon, F. J. Lâeenhardt, R. Martin-Achard, and J. Starobinski, Bibliothique Theologique (Neuchatel: Delachaux et Niestlé, 1971), p. 35.

19. Fokkelman, *Narrative Art in Genesis*, p. 211.

20. The River Jabbok is the *Wadi ez-Zerka,"* the blue," that is, a clear mountain stream. It is on the frontier of the land.

21. Fokkelman, *Narrative Art in Genesis*, p. 211.

22. A. Dillmann, *Genesis, Critically and Exegetically Expounded*, trans. B. Stevenson, 2 vols. (Edinburgh: Clark, 1897), 2:281.

23. G. J. Spurrell, *Notes on the Text of the Book of Genesis*, 2d ed. (Oxford: Clarendon, 1906), p. 282.

24. R. Martin-Achard, "Un Exegete Devant Genesis 32:23–33," *Analyse structurale et Exégèse Biblique*, p. 60.

25. Gunkel says, "*Ye'abeq*—das Wort nur hier und 26; Anspielusig und wisprünglich wol Erklärungs versuch des Namens Yabboq" (*Genesis*, p. 326).

26. Fokkelman, *Narrative Art in Genesis*, p. 213.

27. Von Rad, *Genesis: A Commentary*, p. 320.

28. The verb יָקַע implies a separation or dislocation. It is used figuratively in Jeremiah 6:8 and Ezekiel 23:18. In the Hiphil it represents some form of execution, but its precise form is uncertain. The solemn execution of the seven men in 2 Samuel 21:6 may be a hanging or an impaling.

29. E. A. Speiser, *Genesis* (Garden City, NY: Doubleday, 1971), p. 255.

30. Von Rad suggests that this is a basic feature of human nature. In desperation Jacob clung to the divine for help (*Genesis*, p. 321).

31. It may be observed that the praying began after the fight was over. So the fighting cannot signify intense praying.

32. Fokkelman, *Narrative Art in Genesis*, p. 215.

33. The name Jacob has as its probable meaning "May he protect" or in its fullest form, Jacob-el, "may God protect" (Martin Noth, *Die israelitischen Personennamen im Rahmen der gemeinsemitischen Namengebung* [Stuttgart: Kohlhanmer, 1928], pp. 177–78; also see W. F. Albright, *From the Stone Age to Christianity* [Garden City, NY: Doubleday, 1957], p. 237, n. 51). The protection is that of a rearguard, one who follows behind the group. In the naming of the infant (Gen. 25), the mother selected a name that would instantly recall how the younger child grasped the heel of his brother (עֲקֹב/יַעֲקֹב)—after all, the mother had received the oracle about the twins and so would note such unusual developments. But the parents would in no wise name a child "overreacher" or "deceitful." But in his lifetime Jacob "tripped" his brother twice, prompting Esau to reinterpret his name: "Is he not rightly called Jacob? He has deceived me these two times" (Gen. 27:36, author's translation). After those incidents the significance of the name became that of a deceiver, one who dogged the heels of another to trip him and take unfair advantage. Jeremiah later would say, "Every brother is a 'Jacob'" (Jer. 9:4, author's translation).

34. R. B. Coote, "Hosea XII," *Vetus Testamentum* 21 (1971): 394.

35. Taken after the analogy of other names, יִשְׂרָאֵל may be a jussive, "Let God fight," or a simple imperfect, "God fights/will fight" (G.H. Skipworth, "The Tetragrammaton: Its Meaning and Origin," *Jewish Quarterly Review* 10 [1897–98]: 66). Also see Th. Noldeke, "Personal Names," in *Encyclopedia Biblica*, 3:3271–3307.

36. Robert Coote, "The Meaning of the Name Israel," *Harvard Theological Review* 65 (1972): 137.
37. Cyrus Gordon, *Ugaritic Textbook* (Rome: Pontifical Biblical Institute, 1965), par. 1334. See also James L. Kugel, *The Idea of Biblical Poetry* (New Haven, CT: Yale University Press, 1981), pp. 19–23.
38. Coote, "Hosea XII," p. 394.
39. Robertson Smith writes: "The very name of Israel is martial, and means 'God (El) fighteth,' and Jehovah in the Old Testament is *Iahwe Çebaoth*, the Jehovah of the armies of Israel. It was on the battlefield that Jehovah's presence was most clearly realized . . ." (*The Prophets of Israel* [Edinburgh: Black, 1882], p. 36).
40. John Skinner, *Genesis* (Edinburgh: Clark, 1913), p. 409.
41. Gunkel writes, "Es ist ein grossartiger und sicherlich uralter Gedanke Israels, es sei im Stande, nicht nur die ganze Welt mit Gottes Hülfe, sondern auch, wo nötig Gott selber zu bekampfen und zu überwinden" (*Genesis*, p. 328). Gunkel restated this in the 1917 edition: "denn wen selbst die Gottheit nicht bezwingen konnte, den wird kein Feind bawältigen!"
42. Martin Noth, *Die israelitischen Personennamen*, p. 208.
43. W. F. Albright, "The Names 'Israel' and 'Judah' with an Excursus on the Etymology of Todah and Torah," *Journal of Biblical Literature* 46 (1927): 159. Nestle's discussion was in *Die israelitischen Eigennamen*. There are exceptions, of course, such as יְהַלֶּלְאֵל in 2 Chronicles 29:12.
44. Albright, "The Names 'Israel' and 'Judah.'"
45. The pointing of יִשְׂרָאֵל is in itself unexpected; a shewa would be expected under the ר. Albright suggests a secondary development under the influence of the Greek tradition (Albright follows Max Margolis, "The Pronunciation of the שְׁוָא according to New Hexaplaric Material," *American Journal of Semitic Languages and Literature* [1909]: 66). When the shewa is followed by a laryngeal we have an *a* vowel in Greek (Ἰσραηλ). So the shewa had an a coloring before the weak laryngeal in the pre-Masoretic age. The Masoretes, under the influence of Aramaic reduced a short *a* in the open syllable to shewa, except in two well-known names, יִשְׂרָאֵל, and יִשְׁמָעֵאל where it was too well established to be eliminated (Albright. "The Names of 'Israel' and 'Judah,'" p. 161).
46. For a thorough discussion, see G. A. Danell, *Studies in the Name Israel in the Old Testament* (Uppsala: Appelbergs Boktryckeri, 1946), pp. 22–28.
47. *Interpreter's Dictionary of the Bible*, s.v. "Israel, Name and

Associations of," by A. Haldar (Nashville: Abingdon, 1962), 2:765.

48. "El est droit on juste" (Edmond Jacob, *Theológie de L'Ancient Testament* [Neuchâtel: Delachaux et Niestlé, 1955], p. 155 [p. 203 in the English translation]). Jacob says that the explanation given in Genesis is philologically untenable.

49. Ibid., p. 50.

50. Albright, "The Names 'Israel' and 'Judah,'" p. 166.

51. Ibid., p. 168. Of course the fact that a root שָׂרָה, meaning "fight," is rare was taken as an objection to that meaning. Argument based on rarity loses its force.

52. Coote, "The Meaning of the Name Israel," p. 139.

53. Noth, *Die israelitischen Personennamen*, pp. 191, 208.

54. Giovanni Pettinato, *The Archives of Ebla* (Garden City, NY: Doubleday, 1981), p. 249.

55. Popular etymologies are satisfied with a loose connection between the words. Rarely are they precise etymologies such as with the explanation of Joseph in Genesis 30:23–24 (יֹסֵף, "may he add"). Most often they express a wish or sentiment that is loosely connected by a word play. For example Seth is explained with שָׁת, "he appointed"; Simeon with שָׁמַע, "he heard"; Ephraim with הִפְרַנִי, "he made me fruitful"; Levi with יִלָּוֶה, "he will be attached"; Judah with אוֹדֶה, "I will praise." On occasion the popular etymology employs a completely different root. For example, Jabez (יַעְבֵּץ) is explained with the word עֹצֶב), and Reuben is explained with רָאָה בְעָנְיִי, "he has looked on my affliction." Such popular etymologies are more interested in the significance of the name than in the technical etymology.

56. Von Rad, *Genesis*, p. 322.

57. Dillmann, *Genesis*, 2:279.

58. Fokkelman, *Narrative Art in Genesis*, p. 218.

59. A. S. Herbert, *Genesis 12–50: Introduction and Commentary* (London: SCM, 1962), p. 108.

60. Here the word is spelled פְּנִיאֵל, but later פְּנוּאֵל (LXX has Εἶδοςθεοῦ). The ו and the י that serve as binding vowels are probably old case endings (see E. Kautzsch and A. E. Cowley, eds., *Gesenius' Hebrew Grammar*, 2d ed. [Oxford: Clarendon, 1910], p. 254, para. 90o, and Spurrell, *Notes on the Text of the Book of Genesis*, p. 284). Skinner suggests that it is not improbable that the place is named for its resemblance to a face (*Genesis*, p. 410; Strabo mentions such a Phoenician promontory θεοῦ πρόσωπον [16. 2. 15–16]). The story would then be an etiological narrative designed to explain such a phenomenon. More

likely the name was used to fit the experience rather than the experience to fit the name.

61. Fokkelman, *Narrative Art in Genesis*, p. 219.
62. Heinrich Ewald, *The History of Israel*, trans. R. Martineau, 8 vols. (London: Longmans, Green, 1876), 1:358.
63. Brevard S. Childs, "A Study of the Formula, 'Until This Day,'" *Journal of Biblical Literature* 82 (1963): 292.
64. Ibid., p. 288.
65. Marcus Dods, *The Book of Genesis* (London: Hodder & Stoughton, 1892), p. 300.
66. Dillmann, *Genesis* 2:280.
67. The figure of Jacob is exalted in Isaiah 41:8; 44:1, 2, 21; 48:20; and 49:3. Compare, however, the juxtaposition of Jacob and Israel in 1 Kings 18:31.
68. Von Rad, *Genesis*, p. 325.
69. But the direction Gevirtz takes on this is surely extreme. He argues that the sinew of the hip (גִּיד הַנָּשֶׁה) is an allusion to Gad and Manasseh, who had the Jabbok as their common border. The lesson of the allusion was then that the emergence of Israel depended on the confederation of Gad and Manasseh.

Chapter 4

1. One recent theory is that advanced by Hans Goedicke which places the Exodus in 1477 B.C. during the reign of Queen Hatshepsut (Hershel Shanks, "The Exodus and the Crossing of the Red Sea According to Hans Goedicke," *Biblical Archaeology Review* 7 [September–October 1981]: 42–50). This position was popularized in a recent issue of *Reader's Digest* (Ronald Schiller, "The Biblical Exodus: Fact or Fiction," *Reader's Digest*, April 1983, pp. 133–38). For a critique of the new theory see Eliezer D. Oren, "How Not to Create a History of the Exodus— A Critique of Professor Goedicke's Theories," *Biblical Archaeology Review* 7 (November–December 1981): 46–53.
2. Kenneth A. Kitchen, *Ancient Orient and Old Testament* (Downers Grove, IL: InterVarsity, 1966), pp. 57–59.
3. Merrill F. Unger, *Archaeology and the Old Testament* (Grand Rapids: Zondervan, 1954), pp. 149–50.
4. John H. Walton, *Chronological Charts of the Old Testament* (Grand Rapids: Zondervan, 1978), p. 31.
5. Eugene H. Merrill, *An Historical Survey of the Old Testament* (Grand Rapids: Baker, 1966), p. 107.
6. Nelson Glueck, *The Other Side of the Jordan* (New Haven, CT: American Schools of Oriental Research, 1940), pp. 125–47.

7. Siegfried J. Schwantes, *A Short History of the Ancient Near East* (Grand Rapids: Baker, 1965), p. 158.

8. Clyde T. Francisco, "The Exodus in its Historical Setting," *Southwestern Journal of Theology* 20 (Fall 1977): 12.

9. Merrill, *An Historical Survey of the Old Testament*, p. 108.

10. Kitchen, *Ancient Orient and the Old Testament*, pp. 61–62.

11. Kenneth A. Kitchen, *The Bible in Its World: The Bible and Archaeology Today* (Downers Grove, IL: InterVarsity, 1977), p. 88 (italics added).

12. Gleason L. Archer, Jr., *A Survey of Old Testament Introduction*, rev. ed. (Chicago: Moody, 1974), pp. 225–26.

13. Kenneth A. Kitchen and T. C. Mitchell, "Chronology (OT)," in *The Illustrated Bible Dictionary*, 1:275.

14. John Garstang and J. B. E. Garstang, *The Story of Jericho*, rev. ed. (London: Marshall, Morgan, & Scott, 1948), p. 179.

15. Unger, *Archaeology and the Old Testament*, pp. 146–48. See also Archer, *Survey of Old Testament Introduction*, pp. 223–24.

16. Kathleen M. Kenyon, "Some Notes on the History of Jericho in the Second Millennium B.C.," *Palestinian Exploration Quarterly* 83 (1951): 121–22.

17. Kitchen, *Ancient Orient and the Old Testament*, p. 62.

18. Waltke, "Palestinian Artifactual Evidence Supporting the Early Date of the Exodus," *Bibliotheca Sacra* 129 (January–March 1972): 40–41.

19. Kenyon, "Notes on the History of Jericho," p. 117.

20. Yigael Yadin, "The Fourth Season of Excavation at Hazor," *Biblical Archaeologist* 22 (February 1959): 3.

21. Ibid., p. 4.

22. Ibid., p. 8.

23. Ibid., p. 9 (italics added).

24. Walton, *Chronological Charts of the Old Testament*, p. 28.

25. Waltke, "Palestinian Artifactual Evidence Supporting the Early Date of the Exodus," p. 44.

26. John C. Whitcomb, *Chart of the Old Testament Patriarchs and Judges* (Chicago: Moody, 1968).

27. Waltke, "Palestinian Artifactual Evidence Supporting the Early Date of the Exodus," p. 44.

28. J. A. Thompson, *The Bible and Archaeology*, 3d ed. (Grand Rapids: Eerdmans, 1982), pp. 60–62.

29. Kitchen, *Ancient Orient and the Old Testament*, p. 59, n. 11.

30. John J. Davis, *Moses and the Gods of Egypt* (Grand Rapids: Baker, 1971), p. 27.

31. James B. Pritchard, *Ancient Near Eastern Texts Relating to the*

Old Testament, 3d ed. (Princeton, NJ: Princeton University Press, 1969), p. 246.

32. John C. Whitcomb, *Chart of the Old Testament Kings and Prophets* (Chicago: Moody, 1968).
33. J. N. Oswalt, "Chronology of the Old Testament," *International Standard Bible Encyclopedia*, 1979 ed., 1:677.
34. Leon J. Wood, *A Survey of Israel's History* (Grand Rapids: Zondervan, 1970), p. 89.
35. Kitchen, *Ancient Orient and the Old Testament*, pp. 74–75.
36. Davis, *Moses and the Gods of Egypt*, p. 31.
37. Pritchard, *Ancient Near Eastern Texts Relating to the Old Testament*, p. 449.
38. Archer, *Survey of Old Testament Introduction*, pp. 229–30.
39. Charles F. Aling, "The Sphinx Stele of Thutmose IV and the Date of the Exodus," *Journal of the Evangelical Theological Society* 22 (June 1979): 98.
40. Unger, *Archaeology and the Old Testament*, pp. 145–46.
41. Pritchard, *Ancient Near Eastern Texts Relating to the Old Testament*, pp. 486–87.
42. Ibid., p. 488.
43. Charles F. Pfeiffer, *Tell El Amarna and the Bible* (Grand Rapids: Baker, 1963), pp. 52–54.
44. Josephus *Contra Apionem* 1. 26.
45. Adam William Fisher, "The Argument for the Early Date of the Exodus," Th.M. thesis, Dallas Theological Seminary, May 1968, pp. 32–35.
46. J. Maxwell Miller, "Archaeology and the Israelite Conquest of Canaan: Some Methodological Observations," *Palestinian Exploration Quarterly* 109 (July–December 1977): 88.

Chapter 5

1. These elements may be described briefly as follows. *Romance* is literature that depicts an ideal human society; joy and harmony pervade the atmosphere. *Anti-romance* is the opposite of romance, and portrays a society in bondage; there is a distinct absence of joy and harmony. *Tragedy* is an event that drags the romantic ideal down into the anti-romantic unideal; the tragic element is in this sense transitional. *Comedy* is also transitional and is the opposite of the tragic element in that it pulls the movement up from the bondage of joyless anti-romance into the freedom of joyful romance. The monomyth is the cyclic composite narrative comprising the four elements just described; it is the archetypal pattern true of all literature. For detailed definitions and analyses of

these components of literary analysis, see Northrop Frye, _Anatomy of Criticism_ (Princeton, NJ: Princeton University Press, 1973); and idem, _The Great Code: The Bible and Literature_ (New York: Harcourt Brace Jovanovich, 1981).

2. The tragic element can only be defined in terms of its cause and effect, because the precise moment of transition can seldom be captured in and of itself. Both the cause and the effect are often expressed in terms of archetypes of ideal or unideal experience, or in language expressive of a pivotal decision (= transition). The famine in Judah was not tragic in and of itself, and so is not transitional. It was merely the instrument God used to initiate a transition that eventuated in anti-romance.

3. While the Book of Judges does not come immediately before the Book of Ruth in the Hebrew Bible (Proverbs precedes Ruth in the Massoretic Text), it does provide the historical setting for the events of Ruth. In fact the narrator invited a comparison with the period of the Judges (Ruth 1:1), the most natural book to consult for a record of that time. Literary connections must certainly have been explored in light of the vivid contrasts between the key elements in each book. Disregarding the chronological connection, the contrast in moral climates alone would have been sufficient to invite further literary comparison.

4. Merrill has given an excellent analysis of the features of the trilogy (Eugene H. Merrill, "The Book of Ruth: Narration and Shared Themes," _Bibliotheca Sacra_ 142 [April–June 1985]: 130–41).

5. Note the emphasis on Jonathan's levitical and geographical origins, as well as the connection with Ephraim: "Now there was a young man from Bethlehem in Judah, of the family of Judah, who was a Levite; and he was staying there. Then the man departed from the city, from Bethlehem in Judah . . . he came to the hill country of Ephraim to the house of Micah. And Micah said to him, 'Where do you come from?' And he said to him, 'I am a Levite from Bethlehem in Judah.' . . . So the Levite went in. And the Levite agreed to live with the man. . . . So Micah consecrated the Levite. . . . Then Micah said, 'Now I know that the Lord will prosper me, seeing I have a Levite as priest'" (Judg. 17:7–13). The emphasis on the levitical origin of this descendant of Moses as well as the Bethlehem-Ephraim connection is important as the author of Judges developed by implication a subtly pro-Davidic/anti-Saulide emphasis. This emphasis is increasingly evident in the second and third narratives of the trilogy. For a consideration of this, see the discussion below on the romantic element.

6. It is interesting to note an "emptiness" motif here as well. In Judges 18:24 Micah bemoaned his loss: "You have taken away my gods which I made, and the priest, and have gone away, and what do I have besides?" Micah had lost his gods, while Naomi felt that God had deserted her. Also Micah returned to his house (unideal experience) once he realized his cause was hopeless (18:26). This "return" motif is dominant early in the Book of Ruth.

7. Cf. Merrill, "The Book of Ruth: Narration and Shared Themes," p. 131.

8. The shift is subtle. Later readers may suspect a potential resolution because of recognizing the phrase "the Lord had visited [פקד] His people" as a clue to a positive outcome (cf. 1 Sam. 2:21; this is of particular interest in light of the possibility that Samuel may have written both 1 Sam. 1:1–25:1 and Ruth and that the same construction is used in both places to describe the Lord's making fruitful what was barren). Note also Genesis 21:1; 50:24–25. From the character's point of view the situation is irredeemably tragic. It is also true that the good news from Judah is unsubstantiated for both Naomi and the reader. It is only something she heard about (1:6), and so the possibility exists that her return could be based on a vain hope.

9. This aspect of the development of the plot is considered later under the romantic element.

10. There is no mention of Naomi being bereft of grandchildren, a detail the writer certainly would not have overlooked in view of his emphasis on personal loss. Also the phrase in 4:13, "And the Lord enabled her to conceive," suggests that Ruth had not previously been able to have children.

11. The significance of the Feast of Pentecost, linked with the end of the barley and wheat harvests, will be discussed later with the development of the fourth structural element.

12. There is no direct mention of any of the feasts in the Book of Ruth. However, is the reader to take the pointed seasonal references in 1:22 and 2:23 as merely temporal indicators? Do the prominent agricultural images of famine, harvest, wheat, and barley serve no other purpose than to reinforce metaphorical parallels with the main characters? Could not these and other such references be a subtle artistic device that draws attention to a significance in the feasts that lies beyond surface observations? In fact could not the book's lack of explicit mention of the feasts be taken as an indirect commentary on their significance, especially in light of these other considerations? It is as if the author were "talking around" the feasts, noting the times

of year in which Passover, Unleavened Bread, and Firstfruits were celebrated; noting the harvesting of particular crops of barley and wheat; tying the agricultural motif into the lives of the characters in an essential way; and emphasizing the blessing of God as He made fruitful what had been barren. It seems, therefore, that a consideration of the significance of the festal cycle as it relates to the events in the Book of Ruth is called for.

The absence of direct reference to the feasts does not automatically suggest that they were not being observed. Unless one holds that the lineage leading to David in Ruth 4:18–22 is a historical gloss or other type of conflation, there is some biblical evidence to suggest that at least some of the annual feasts were being observed at or near the time of writing (probably the early monarchical period): Joshua 5:10–12 records the observance of the Passover at Gilgal when Joshua brought the people into Canaan; the celebration of Tabernacles during the time of Ezra is said to have been different from anything done since the days of Joshua (Neh. 8:13–18), suggesting there had been at least some observance of the feast in the interim; the feast mentioned in Judges 21:19 is almost certainly one of the annual feasts and could have been the Passover ("behold, there is a feast of the Lord from year to year in Shiloh"; the dancing of the women [v. 21] may imitate the celebratory dance of the women following the first Passover after the deliverance from the Egyptians through the Red Sea [Ex. 15]); the feast that is mentioned without elucidation in 1 Kings 8:2 is almost certainly the Feast of Tabernacles (1 Kings 8:65; 2 Chron. 7:9–10), since it occurred in the seventh month (cf. Lev. 23:33–36). In 2 Chronicles 8:12–13 Solomon is said to have offered burnt offerings to the Lord for the three annual feasts (among others). There can be little doubt that at least some of the feasts were being celebrated, if not during the time of Ruth, then certainly during the monarchy, when the audience would have noted not only the significance of the calendrical references but also the absence of any direct reference to the feasts.

13. For an extended discussion, see Terry C. Hulbert, "The Eschatological Significance of Israel's Annual Feasts" (Th.D. diss., Dallas Theological Seminary, 1965).

14. In 1:22a the word "returned" (שׁוּב) is used once as a verb and once as a participle. This repetition mirrors the double statement of Naomi's return with her daughters-in-law which closed out the first scene (1:6–7).

15. Müller suggests the following translations: "terrified" (1 Sam. 4:5), "uproar" (1 Kings 1:45), "uproar" (Ruth 1:19). In each

case the context helps determine the translation of the *niphal*. The 1 Samuel context is positive, as is the 1 Kings context. It seems that after Naomi's arrival, the initial atmosphere—that is, the one in which the exclamation of the townsfolk was made— was also positive. However, Naomi quickly reversed the mood in her insistence on being called "Mara" (H.–P. Müller, "המם," in *Theological Dictionary of the Old Testament*, 3 [1974]: 422).

16. Edward F. Campbell, Jr., *Ruth: A New Translation with Introduction, Notes, and Commentary*, Anchor Bible (Garden City, NY: Doubleday, 1975), p. 75.

17. Naomi's familiarity with God's revelation of Himself as the covenant-keeping God of Israel is evident in her repeated use of His covenant name Yahweh (1:6, reported conversation from the narrator's point of view; 1:8–9, 13, 21). This does not suggest she was unfamiliar with other names for God. For example she used אֱלֹהִים in reference to the gods of Moab in 1:15. Ruth referred to "your God" (וֵאלֹהַיִךְ), the one true God (1:16). Naomi used another name for God in 1:20–21: "Call me Mara, for the Almighty (שַׁדַּי) has dealt very bitterly with me . . . and the Almighty (וְשַׁדַּי) has afflicted me." That Naomi fully understood the covenant-keeping nature of the Lord is also evident in her declaration of 2:20: "May he be blessed of the Lord [Yahweh] who has not withdrawn his kindness to the living and to the dead." The word translated "withdrawn" is עָזַב. A better translation in this context would be "forsaken," the idea being that Yahweh has not "forsaken" the "kindness" (חֶסֶד) on which His unilateral covenant is at least partially predicated, by which it is sustained, and through which it is revealed in His covenant-keeping name. The use of עָזַב here anticipates David's use of the same word when he reminded his readers of God's promise never to forsake the righteous by allowing him to fall into the hands of the wicked (Ps. 37:25, 33). Neither do the poor and the oppressed have anything to fear, since the Lord has not forsaken them: "The Lord [Yahweh] also will be a stronghold for the oppressed, a stronghold in times of trouble, and those who know Thy name will put their trust in Thee; for Thou, O Lord [Yahweh], hast not forsaken those who seek Thee" (Ps. 9:9–10). Of particular note in light of the Ruth narrative is Ethan's use of the word in Psalm 89:30–37. Even if David's descendants forsake (עָזַב) Yahweh's law, still He will not break off (v. 33) His lovingkindness (חֶסֶד; cf. Ruth 2:20), nor will He violate His covenant (Ps. 89:34) with the Davidic dynasty. Given the author's definite interest in presenting the Davidic line in a posi-

tive light (Ruth 4:18–22), Naomi's recognition in 2:20 of the Lord's guiding hand is all the more significant.

18. Robert Alter has similarly observed, "In this elliptical version, the author has rotated the betrothal type-scene 180 degrees on the axes of gender and geography" (*The Art of Biblical Narrative* [New York: Basic, 1981], p. 58).

19. Cf. Walter Arend, *Die typischen Szenen bei Homer,* Forschungen zur klassischen Philologie 7 (Berlin: Weidmann, 1933).

20. Alter, *The Art of Biblical Narrative,* p. 50. Regarding the audience expectation of certain archetypal ingredients, Alter writes, "What I would suggest is that when a biblical narrator—and he might have originally been an oral storyteller, though that remains a matter of conjecture—came to the moment of his hero's betrothal, both he and his audience were aware that the scene had to unfold in particular circumstances, according to a fixed order. If some of those circumstances were altered or suppressed, or if the scene were actually omitted, that communicated something to the audience" (ibid., p. 52).

21. Alter's type-scenes are defined in terms of archetypal content as well as the structure of that content and the ordered movement within that structure (from one archetype to the next). While he does not go far enough in defining the structure as such (he seems to assume fixed archetypes), still Alter offers a summary of the essential components (along with archetypal significance) of the traditional betrothal type-scene based on observed structural and archetypal similarities in Homeric epic. The summary is of interest here, since his study reflects a comparative analysis of exclusively biblical texts: "The betrothal type-scene, then, must take place with the future bridegroom, or his surrogate, having journeyed to a foreign land. There he encounters a girl—the term 'na`arah' invariably occurs unless the maiden is identified as so-and-so's daughter—or girls at a well. Someone, either the man or the girl, then draws water from the well; afterward, the girl or girls rush to bring home the news of the stranger's arrival (the verbs 'hurry' and 'run' are given recurrent emphasis at this junction of the type-scene); finally, a betrothal is concluded between the stranger and the girl, in the majority of instances, only after he has been invited to a meal.

"The archetypal expressiveness of this whole type-scene is clear enough. The hero's emergence from the immediate family circle—though two of the most famous betrothal scenes stress endogamy (Gen. 24:10–61; Gen. 29:1–20)—to discover a mate in the world outside is figured in the young man's journey to a foreign land; or perhaps the foreign land is chiefly a geographical correlative for sheer female otherness of the prospective wife. The well at an oasis is obviously a symbol of fertility and, in all likelihood, also a female symbol. The drawing of water from the well is the act that emblematically establishes a bond—male-female, host-guest, benefactor-benefited—between the stranger and the girl, and its apt result is the excited running to bring the news, the gestures of hospitality, the actual bretrothal. The plot of the type-scene, then, dramatically enacts the coming together of mutually unknown parties in the marriage" (ibid., p. 52).

22. There are, of course, others, including David's obtaining of three of his wives (though these narratives contain a number of ambiguities and so are suspect as legitimate betrothal type-scenes). Samson's "betrothal scene" in Judges 14 is almost heavy-handed in its obvious omission of the "proper" channels of courtship (underscoring his impetuosity; see Alter, *The Art of Biblical Narrative*, p. 61).

23. Ibid., p. 59.

24. Ibid.

25. The significance of Abraham's insistence will be discussed under the romantic element.

26. Ibid., p. 59. Alter allows for "significant playful activity on the part of the Hebrew writers" (ibid., p. 60).

27. It should be noted as well that it is not merely a question of being exposed to previous narratives with a similar structure and archetypal content. The fact is that the betrothal scene of Isaac and Rebekah sets the archetypal pattern for the scenes that follow by virtue of the fact that they were the first children to marry under the canopy of the Abrahamic Covenant. All subsequent betrothals would necessarily be measured against the original (cf. ibid., p. 60).

28. Those structures contrast not in the sense of violating the structural conventions associated with tragedy, but in the sense of injecting an unexpected comic structure. This structure is particularly deceptive due to the introductory archetypes of the unideal experience that had just been employed at the outset of the previous two tragic narratives (Judg. 17–18; 19–21).

29. "Birth" is anticipated in the blessing in 4:11c–12 and is realized and emphasized in 4:13–22. The word for "birth" (יָלַד) is repeated in several forms 12 times, not including the derivatives תּוֹלְדוֹת ("generations," which occurs once), and יֶלֶד ("child," which occurs once).

30. Ruth's literary connection with Abraham in 2:11 is especially interesting in this light.

31. Another explanation is that this Rahab is in fact the mother of Boaz and thereby is not the same person as the prostitute in Joshua 2.

32. Merrill points out that the selection of David himself was "contrary to all convention since he was not the eldest son of Jesse but, to the contrary, the youngest. Beyond the confines of the genealogy proper it is significant finally that David's own dynastic heir, Solomon, was born to a royal wife who had become such under most inauspicious circumstances. And he was not the eldest son of David, not the one who by every traditional criterion should have become heir apparent. Moreover, he was the son of a foreigner, a Hittite" (Merrill, "The Book of Ruth: Narration and Shared Themes," pp. 134–35). Merrill also demonstrates the regal link to Messiah through the continuum, Abraham–David–Christ (evident in the Book of Ruth), as well as the priestly link with Messiah through the Melchizedek–David–Christ continuum, neither of which is interrupted by Mosaism (ibid., p. 137). This means that in David's functioning as a priest after the order of Melchizedek (1 Chron. 15:25–28; 16:1–3, 8–36; cf. Ps. 110; he could not have functioned as an Aaronic priest since he was of the tribe of Judah [Matt. 1:1–6]), he did so "outside the Mosaic priestly order and in an inherently more universal and comprehensive way since, as Hebrews argued, even Levi in Abraham's loins paid tithe to Melchizedek" (ibid.). This is especially interesting in light of the Tamar/Judah connection in Ruth 4:18, but it is beyond the scope of this article to explore the New Testament connection with Messiah in any depth.

33. The point of discovery comes when the content of the exegetically analyzed text (consisting of archetypes of ideal or unideal experience, motifs, "incidental data," etc.) assumes the "shape" of one of the four recognizable structures. It is at this point that the focus narrows to a search for the transitional or static element that is the *sine qua non* of that structure.

34. Individual structures are initially defined in terms of their relationships with other structures; however, once the overall structure of the entire narrative has been discovered, one may return to individual structures or even to the structural elements themselves (as they occur in context) for insight. It is also important to remember the nature of the individual structures: the ideal and unideal structures are static, while the tragic and comic structures are transitional. This means that one can analyze the static structures as they are, but one can only analyze the transitional structures in terms of "having been" and "becoming."

Chapter 6

1. David Noel Freedman, "The Chronicler's Purpose," *Catholic Biblical Quarterly* 23 (October 1961): 436.
2. For an explanation of why 1 Chronicles 3:19–24 need not be taken as a genealogy to the sixth generation after Zerubbabel (11th generation in the Septuagint, the Vulgate, and the Syriac), see Edward J. Young, *An Introduction to the Old Testament*, rev. ed. (Grand Rapids: Eerdmans, 1960), p. 414; and Gleason L. Archer, Jr., *A Survey of Old Testament Introduction* (Chicago: Moody, 1964), pp. 391–92. Many scholars, however, reject this view.
3. Freedman suggests an even earlier date shortly after the completion of the temple, around 515 B.C., based on parallels with Haggai-Zechariah and the assumption that at least parts of 1 Chronicles 1–9 constitute a later addition to the original work ("The Chronicler's Purpose," p. 441).
4. Cf. Archer, *A Survey of Old Testament Introduction*, p. 390.
5. R. K. Harrison, *Introduction to the Old Testament: With a Comprehensive Review of Old Testament Studies and a Special Supplement on the Apocrypha* (Grand Rapids: Eerdmans, 1969), p. 1157.
6. For an answer to the late-date argument based on the reference to "darics of gold" in 1 Chronicles 29:7, see Harrison, *Introduction to the Old Testament*, p. 1157.
7. Cf. Bruce K. Waltke, "The Samaritan Pentateuch and the Text of the Old Testament," in *New Perspectives on the Old Testament*, ed. J. Barton Payne (Waco, TX: Word, 1970), pp. 212–39.
8. This writer prefers a date closer to the construction of the temple because of the messianic parallels between Chronicles and Haggai-Zechariah. Though the question of whether the chronicler wrote Ezra-Nehemiah is not discussed here, this writer agrees with the recent trend away from seeing the chronicler as the author of Ezra-Nehemiah (see, e.g., H. G. M. Williamson, *Israel in the Books of Chronicles* [London: Cambridge University Press, 1977]).
9. John Sailhamer, *First and Second Chronicles*, Everyman's Bible Commentary (Chicago: Moody, 1983), p. 13.
10. For a recent presentation of this midrashic view of Chronicles see Jacob M. Myers, *1 Chronicles*, Anchor Bible (Garden City, NY: Doubleday, 1965), pp. xviii, xxx, lxiii.
11. Cf. Bruce K. Waltke, "The Textual Criticism of the Old Testament," in *The Expositor's Bible Commentary*, ed. Frank E. Gaebelein, 12 vols. (Grand Rapids: Zondervan, 1979–), 1 (1979): 214–16.

12. So Leland Ryken, *The Literature of the Bible* (Grand Rapids: Zondervan, 1974), p. 78.

13. Sailhamer, *First and Second Chronicles,* p. 9.

14. Adapted from Roy B. Zuck, "1 and 2 Chronicles" (unpublished class notes in 303 Bible, Dallas Theological Seminary), pp. 4–5.

15. Ibid., p. 5.

16. Elliott E. Johnson (unpublished class notes in 303 Bible, Dallas Theological Seminary).

17. Raymond Dillard, "The Reign of Asa (2 Chronicles 14–16): An Example of the Chronicler's Theological Method," *Journal of the Evangelical Theological Society* 23 (September 1980): 208.

18. As in the unconditional Abrahamic Covenant so in the unconditional Davidic Covenant obedience determined individual blessing under the covenant without invalidating the fact that Yahweh would eventually keep His promises to Abraham and to David. In Chronicles the condition of obedience for prosperity in the covenant is employed as a means of showing the remnant, on the basis of the record of each Davidic king, that the promised, obedient Son was yet to come.

19. George M. Harton, "Fulfillment of Deuteronomy 28–30 in History and in Eschatology" (Th.D. diss., Dallas Theological Seminary, 1981), p. 190.

20. A chart showing this detail can be found in *Understanding 1 & 2 Chronicles: The House of God and Its Service*, by John Heading (Kansas City: Walterick Publishers, 1980).

21. The genealogies of Dan and Zebulun are missing, perhaps through textual transmission (so H. G. M. Williamson, *1 and 2 Chronicles,* New Century Bible Commentary [Grand Rapids: Eerdmans, 1982], pp. 47–48) or through a desire to maintain the idea of 12 tribes since the half-tribes of Manasseh and Ephraim are included (Sailhamer, *First and Second Chronicles,* p. 26).

22. Harton, "Fulfillment of Deuteronomy 28–30 in History and in Eschatology," p. 188.

23. Sailhamer, *First and Second Chronicles,* p. 68.

24. For a discussion of the critical problems raised by these differences see Dillard, "The Reign of Asa (2 Chronicles 14–16): An Example of the Chronicler's Theological Method," pp. 213–18.

25. Harton, "Fulfillment of Deuteronomy 28–30 in History and in Eschatology," p. 190.

26. Dillard, "The Reign of Asa (2 Chronicles 14–16): An Example of the Chronicler's Theological Method," p. 208, n. 5.

27. Freedman, "The Chronicler's Purpose."

28. Magne Saebo, "Messianism in Chronicles?: Some Remarks to

the Old Testament Background of the New Testament Christology," *Horizons in Biblical Theology* 2 (1980): 85–109.
29. Sailhamer, *First and Second Chronicles.*
30. Johnson, unpublished class notes.
31. James D. Newsome, Jr., "Toward an Understanding of the Chronicler and His Purposes," *Journal of Biblical Literature* 94 (June 1975): 201–17.
32. Zuck, "1 and 2 Chronicles."

Chapter 7

1. J. Chr. R. von Hofmann, *Schriftbeweis* (Nördlingen: C. H. Bed'schen, 1960), p. 404.
2. R. B. Y. Scott, *The Way of Wisdom in the Old Testament* (New York: Macmillan, 1971), p. 86.
3. Margaret B. Crook, "The Marriageable Maiden of Prov. 31:10–31," *Journal of Near Eastern Studies* 13 (1954): 140.
4. R. N. Whybray, *Book of Proverbs*, Cambridge Bible Commentary (Cambridge University Press, 1972), p. 184.
5. Roland E. Murphy, *Wisdom Literature: Job, Proverbs, Ruth, Canticles, Ecclesiastes and Esther*, Forms of Old Testament Literature, ed. Rolf Kneirim and Gene M. Tucker (Grand Rapids: Eerdmans, 1981), p. 82.
6. For an examination of this and other shades of meaning of this often-used word in the Old Testament see Tom R. Hawkins, "The Meaning and Function of Proverbs 31:10–31 in the Book of Proverbs" (Ph.D. diss., Dallas Theological Seminary, 1995), pp. 62–76.
7. "An excellent wife [אֵשֶׁת־חַיִל] is the crown of her husband, but she who shames him is as rottenness in his bones."
8. Hanneke van der Sluis-van der Korst and Douwe van der Sluis, "De deugdelijke huisvrouw in opspraak: een interpretatie van spreuken 31:10–31," *Schrift* 69 (1980): 94.
9. Ibid.
10. Ibid., p. 95.
11. Ibid., p. 96.
12. Ibid.
13. Thomas P. McCreesh, "Wisdom as Wife: Proverbs 31:10–31," *Revue Biblique* 92 (1985): 28.
14. Claudia Camp, *Wisdom and the Feminine in the Book of Proverbs* (Decatur, GA: Almond, 1985), p. 83.
15. Hermanson called her a "prostitute," but the better term is "adulteress" (Michael R. Hermanson, "The Personification of Wisdom in Proverbs 31:10–31" [Th.M. thesis, Dallas Theological Seminary, 1983], p. 40).

Vital Old Testament Issues

16. Ibid., p. 42.
17. Ibid., p. 44.
18. Job 28:18 uses the same word in describing the price of wisdom.
19. Proverbs 31:23 says that one of the "good" things he enjoys is respect in "the gates."
20. Most of these suggestions on the comparison of Lady Wisdom and the אֵשֶׁת־חַיִל are found in McCreesh, "Wisdom as Wife," pp. 41–43.
21. Ibid., p. 30. It could be questioned, however, that his phrase "make their home with her in chapter 9" is an accurate portrayal of her invitation to a meal.
22. Ibid., p. 44.
23. In addition several verses could be viewed as allusions to her activities as a mother (vv. 15, 21, 27).
24. Roy B. Zuck, "A Theology of the Wisdom Books and the Song of Songs," in *A Biblical Theology of the Old Testament*, ed. Roy B. Zuck (Chicago: Moody, 1991), p. 237.
25. Ibid. (italics his).
26. Ibid., pp. 237–38.
27. Duane A. Garrett, *Proverbs,* New American Commentary (Nashville: Broadman, 1993), p. 249; Helmer Ringgren, Artur Weiser, and Walther Zimmerli, *Sprüche, Prediger, Das Hohe Lied, Klagelieder, Das Buch Esther* (Göttingen: Vandenhoeck & Ruprecht, 1980), p. 121; and Al Wolters, "Ṣopîyyâ (Prov. 31:27) as Hymnic Participle and Play on *Sophia,*" *Journal of Biblical Literature* 104 (1985): 581.
28. Wolters, "Ṣopîyyâ (Prov 31:27) as Hymnic Participle and Play on *Sophia,*" p. 581.
29. Ibid., pp. 581–82.
30. John J. Collins, *Proverbs, Ecclesiastes*, Knox Preaching Guides (Atlanta: Knox, 1980), pp. 69–70.
31. Robina Drakeford and John W. Drakeford, *In Praise of Women: A Christian Approach to Love, Marriage and Equality* (San Francisco: Harper & Row, 1980), p. 26.

Chapter 8

1. For a helpful summary article, see Roy H. Campbell, "Social Gospel," in *The International Dictionary of the Christian Church,* p. 911.
2. "Global Camp Meeting," *Christianity Today,* August 18, 1989, pp. 39–40.
3. Willis Judson Beecher, *The Prophets and the Promise* (New York: Cromwell, 1905), p. 98.

4. Emil G. Kraeling, *The Prophets* (New York: Rand McNally, 1969), p. 15.
5. Beecher, *The Prophets and the Promise,* p. 97.
6. C. Hassell Bullock, *An Introduction to the Old Testament Prophetic Books* (Chicago: Moody, 1986), p. 25.
7. Abraham J. Heschel, *The Prophets,* 2 vols. (New York: Harper & Row, 1962), 1:198.
8. Bullock, *An Introduction to the Old Testament Prophetic Books,* p. 25.
9. E. Hammershaimb, *Some Aspects of Old Testament Prophets from Isaiah to Malachi* (Denmark: Rosenkilde Og Bagger, 1966), p. 71.
10. Yehezkel Kaufmann, *The Religion of Israel,* trans. Moshe Greenberg (London: Allen & Unwin, 1960), p. 365.
11. Samuel J. Shultz, *The Prophets Speak* (New York: Harper & Row, 1968), p. 36.
12. Bullock, *An Introduction to the Old Testament Prophetic Books,* p. 19.
13. Though the theme of social concern is reflected throughout the prophets, three major prophets (Isaiah, Jeremiah, and Ezekiel) and seven minor prophets (Hosea, Amos, Micah, Habakkuk, Zephaniah, Zechariah, and Malachi) illustrate this emphasis.
14. Kaufmann, *The Religion of Israel,* p. 366.
15. R. D. Culver, "מִשְׁפָּט," in *Theological Wordbook of the Old Testament,* 1:949.
16. H. G. Stigers, "צָדֵק," in *Theological Wordbook of the Old Testament,* 2:753.
17. John Paterson, *The Godly Fellowship of the Prophets* (New York: Scribner's Sons, 1948), p. 47.
18. H. L. Ellisen, *The Old Testament Prophets,* 2d ed. (Grand Rapids: Zondervan, 1966), p. 63.
19. Quoted by Ruth A. Tucker in *Guardians of the Great Commission* (Grand Rapids: Zondervan, 1988), p. 134.

Chapter 9

1. See Wilfred G. E. Watson, *Classical Hebrew Poetry: A Guide to Its Techniques,* JSOT Supplement Series 26 (Sheffield: JSOT, 1984), p. 238, as well as the sources cited there.
2. For a discussion of explicit and implicit polysemantic wordplay, see Stephen Ullmann, *Semantics: An Introduction to the Science of Meaning* (Oxford: Basil Blackwell, 1977), pp. 188–89.
3. Ibid.
4. God is the implied subject of the third masculine singular verb

form in the Masoretic text (cf. NASB). Since God is speaking in
the context, some prefer to read an imperatival form (*zᵉpaḥ*),
which is presupposed by the Septuagint, Aquila, and Theodotion
(cf. NIV). This reading, while preserving the wordplay with verse
3, demands a different force for it, namely, the people should
have experienced a reversal in their attitude, demonstrating the
same antipathy for their idols as they had for what is good. However, the reading of the Masoretic text, though the more difficult
one, is not impossible. Elsewhere in Hosea third person references to God occur in divine speeches rather frequently (cf. 1:7; 4:6,
10, 12; 8:13–14). Another possibility is to emend to a first person
form (cf. the apparatus of *Biblia Hebraica Stuttgartensia*) or re-
point it as an infinitive absolute functioning as a finite verb (cf.
Francis I. Andersen and David Noel Freedman, *Hosea,* Anchor
Bible [Garden City, NY: Doubleday, 1980], p. 494).

5. The translation is that of Leslie C. Allen, *The Books of Joel,
    Obadiah, Jonah and Micah,* New International Commentary on
    the Old Testament (Grand Rapids: Eerdmans, 1976), p. 334.

6. The verb *ʾāsap* is used elsewhere in harvesting/threshing con-
    texts (cf. Ex. 23:10, 16; Lev. 23:39; 25:3, 20; Deut. 11:14;
    16:13; 28:38; Job 39:12; Isa. 17:5; Jer. 40:10, 12). Note also the
    use of the related noun *ʾōsep* in Micah 7:1.

7. For further discussion of the wordplay here, see Hans Walter
    Wolff, *Joel and Amos* (Philadelphia: Fortress, 1977), pp. 197–
    98; James Luther Mays, *Amos* (Philadelphia: Westminster, 1969),
    p. 67; and Gerhard Hasel, *The Remnant,* Andrews University
    Monographs, Studies in Religion 5, 3d ed. (Berrien Springs,
    MI: Andrews University Press, 1980), pp. 180–81.

8. This is the meaning given in Francis Brown, S. R. Driver, and
    Charles A. Briggs, *A Hebrew and English Lexicon of the Old Tes-
    tament* (Oxford: Clarendon, 1907), p. 705. They relate the word to
    the root *sph*, an *s/ś* interchange being proposed. Walter Baumgart-
    ner offers the meaning "lawbreaking" (*Rechtsbruch*), deriving the
    word from the root *pśh* (a metathesis of *p/ś*; being proposed for
    miśpāḥ). See his *Hebräisches und aramäisches Lexikon zum Alten
    Testament,* 3 vols. (Leiden: Brill, 1967–83), p. 606.

9. For further discussion of the poetic justice theme in these vers-
    es, see Patrick D. Miller, Jr., *Sin and Judgment in the Prophets,*
    Society of Biblical Literature Monograph Series 27 (Chico, CA:
    Scholars, 1982), pp. 29–31.

10. Brown, Driver, and Briggs, *A Hebrew and English Lexicon of
    the Old Testament,* pp. 266–67. Baumgartner takes the root as
    zrr, rather than *zwr* (*Hebräisches und aramäisches Lexikon zum*

Alten Testament, p. 272). In this case the root would still be virtually homonymic to *zûr*, "be a stranger."

11. For further discussion of the relationship between wordplay and the theme of poetic justice in this passage, see Miller, *Sin and Judgment in the Prophets,* p. 23.

12. For a list of these, see Watson, *Classical Hebrew Poetry: A Guide to Its Techniques,* pp. 245–46.

Chapter 10

1. See Leland Ryken, *How to Read the Bible as Literature* (Grand Rapids: Zondervan, 1984), esp. pp. 11–32.

2. Studies dealing with the definition and method of biblical rhetorical criticism include among others the following: James Muilenburg, "Form Criticism and Beyond," *Journal of Biblical Literature* 88 (1969): 1–18; David Greenwood, "Rhetorical Criticism and Formgeschichte: Some Methodological Considerations," *Journal of Biblical Literature* 89 (1970): 418–26; Martin Kessler, "A Methodological Setting for Rhetorical Criticism," *Semitics* 4 (1974): 22–36; idem, "An Introduction to Rhetorical Criticism of the Bible: Prolegomena," *Semitics* 7 (1980): 1–27; Isaac M. Kikawada, "Some Proposals for the Definition of Rhetorical Criticism," *Semitics* 5 (1977): 67–91; Yehoshua Gitay, *Prophecy and Persuasion* (Bonn: Linguistica Biblica, 1981). esp. pp. 34–49; George A. Kennedy, *New Testament Interpretation through Rhetorical Criticism* (Chapel Hill, NC: University of North Carolina Press, 1984), esp. pp. 3–38; and N. J. Tromp, "Amos 5:1–17: Towards a Stylistic and Rhetorical Analysis," *Oudtestamentische Studiën* 23 (1984): 56–84.

3. Such an approach is illustrated by the work of Muilenburg and his followers. In describing rhetorical criticism Muilenburg stated, "What I am interested in, above all, is in understanding the nature of Hebrew literary composition, in exhibiting the structural patterns that are employed for the fashioning of a literary unit . . . and in discerning the many and varied devices by which the predications are formulated and ordered into a unified whole" ("Form Criticism and Beyond," p. 8). Several studies by his followers are collected in Jared J. Jackson and Martin Kessler, eds., *Rhetorical Criticism: Essays in Honor of James Muilenburg* (Pittsburgh: Pickwick, 1974).

4. For examples of such studies see the works of Gitay, Kennedy, and Tromp mentioned in note 2. For a brief comparison of the two basic approaches mentioned here, see Gitay, *Prophecy and Persuasion,* p. 27.

5. Gitay, *Prophecy and Persuasion*, p. 45.
6. On the subject of the oral character of ancient texts, see Yehoshua Gitay, "Deutero-Isaiah: Oral or Written?" *Journal of Biblical Literature* 99 (1980): 190–97; H. van Dyke Parunak, "Some Axioms for Literary Architecture," *Semitics* 8 (1982): 2–4; and Kennedy, *New Testament Interpretation through Rhetorical Criticism*, pp. 5–6.
7. See Herbert M. Wolf, "Implications of Form Criticism for Old Testament Studies," *Bibliotheca Sacra* 127 (1970): 299–307.
8. See the critiques offered by Muilenburg, "Form Criticism and Beyond," pp. 1–7; Greenwood, "Rhetorical Criticism and Formgeschichte: Some Methodological Considerations," pp. 418–26; and Rolf Knierim, "Old Testament Form Criticism Reconsidered, " *Interpretation* 27 (1973): 435–68.
9. The limits proposed are well defined. Verses 8–30 are clearly structurally distinct from the preceding "song of the vineyard" (5:1–7) and the following call narrative (chap. 6).
10. On this positive, persuasive goal of chapters 1–12 as a whole, see Yehoshua Gitay, "Isaiah and His Audience," *Prooftexts* 3 (1983): 223–30.
11. For example see Edward J. Young, *The Book of Isaiah*, 3 vols. (Grand Rapids: Eerdmans, 1965, 1969, 1972), 1:205–6; Hans Wildberger, *Jesaja 1–12*, Biblischer Kommentar, Altes Testament, 2d ed. (Neukirchen-Vluyn: Neukirchener, 1980), pp. 181–82; Ronald E. Clements, *Isaiah 1–39*, New Century Bible Commentary (Grand Rapids: Eerdmans, 1980), pp. 60–66; Otto Kaiser, *Isaiah 1–12*, Old Testament Library, 2d ed. (Philadelphia: Westminster, 1983), pp. 96–109. Isaiah 10:1–4, also introduced by הוי, is often combined with 5:8–24 to produce a series of seven woes. At the same time, 5:25–30 is frequently combined with 9:8–21 (Heb. vv. 7–20) because of the refrain in 5:25b, which appears as well in 9:12, 17, 21. Finally, several verses within 5:8–24 are considered to be later interpolations, though commentators often disagree on which are to be so labeled. As stated later in this chapter, a rhetorical analysis of the passage makes these conclusions, based on the methods of form and redaction criticism, highly suspect.
12. The literature on woe oracles is quite extensive, including among others: Claus Westermann, *Basic Forms of Prophetic Speech* (London: Lutterworth, 1967), pp. 190–94, Erhard Gerstenberger, "The Woe-Oracles of the Prophets," *Journal of Biblical Literature* 81 (1962): 249–63; Richard J. Clifford, "The Use of *Hôy* in the Prophets," *Catholic Biblical Quarterly* 28 (1966):

458–64; James G. Williams, "The Alas-Oracles of the Eighth Century Prophets," *Hebrew Union College Annual* 38 (1967): 75–91; Waldemar Janzen, *Mourning Cry and Woe Oracle* (Berlin: de Gruyter, 1972); and Ronald E. Clements, "The Form and Character of Prophetic Woe Oracles," *Semitics* 8 (1982): 17–29.

13. Westermann, *Basic Forms of Prophetic Speech*, p. 190.

14. Ibid., pp. 142–61, 169–87.

15. Verse 8, introduced by הוֹי, is an accusation against the wealthy Judean landowners, while judgment on this same group is announced in verses 9–10. In verses 11–12 another accusation appears, while verses 13–17 contain the accompanying announcement of judgment (note לָכֵן, "therefore," at the beginning of v. 13). In the sixth oracle verses 22–23 are accusatory; in verse 24a (introduced by לָכֵן) judgment is announced.

16. Clements, *Isaiah 1–39*, pp. 64–65.

17. Kaiser, *Isaiah 1–12*, pp. 96–109.

18. Parunak points out "that more than one pattern may be active simultaneously in a passage" ("Some Axioms for Literary Architecture." p. 10). He adds that these alternate patterns may be concurrent with or embedded in another (pp. 10–12). Parunak also points out that chiasmus is one of the basic structural patterns in oral literature (pp. 7–10; see also his "Oral Typesetting: Some Uses of Biblical Structure," *Biblica* 62 [1981]: 153–68).

19. Kaiser speaks of a "circular composition" in the arrangement of woes, though he sees 10:1–2, which in his scheme is the seventh in the list, as corresponding to 5:8. He notes that both are concerned with "transgressors of the law." He sees this same theme in verse 23, which he places after verse 20, making it fourth in the list (*Isaiah 1–12*, pp. 96–97). The chiasmus is apparent as the text stands; one need not rearrange verses or import passages from other chapters as Kaiser has done.

20. Ibid., p. 100. The incident recorded in 1 Kings 21, though occurring at an earlier date (9th century B.C.) and in a different place (the Northern Kingdom), provides a vivid illustration of how these "land deals" may have worked. For a detailed study of the socioeconomic setting of Isaiah 5:8–10, see Eryl Davies, *Prophecy and Ethics* (Sheffield: JSOT, 1981), pp. 65–89.

21. Cf. Kaiser, *Isaiah 1–12*, p. 100. On the importance of the Lord's ownership of the land to Old Testament thought, see Christopher J. H. Wright, *An Eye for an Eye* (Downers Grove, IL: InterVarsity, 1983), pp. 46–62.

22. On the relationship between the judicial system and socioeconomic exploitation in ancient Israel, see Davies, *Prophecy and*

Ethics, pp. 90–112.

23. In verse 13 the scope expands to include the entire nation (cf. "My people"), though the nobility (the focus of attention in vv. 8–12) may still be singled out for special consideration (cf. כְּבוֹדוֹ, "its [the nation's] glory," which possibly refers to the upper crust of society in contrast to its masses, to which הֲמוֹנוֹ probably refers here).

24. The word הִרְחִיבָה is a prophetic perfect, followed up by two perfects (with *waw* consecutive) carrying a specific future nuance. Cf. E. Kautzsch, ed., *Gesenius' Hebrew Grammar*, 2d Eng. ed. (Oxford: Clarendon, 1910), p. 333 (sec. 112s). In verses 15–16 the *yiqtōl* forms (with *waw* consecutive) also have a future sense (note the imperfect תִּשְׁפַּלְנָה in v. 15b; cf. ibid., p. 329, sec. 111w). With וְרָעוּ (perfect with *waw* consecutive) in verse 17 the author returns to the pattern of verse 14.

25. The carousers are not specifically identified as the subject in verse 14b, but הֲדָרָהּ, "its [prob. Jerusalem's] splendor," probably alludes to them (the contrasting הֲמוֹנָהּ, "its teeming masses," follows). The words שְׁאוֹנָהּ, "its uproar," and עָלֵז, "the one who exults," probably refer to the revelry described in verses 11–12 (both roots are used in 24:8, where drunken revelry is clearly in view).

26. For this same picture of death as having a voracious appetite, see Proverbs 30:15–16 and Habakkuk 2:5. The background for the imagery can be found in Canaanite myth, where deified Death is pictured as one who opens his mouth wide to swallow his hapless victims. See J. C. L. Gibson, *Canaanite Myths and Legends*, 2d ed. (Edinburgh: Clark, 1978), pp. 68–69, for a particularly illustrative text in this regard.

27. The Masoretic text has גָּרִים, a participle, "resident aliens," in verse 17b (cf. NASB, "strangers"). This reading would make sense contextually since the גֵרִים are often mentioned as oppressed elements in society. The picture is that of the oppressed outliving their oppressors. However, tighter parallelism is achieved (cf. כְבָשִׂים, "lambs," in v. 17a) if the word is גְּדָיִים, "kids" (this word occurs twice in the construct . . . , but note the absolute form in 1 Sam. 10:3)

28. This writer understands מֵחִים, "fatlings," as a genitive of possession following the construct חָרְבוֹת, "ruins" (which is an adverbial accusative of location here). Attested elsewhere only in Psalm 66:15, מֵחַ is used of sacrificial animals. Here it is apparently a derogatory reference to the well-fed, rich carousers (cf. Amos 4:1 for similar imagery) who, ironically, are devoured by Sheol as if they were sacrificial animals.

29. See note 11.

30. On the theme of appropriate punishment in these verses, see Patrick D. Miller, Jr., *Sin and Judgment in the Prophets* (Chico, CA: Scholars, 1982), pp. 42–43.

31. On the irony inherent in their arrogant words, see Edwin M. Good, *Irony in the Old Testament* (Philadelphia: Westminster, 1965), pp. 119–20.

32. For some of the literature on the woe oracles, see note 12. Among the proposed backgrounds for the oracle are popular wisdom (Gerstenberger), curse formulae (Westermann), and mourning rites (Clifford, Williams, Janzen).

33. Also see Jeremiah 22:18; 34:5; Amos 5:16.

34. This need not imply that the prophet experienced psychological sorrow over the impending death of the sinners. Ritual mourning was an accepted practice in the biblical world, even to the point that professionals were hired. On this point Clifford writes, "When the prophet hears of impending disaster from Yahweh, he utters a ritual *hôy* in automatic lament, a cry borrowed from the funeral customs of his milieu. The prophet need not feel a psychological drive, but only an 'ontological' one—the situation demands it" ("The Use of *Hôy* in the Prophets," p. 464).

35. Cf. Williams, "The Alas-Oracles of the Eighth Century Prophets," p. 86.

36. The technical term for this device is *hypotyposis* (E. W. Bullinger, *Figures of Speech Used in the Bible* [1898; reprint, Grand Rapids: Baker, 1968], pp. 444–45).

37. Cf. Wildberger, *Jesaja 1–12*, pp. 223–24.

38. Note the appearance of the phrases מֵרָחֹק and מִקְצֵה הָאָרֶץ in both Deuteronomy 28:49 and Isaiah 5:26.

39. The description is, of course, hyperbolic, but also quite realistic in many respects, as a comparison with Assyrian sculpture (which has its hyperbolic elements as well) indicates. On the sculptural evidence, see Julian Reade, "The Neo-Assyrian Court and Army: Evidence from the Sculptures," *Iraq* 34 (1972): 87–112.

40. Public awareness of Assyrian military power and practice would have steadily increased from around 743 B.C. due to increased Assyrian military involvement in the west during the last half of the 8th century B.C. The precise date of origin for Isaiah 5:8–30 is not known. Even if originally proclaimed early in Isaiah's career, it was probably repeated and/or recalled periodically. The description in verses 26–30 would have been especially effective in conjunction with or after Tiglath-pileser's campaign against Damascus and Samaria (ca. 734–732), which reduced the latter to a puppet state, the conquest of Samaria (722), Sar-

gon's Ashdod campaign of 712, and Sennacherib's invasion of
Judah (701).
41. Daniel D. Luckenbill, *Ancient Records of Assyria and Babylonia,* 2 vols. (Chicago: University of Chicago Press, 1926–27),
2:27 (par. 56).
42. Ibid., 2:126 (par. 253).
43. Clements, *Isaiah 1–39,* p. 70.
44. Luckenbill, *Ancient Records of Assyria and Babylonia,* 2:94
(par. 171).
45. Ibid., 2:89 (par. 163). Cf. Sennacherib's description of the invading Elamite army (2:126, par. 252): "Like the onset of the
locust swarms of the springtime they kept steadily coming on
against me to offer battle. With the dust of their feet covering
the wide heavens, like a mighty storm with (its) masses of dense
clouds, they drew up in battle array."
46. Peter Machinist explores this possibility in "Assyria and Its Image
in the First Isaiah," *Journal of the American Oriental Society* 103
(1983): 719–37. He concludes that Assyrian propaganda did influence Isaiah's view of Assyria, though he recognizes that general
ancient Near Eastern use may account for similarities (note esp. his
reservations with respect to the "lion" imagery of Isa. 5:29, pp.
728–29). He discusses possible ways in which Judeans like Isaiah
could have become aware of Assyrian propaganda (pp. 728–34).

Chapter 11

1. Eugene H. Merrill, "Survey of a Century of Studies on Isaiah
40–55," *Bibliotheca Sacra* 144 (January–March 1987): 24–43.
2. Hugo Gressmann, "Die literarische Analyse Deuterojesajas," *Zeitschrift
für die alttestamentliche Wissenschaft* 34 (1914): 284–95.
3. Ibid., pp. 286–87.
4. Isaiah 44:23; 45:8; 45:15–17; 48:20–21; 49:13; 50:2b–3; 51:3;
52:9–10; 54:1–3.
5. Isaiah 40:12–16; 42:10–13.
6. Sigmund Mowinckel, *The Psalms in Israel's Worship,* trans.
D. R. Ap-Thomas, 2 vols. (Nashville: Abingdon, 1962), 1:81–105.
Also see A. A. Anderson, *The Book of Psalms,* New Century
Bible, 2 vols. (Greenwood, SC: Attic, 1972), pp. 32–36; Artur
Weiser, *The Psalms: A Commentary,* trans. Herbert Hartwell
(Philadelphia: Westminster, 1962), pp. 52–66; Hermann Gunkel,
The Psalms: A Form-Critical Introduction, trans. Thomas M.
Horner (Philadelphia: Fortress, 1967), pp. 10–13; and Claus
Westermann, *The Praise of God in the Psalms,* trans. K. Crim
(Richmond, VA: Knox, 1965).

7. Mowinckel, *Psalms*, p. 93; cf. p. 97. H. E. von Waldow limits the self-praise of God to only Isaiah in the Old Testament but points out that it is well known in the Mesopotamian world ("The Message of Deutero-Isaiah," *Interpretation* 22 [1968]: 273, n. 46).

8. James Muilenburg, "The Book of Isaiah. Chapters 40–66," in *The Interpreter's Bible*, ed. G. A. Buttrick, 12 vols. (New York: Abingdon, 1956), 5:390.

9. Claus Westermann, *Isaiah 40–66: A Commentary*, trans. David M. G. Stalker (Philadelphia: Westminster, 1969), p. 102.

10. Frank Crüsemann, *Studien zur Formgeschichte von Hymnus und Danklied im Israel* (Neukirchen-Vluyn: Neukirchener, 1969), pp. 40–49.

11. Lynne M. Deming, "Hymnic Language in Deutero-Isaiah: The Calls to Praise and Their Function in the Book" (Ph.D. diss., Emory University, 1978).

12. Ibid., pp. 82–84.

13. Ibid., pp. 138–48.

14. Ibid., pp. 154–66.

15. Ibid., p. 174. See also von Waldow, "The Message of Deutero–Isaiah," p. 269.

16. This is the well-chosen term used by Antoon Schoors to describe the trial speech *(Gerichtsrede)* and disputation *(Streitgesprach)*. See his work, *I Am God Your Saviour: A Form-Critical Study of the Main Genres in Is. XL-LV* (Leiden: Brill, 1973), p. 176.

17. Ralph W. Klein, *Israel in Exile: A Theological Interpretation* (Philadelphia: Fortress, 1979), p. 101; see also Westermann, *Isaiah 40–66: A Commentary*, p. 63.

18. Ibid.

19. Gressmann, "Die literarische Analyse Deuterojesajas," pp. 254–97.

20. Ludwig Köhler, "Deuterojesaja stilkritisch untersucht," *Beihefte zur Zeitschrift für die alttestamentliche Wissenschaft* 37 (1923).

21. Hermann Gunkel and Joachim Begrich, *Einleitung im die Psalmen: Die Gattungen der religiösen Lyrik Israels* (Göttingen: Vandenhoeck & Ruprecht, 1933), pp. 364–65.

22. H. E. von Waldow, *Anlass und Hintergrund der Verkündigung des Deuterojesaja* (Ph.D. diss., Bonn University, 1953). Also see his "The Message of Dt.-Is.," *Interpretation* 22 (1968): 259–87.

23. Julien Harvey, "Le 'Rib-Pattern', Requisitoire prophetique sur la rupture de l'Alliance," *Biblica* 43 (1962): 172–96. Also see J. Limburg, "The Root ריב and the Prophetic Lawsuit Speeches," *Journal of Biblical Literature* 88 (1969): 304.

24. Berend Gemser, "The *RIB*—or Controversy—Pattern in Hebrew Mentality," *Vetus Testamentum* Supplement 3 (1955): 128.
25. Ibid., p. 131.
26. Schoors, *I Am God Your Saviour*, p. 181 and *passim*.
27. Ibid., p. 188.
28. Ibid., p. 244. Also see Kirsten Nielsen, *Yahweh as Prosecutor and Judge: An Investigation of the Prophetic Lawsuit (Rib-Pattern)*, trans. Frederick Cryer, *JSOT* Supplement 9 (Sheffield: JSOT, 1978), p. 73.
29. Ibid., p. 239.
30. Roy Melugin, *The Formation of Isaiah 40–55* (New York: de Gruyter, 1976), pp. 57–58.
31. Ibid., p. 47.
32. Nielsen, *Yahweh as Prosecutor and Judge.*
33. See Westermann, *Isaiah*, p. 63.
34. Nielsen, *Yahweh as Prosecutor and Judge*, p. 67.
35. This is not a disputation in the formal sense, for as virtually all scholars have noted this is a classic trial speech.
36. Ibid., p. 69.
37. Schoors, *I Am God Your Saviour*, p. 188.
38. Isaiah 40:26, 28; 45:12.
39. Isaiah 46:9–10; 48:3.
40. Isaiah 40:12–14, 22–23; 44:24–26a; 48:12–14a.
41. Isaiah 40:15–17, 19–20, 21–24, 26; 48:5b, 14a.
42. Isaiah 40:27–31; 48:1–11; 55:8–13.
43. Melugin, *The Formation of Isaiah 40–55*, p. 44.
44. J. Begrich, "Das priesterliche Heilsorakel," *Zeitschrift für die alttestamentliche Wissenschaft* 52 (1934): 81–92.
45. Ibid., p. 82.
46. Melugin, *The Formation of Isaiah 40–55*, pp. 13–14.
47. P. B. Harner, "The Salvation Oracle in Second Isaiah," *Journal of Biblical Literature* 88 (1969): 418–34.
48. Ibid., p. 419. Another important study by H. E. von Waldow recognizes three parts to the body of the oracle: (a) the intervention of God in which He is the grammatical subject speaking in the first person; (b) the consequences of God's intervention in which God is no longer the subject; and (c) the objective of God's intervention, usually His honor or recognition ("The Message of Deutero-Isaiah," *Interpretation* 22 [1968], pp. 266–67).
49. Ibid., pp. 430, 434. It is well to heed Dion's reminder, however, that the typical formulae of the salvation oracle are found as early as the Zakir stele of the 8th century, though, indeed, they are more common and refined in the 7th-century oracles to

Esarhaddon and Ashurbanipal (P. E. Dion, "The Patriarchal Traditions and the Literary Form of the 'Oracle of Salvation,'" *Catholic Biblical Quarterly* 29 [1967]: 200–201).

50. Schoors, *I Am God Your Saviour*, p. 47.
51. Ibid., pp. 33–34.
52. Claus Westermann, "Das Heilswort bei Deutero-jesaja," *Evangelische Theologie* 7 (1964): 355–75. Cf. also von Waldow, who fails to see this distinction because it involves two kinds of *Sitz im Leben,* private and public penitence, for which von Waldow can find no basis ("The Message of Deutero-Isaiah," pp. 266–68).
53. Westermann, "Das Heilswort bei Deutero-jesaja," pp. 365–67.
54. Ibid., pp. 365–66; Westermann, *Isaiah,* pp. 13–14.
55. Schoors, *I Am God Your Saviour*, pp. 297–98.

Chapter 12

1. This article follows Watson's terminology. A "poem" is an alphabetic unit; a "stanza" is a subsection of the poem; a "strophe" is one or more cola; a "colon" is a single line of poetry (W. G. E. Watson, *Classical Hebrew Poetry*, JSOT Supplement 26 [Sheffield: JSOT, 1984], pp. 7, 12–15; see also pp. 190–200).
2. A fourth line appears in 1:7 and in 2:19. While some excise the lines, S. J. Renkema defends their integrity ("The Literary Structure of Lamentations," in *The Structural Analysis of Biblical and Canaanite Poetry,* ed. W. van der Meer and J. C. de Moor, JSOT Supplement 74 [Sheffield: JSOT, 1988], p. 316). Freedman is cautious and shows the possibility of their validity (David Noel Freedman, *Poetry, Pottery and Prophecy* [Winona Lake, IN: Eisenbrauns, 1980], pp. 64–65).
3. Norman K. Gottwald, *Studies in the Book of Lamentations,* Studies in Biblical Theology 14 (London: SCM, 1954), p. 30.
4. More recently Iain Provan displays an excessive skepticism as to what can be known about the historical setting of the book (*Lamentations,* New Century Bible Commentary [Grand Rapids: Eerdmans, 1991], pp. 11–12).
5. Delbert R. Hillers, *Lamentations,* Anchor Bible (Garden City, NY: Doubleday, 1972), p. 370. Gordis writes, "The book consists of five elegies, three of which (chaps. 1, 2, 4) are laments on the burning of the Temple and the destruction of Jerusalem by the Babylonians, as well as on the national devastation that followed the calamities of 587 B.C.E." (Robert Gordis, "A Commentary on the Text of Lamentations," *Jewish Quarterly Review* [1967]: 267).
6. Renkema, "The Literary Structure of Lamentations," pp. 390–91. Working from a different point of view, Marcus agrees (David

Marcus, "Non-Recurring Doublets in the Book of Lamentations," *Hebrew Annual Review* 10 [1986]: 177–94).

7. See, for example, Renkema, "The Literary Structure of Lamentations," p. 333. As Renkema acknowledges, much of his work on chapters 1 and 2 was done by A. Condamin ("Symmetrical Repetitions in *Lamentations* Chapters I and II," *Journal of Theological Studies* 7 [1906]: 137–40), though Renkema cites him from his *Poèmes de la Bible*.

8. Gottwald, *Studies in the Book of Lamentations*, p. 111. Dahood remarks that "the textual discoveries at Ras Shamra-Ugarit in 1929 on revealed a highly refined and elliptical poetry around 1350 B.C., the poetic matrix from which biblical poetry took its origins. Now the recovery of the Ebla tablets of circa 2500 B.C. carries the Canaanite literary tradition back into the third millennium. With this long literary tradition at their disposition, biblical poets surely possessed a formation and technical capacity that modern critics underestimate at their own peril" (Mitchell Dahood, "New Readings in Lamentations," *Biblica* 59 [1978]: 197). Marcus argues for 183 doublets that he believes lend credence to the idea of one author and to the sophistication of the poet ("Non-Recurring Doublets in the Book of Lamentations").

9. For a similar discussion on chapter 1 and the structure of the book, see Bo Johnson, "Form and Message in Lamentations," *Zeitschrift für alttestamentliche Wissenschaft* 97 (1985): 58–73.

10. The phrase, "Our fathers sinned, and are no more. It is we who have borne their iniquities" (5:7), goes against this statement. However, according to Hillers, "fathers" could refer to the sins of the prophets and priests and to the sinful policy of foreign alliances (Delbert Hillers, "History and Poetry in Lamentations," *Currents in Theology and Missions* 10 [1983]: 161). Renkema argues for a similar interpretation ("The Literary Structure of Lamentations," p. 357, n.). Brunet agrees, but from a different point of view: These weepers are probably sons of men who belonged to the old party in power. They are expiating their fathers' sins (Gilbert Brunet, "La Cinquième Lamentation," *Vetus Testamentum* 33 [1983]: 149–70).

11. See Walter Brueggemann for an excellent discussion of the place of lament in the approach of the lesser member of the covenant to the greater ("The Costly Loss of Lament," *Journal for the Study of the Old Testament* 36 [1986]: 57–71).

12. The language changes at 1:12, thus providing a natural break apart from alphabetic considerations. See Hillers, *Lamentations*, pp. 17, 25, for the outline.

13. Renkema, "The Literary Structure of Lamentations," p. 297.

14. Renkema argues for a detailed interdependence of the book that is arranged concentrically. Ultimately he focuses on chapter 3 as presenting the main theme of the book ("The Literary Structure of Lamentations," pp. 321–24).

15. Brunet argues that the first four laments were composed, not by Jeremiah, who was opposed to the corrupt leadership, but by a member of the aristocracy writing between the fall of Jerusalem in 586 and its destruction by Nebuzaradan. He further believes it was the high priest Seraiah who was executed by the Chaldeans after the liquidation of the provisional regime and the destruction of the city (2 Kings 25:18–21; Jer. 52:24–27) (Brunet, "La Cinquième Lamentation," pp. 149–70). However, Jeremiah, not the aristocracy, suffered this way (the priest Pashhur abused Jeremiah by putting him in the stocks, Jer. 20:1–6).

16. Six strophes each use the same word twice (vv. 7, 9; 19, 20; 29, 30; 43, 44; 49, 51; 59, 60).

17. Some argue that Jeremiah's antipathy toward efforts to acquire Egyptian help and toward King Zedekiah show that Jeremiah could not have written these verses, but he or any other poet may simply have been joining in the lament of the people.

18. Renkema, "The Literary Structure of Lamentations," pp. 365–66.

19. Hillers refers to verse 19 as a "little hymn-like verse." He says, "Even in the deepest trouble Israel did not forget to hymn God's praises" (*Lamentations*, pp. 105–6).

20. As stated in note 2, Lamentations 1:7 and 2:19 have four lines each, thus making a total of 67 lines for both of those chapters.

21. Bergler agrees with Bickel that chapter 5 is used simply as the conclusion of the acrostics of chapters 1–4 (S. Bergler, "Threni V—nur ein alphabetisierendes Lied? Versuch einer Deutung," *Vetus Testamentum* 37 [1977]: 304–20). Landy, however, says, "The discourse attempts to explain, illustrate, and thus mitigate the catastrophe, to house it in a familiar literary framework; it must also communicate its own inadequacy. Its success, in a sense, depends on its failure. This happens, for example, if a poem fades out in a whimper or an ineffectual cry for revenge, and it has to recognize the silence that exhausts it, the power of the enemy, and the necessity of starting again" (F. Landy, "Lamentations," in *The Literary Guide to the Bible,* ed. Robert Alter and Frank Kermode [London: Collins, 1987], 329).

22. Hillers, *Lamentations*, pp. 100–101.

23. Robert Gordis, "Critical Notes: The Conclusion of the Book of Lamentations (5:22)," *Journal of Biblical Literature* 93 (1974): 289–93.

24. Kennicott shows that four Hebrew manuscripts have changed 2:16–17 to their normal alphabetical order; two manuscripts have done the same with 3:46–51; and five manuscripts have done so with 4:16–17. There is no evidence that 1:16–17 was changed from the normal order existing in the Masoretic text to the reversed order of chapters 2–4 (B. Kennicott, *Vetus Testamentum; cum Variis Lectionibus,* 2 vols. [Oxford: Clarendon, 1880]). Ziegler indicates that the Septuagint follows the Masoretic text, but that the inverted units in chapters 2 and 3 have been returned to the correct order in Syh, L', Arm=Pesch (J. Ziegler, *Ieremias, Baruch, Threni, Epistula Ieremiae,* 15 in Septuaginta, Vetus Testamentum Graecum, Auctoritate Societatis Litterarum Gottingensis [Göttingen: Vandenhoeck & Ruprecht, 1957]). There are no Septuagint variants on 4:16–17. Thus it seems that the *peh* before *'ayin* order in chapters 2–4 is original.

25. Hillers, *Lamentations,* p. xxvii.

26. H. Wiesmann, *Die Klagelieder* (Frankfurt: Philosophischtheologische Hochschule Sankt Georgen, 1954), pp. 32–33.

27. Provan (*Lamentations,* p. 4) cites Frank Cross ("Newly Found Inscriptions in Old Canaanite and Early Phoenician Scripts," *Bulletin of the American Schools of Oriental Research* 238 [1980]: 1–20) for the inversion of these letters in extrabiblical inscriptions. However, the nature of the 'Izbet Ṣarṭah ostracon precludes its use as an example. Cross himself does not mention the order.

28. Hillers, *Lamentations,* p. xxvii.

29. Wiesmann is not entirely fair with Boehmer's argument (J. Boehmer, "Ein alphabetisch-akrostichisches Rätsel und ein Versuch es zu lösen," *Zeitschrift für die alttestamentliche Wissenschaft* 28 [1908]: 53–57). Boehmer shows that by combining each letter with its following (e.g., אב "father"; גד, "luck"; etc.), a meaning can be found everywhere except where ס, ע, פ, and צ occur. By inverting *'ayin* and *peh,* meanings can be derived for each form.

30. Wiesmann, *Die Klagelieder,* p. 33.

31. Gottwald, *Studies in the Book of Lamentations,* p. 53.

32. Hedwig Jahnow, *Das hebräische Leichenlied im Rahmen der Völkerdichtung* (Giessen: Töpelmann, 1923).

33. Gottwald, *Studies in the Book of Lamentations,* p. 53.

34. This process theoretically could have begun in the *'ayin* strophe of chapter 1. There the triumph of the enemy is stated (1:16) followed by the futility of Zion's plea (v. 17). The phrase "because of these

things" (עַל־אֵלֶּה) gives a conclusion to the preceding section. Perhaps for this reason the writer chose not to invert it.

Chapter 13

1. *Notes on Some Problems in the Book of Daniel* (London: Tyndale, 1965).
2. Edwin R. Thiele, *A Chronology of the Hebrew Kings* (Grand Rapids: Zondervan, 1977), p. 68, n. 3.
3. L. F. Hartman and A. Di Lella, *The Book of Daniel*, Anchor Bible (Garden City, NY: Doubleday, 1978), p. 123.
4. Wiseman et al., *Notes on Some Problems in the Book of Daniel*, pp. 16–18.
5. Hartman and Di Lella, *The Book of Daniel*, p. 48.
6. A. R. Millard, "Daniel 1–6 and History," *Evangelical Quarterly* 49 (1977): 69; and Joyce G. Baldwin, *Daniel: An Introduction and Commentary* (Downers Grove, IL: InterVarsity, 1978), pp. 19–21.
7. Martin McNamara, "Nabonidus and the Book of Daniel," *Irish Theological Quarterly* 37 (1970): 132.
8. Wiseman et al., *Notes on Some Problems in the Book of Daniel*, p. 18.
9. D. J. Wiseman and Edwin M. Yamauchi, *Archaeology and the Bible* (Grand Rapids: Zondervan, 1979), p. 50.
10. In a review of A. K. Grayson, *Assyrian and Babylonian Chronicles* in *Bibliotheca Orientalis* 34 (1977): 336; and Baldwin, *Daniel: An Introduction and Commentary*, p. 35.
11. P.-R. Berger, "Der Kyros-Zylinder . . . und die akkadischen Personennamen im Danielbuch," *Zeitschrift für Assyriologie* 64 (1975): 224–34; and Millard, "Daniel 1–6 and History," p. 72.
12. W. G. Lambert, "Nebuchadnezzar King of Justice," *Iraq* 27 (1965): 8.
13. Archer, "Modern Rationalism and the Book of Daniel," pp. 136–37; and Baldwin, *Daniel: An Introduction and Commentary*, p. 29.
14. Millard, "Daniel 1–6 and History," p. 70.
15. Cited by J. A. Brinkman, *A Political History of Post-Kassite Babylonia 1158–722 B.C.* (Rome: Pontificium Institutum Biblicum, 1968), p. 227.
16. Ibid., pp. 226–27.
17. Franz Cumont, *Astrology and Religion among the Greeks and Romans* (1912; reprint, New York: Dover, 1960), p. 16; and G. Messina, *Der Ursprung der Magier und die zarathuštriche Religion* (Rome: Pontificio Instituto Biblico, 1930).
18. Leonard Woolley and M. E. L. Mallowan, *Ur Excavations IX:*

The Neo-Babylonian and Persian Periods (London: British Museum, 1962), p. 24.

19. Yamauchi, *Greece and Babylon*, p. 79. McNamara, observes, "The Harran Inscription of Nabonidus, narrating his Taima sojourn, changes abruptly from the first to the third person, just as Daniel 4 . . . does" ("Nabonidus and the Book of Daniel," p. 137).

20. Gerhard F. Hasel, "The First and Third Years of Belshazzar (Dan. 7:1; 8:1)," *Andrews University Seminary Studies* 15 (1977): 153–68.

21. It is most improbable that such an unflattering episode would ever have been recorded in royal documents.

22. McNamara, "Nabonidus and the Book of Daniel," p. 134.

23. L. Hartman, "The Great Tree and Nobuchodonosor's Madness," in *The Bible in Current Catholic Thought*, ed. J. L. McKenzie (New York: Herder and Herder, 1962), p. 77; and J. C. Lebram, "Perspektiven der gegenwärtigen Danielforschung," *Journal for the Study of Judaism* 5 (1974): 7–8.

24. J. T. Milik, "Prière de Nabonide," *Revue Biblique* 63 (1956): 407–15.

25. Among the many studies of this text, see R. Meyer, *Das Gebet des Nabonid* (Berlin: Akademie-Verlag, 1962); Alfred Mertens, *Das Buch Daniel im Lichte der Texte vom Toten Meer* (Echter: Katholisches Bibelwerk, 1971), pp. 34–42; and B. Jongeling, C. J. Labauschagne, and A. S. van der Woude, *Aramaic Texts from Qumran I* (Leiden: Brill, 1976), pp. 123–31 (these pages reproduce the Aramaic text).

26. Jongeling, Labauschagne, and van der Woude, *Aramaic Texts from Qumran I*, p. 124.

27. David N. Freedman, "The Prayer of Nabonidus," *Bulletin of the American Schools of Oriental Research* 145 (1957): 31–32.

28. Edwin M. Yamauchi, *The Stones and the Scriptures* (Philadelphia: Lippincott, 1972), p. 89; and Yamauchi, *Greece and Babylon*, p. 89, n. 149.

29. Isaac Jerusalmi, *The Aramaic Sections of Ezra and Daniel* (Cincinnati: Hebrew Union College, 1970), p. 100; and Ernestus Vogt, *Lexicon Linguae Aramaicae Veteris Testamenti* (Rome: Pontificium Institutum Biblicum, 1971), p. 124.

30. For discussion of a modern case of lycanthropy, see R. K. Harrison, *Introduction to the Old Testament* (Grand Rapids: Eerdmans, 1969), pp. 1115–16.

31. Hartman, "The Great Tree," p. 80; McNamara, "Nabonidus and the Book of Daniel," p. 141.

32. Pierre Grelot, "La prière de Nabonide (4QOrNab)," *Revue de Qumran* 9 (1978): 487.
33. Jongeling, Labauschagne, and van der Woude, *Aramaic Texts from Qumran I*, pp. 126–27.
34. Hartman, "The Great Tree," p. 81.
35. Archer, "Modern Rationalism and the Book of Daniel," pp. 135–36.
36. John C. Whitcomb, *Darius the Mede* (Grand Rapids: Eerdmans, 1959).
37. Wiseman et al., *Notes on Some Problems in the Book of Daniel*, pp. 12–16.
38. James M. Bulman, "The Identification of Darius the Mede," *Westminster Theological Journal* 35 (1973): 267.
39. C. Schedl, *History of the Old Testament* (Staten Island, NY: Alba, 1973), 5:51–86, as reported by Hartman and Di Lella, *The Book of Daniel*, p. 50, n. 96.
40. Raymond F Dougherty, *Nabonidus and Belshazzar* (New Haven, CT: Yale University Press, 1929), pp. 13–14.
41. Yamauchi, *The Stones and the Scriptures*, pp. 159–60.
42. Baldwin, *Daniel: An Introduction and Commentary*, p. 29. This recalls Dougherty's verdict: "Of all non-Babylonian records dealing with the situation at the close of the Neo-Babylonian Empire, the fifth chapter of Daniel ranks next to cuneiform literature in accuracy so far as outstanding events are concerned" (*Nabonidus and Belshazzar*, p. 200).
43. Hartman, "The Great Tree," pp. 77–78.
44. Ibid.
45. Ernst F. Weidner, "Jojachin, König von Juda, in Babylonischen Keilschrifttexten," *Mélanges Syriens offerts à M. René Dussaud* (Paris: Geuthner, 1939), 2:930–31; cf. D. J. Wiseman, "Some Egyptians in Babylonia," *Iraq* 26 (1966): 154–58.
46. I. Eph'al, "The Western Minorities in Babylonia in the 6th-5th Centuries B.C.," *Orientalia* 47 (1978): 78.
47. Both the Hebrew and the Akkadian words are derived from the Egyptian ḥry-tp, literally "chief lector priest." See K. A. Kitchen, "Magic and Sorcery," in *The New Bible Dictionary*, ed. J. D. Douglas (Grand Rapids: Eerdmans, 1962), p. 769; and J. Vergote, *Joseph en Égypte* (Louvain: Publications Universitaires, 1959), pp. 80–94, 209.
48. H. H. Rowley, *The Aramaic of the Old Testament* (London: Oxford University Press, 1929).
49. Peter W. Coxon, "The Distribution of Synonyms in Biblical Aramaic in the Light of Official Aramaic and the Aramaic of Qumran," *Revue de Qumran* 9 (1978): 512.

50. J. A. Fitzmyer, *The Genesis Apocryphon of Qumran Cave I*, 2d ed. (Rome: Biblical Institute Press, 1971), pp. 20–21, n. 56; and J. A. Fitzmyer, "The Contribution of Qumran Aramaic to the Study of the New Testament," *New Testament Studies* 20 (1974): 382, n. 4.

51. K. A. Kitchen, "The Aramaic of Daniel," in Wiseman et al., *Notes on Some Problems in the Book of Daniel*, pp. 31–79.

52. H. H. Rowley, "Review of *Notes on Some Problems in the Book of Daniel*, by D. J. Wiseman et al.," *Journal of Semitic Studies* 11 (1966): 112–16.

53. E. Y. Kutscher, "Aramaic," *Current Trends in Linguistics VI*, ed. T. A. Sebeok (The Hague: Mouton, 1970), pp. 347–412, esp. pp. 401–2.

54. E. Y. Kutscher, "The Hermopolis Papyri," *Israel Oriental Studies* 1 (1971): 103–19.

55. Peter W. Coxon, "Greek Loan-Words and Alleged Greek Loan Translations in the Book of Daniel," *Glasgow University Oriental Society Transactions* 25 (1973–74): 24.

56. Hartman and Di Lella, *The Book of Daniel*, p. 13.

57. See T. C. Mitchell and R. Joyce, "The Musical Instruments in Nebuchadnezzar's Orchestra," in Wiseman et al., *Notes on Some Problems in the Book of Daniel*, pp. 19–27.

58. Coxon, "Greek Loan-Words," p. 31.

59. Alfred Sendry, *Music in Ancient Israel* (New York: Philosophical Library, 1969), p. 297.

60. Hartman and DiLella, *The Book of Daniel*, p. 157. See Yamauchi, *Greece and Babylon*, p. 19.

61. Cited by Sendry, who devotes along discussion to this word (*Music in Ancient Israel*, pp. 325–33).

62. Coxon, "Greek Loan-Words," p. 36.

63. Rowley, "Review of *Notes on Some Problems in the Book of Daniel* by D. J. Wiseman, et al.," pp. 114–15.

64. Kutscher, "Aramaic," pp. 401–2.

65. Yamauchi, *Greece and Babylon*, pp. 19–24; and idem, "The Greek Words in Daniel," pp. 176–77.

66. Margaret S. Drower, "Syria *c*. 1550–1400 B.C.," in *The Cambridge Ancient History*, 3d. ed. (Cambridge: University Press, 1970–), vol. 2, pt. 1, p. 482.

67. D. J. Wiseman, "Assyria and Babylonia c. 1200–1000 B.C.," in *The Cambridge Ancient History*, 3d ed. (Cambridge: University Press, 1970–), vol. 2, pt. 2, p. 445.

68. M. E. L. Mallowan, *Nimrud and Its Remains* (New York: Dodd, Mead & Co., 1966), p. 217.

69. Friedrich Ellermeier, *Sibyllen, Musikanten, Haremsfrauen* (Herzberg am Harz: Junger, 1970), pp. 12–19.

Chapter 14

1. James A. Montgomery, *A Critical and Exegetical Commentary on the Book of Daniel*, International Critical Commentary (New York: Scribner's Sons, 1927), pp. 390–401; George A. F. Knight, "The Book of Daniel," in *The Interpreter's One-Volume Commentary of the Bible*, ed. M. Laymon (Nashville: Abingdon, 1971), pp. 447–48.

2. Edward J. Young, *The Messianic Prophecies of Daniel* (Grand Rapids: Eerdmans, 1954), p. 56; cf. H. C. Leupold, *Exposition of Daniel* (Columbus, OH: Wartburg, 1949), pp. 409–10; and C. F. Keil, *Biblical Commentary on the Book of Daniel*, trans. M. G. Easton (Edinburgh: Clark, 1876), pp. 399–402.

3. Leon Wood, *A Commentary on Daniel* (Grand Rapids: Zondervan, 1973), p. 247.

4. Francis Brown, S. R. Driver, and Charles Briggs, *A Hebrew and English Lexicon of the Old Testament* (Oxford: Clarendon, 1907), pp. 988–89; Ludwig Koehler and Walter Baumgartner, eds., *Lexicon in Veteris Testamenti Libros* (Leiden: Brill, 1958), p. 940.

5. Brown, Driver, and Briggs, *A Hebrew and English Lexicon of the Old Testament*, p. 797.

6. Mishnah: Baba Metzia ix. 10; Sanhedrin v. 1.

7. For a fuller discussion of these terms, see E. W. Hengstenberg, *Christology of the Old Testament*, trans. Theodore Meyer and James Martin, 4 vols. (Edinburgh: Clark, 1872–78), 3:115–17.

8. Montgomery, *A Critical and Exegetical Commentary on the Book of Daniel*, p. 380.

9. Brown, Driver, and Briggs, *A Hebrew and English Lexicon of the Old Testament*, p. 358.

10. Joseph Reider, "Etymological Studies in Biblical Hebrew," *Vetus Testamentum* 2 (April 1952): 116–17.

11. Montgomery, *A Critical and Exegetical Commentary on the Book of Daniel*, p. 380.

12. Ibid.

13. M. Baillet, J. T. Milik, et R. de Vaux, *Les "Petites Grottes" de Qumrân*, 2 vols., *Discoveries in the Judean Desert of Jordan: III* (Oxford: Clarendon, 1962), 1:244.

14. Marcus Jastrow, comp., *A Dictionary of the Targumin, the Talmud Bibli Yerushalmi, and the Midrashic Literature*, 2 vols. (London: Luzac, 1903), 1:502; cf. p. 505.

15. Montgomery, *A Critical and Exegetical Commentary on the Book*

of Daniel, p. 380; and Judah J. Slotki, *Daniel, Ezra and Nehemiah* (London: Soncino, 1951), p. 78.

16. Montgomery, *A Critical and Exegetical Commentary on the Book of Daniel*, p. 380.

17. John C. Whitcomb, Jr., *Darius the Mede* (Grand Rapids: Eerdmans, 1959), pp. 70–71.

18. Keil, *Daniel*, pp. 355–56.

19. Leupold, *Exposition of Daniel*, pp. 417–26.

20. Edward J. Young, *The Prophecy of Daniel: A Commentary* (Grand Rapids: Eerdmans, 1949), pp. 202–3.

21. Ibid.

22. Edward J. Young, *An Introduction to the Old Testament*, rev. ed. (Grand Rapids: Eerdmans, 1960), pp. 403–4.

23. Brown, Driver, and Briggs speak of it as a wall of stones without mortar, *Hebrew and English Lexicon of the Old Testament*, p. 173.

24. C. F. Keil, *The Books of Ezra, Nehemiah, and Esther*, trans. Sophia Taylor (Edinburgh: T. & T. Clark, 1873), pp. 120–21; and Slotki, *Daniel, Ezra and Nehemiah*, p. 167.

25. Young, *The Prophecy of Daniel*, pp. 205–6, 220; cf. Young, *Messianic Prophecies*, pp. 67–70.

26. Young, *The Prophecy of Daniel*, pp. 213–21; Young, *Messianic Prophecies*, pp. 69–84.

27. E. B. Pusey, *Daniel the Prophet* (Oxford: Parker, 1876), pp. 164–233, esp. pp. 168–78.

28. Charles Boutflower, *In and Around the Book of Daniel* (London: SPCK, 1923), pp. 168–211.

29. J. Barton Payne, *The Theology of the Older Testament* (Grand Rapids: Zondervan, 1962), pp. 276–78; J. Barton Payne, *The Imminent Appearing of Christ* (Grand Rapids: Eerdmans, 1962), pp. 148–50.

30. Glenn Richard Goss, "The Chronological Problems of the Seventy Weeks of Daniel" (Th.D. diss., Dallas Theological Seminary, 1966), pp. 122–30.

31. Keil, *Daniel*, p. 379; cf. Michael J. Gruenthaner, "The Seventy Weeks," *Catholic Biblical Quarterly* 1 (January 1939): 51.

32. Payne, *The Imminent Appearing of Christ*, p. 148.

33. For a fuller discussion, see Fred Holtzman, "A Re-examination of the Seventy Weeks of Daniel" (Th.M. thesis, Dallas Theological Seminary, 1974), pp. 82–84.

34. Harold W. Hoehner, "Chronological Aspects of the Life of Christ, Part II: The Commencement of Christ's Ministry," *Bibliotheca Sacra* 131 (January–March 1974): 41–54.

35. Harold W. Hoehner, "Chronological Aspects of the Life of Christ,

Part V: The Year of Christ's Crucifixion," *Bibliotheca Sacra* 131 (October–December 1974): 332–48.

36. Harold Hoehner, "Chronology of the Apostolic Age" (Th.D. diss., Dallas Theological Seminary, 1965), pp. 200–204; George Ogg, *The Odyssey of Paul* (Old Tappan, NJ: Revell, 1968), pp. 24–30.

37. Cf. Albert Barnes, *Notes, Critical, Illustrative, and Practical, on the Book of Daniel* (New York: Worthington, 1881), p. 390.

38. Keil, *Daniel*, pp. 379–80.

39. Goss, "The Chronological Problems of the Seventy Weeks of Daniel," p. 120.

40. Edwin R. Thiele, *The Mysterious Numbers of the Hebrew Kings*, rev. ed. (Grand Rapids: Eerdmans, 1965), pp. 28–30, 161.

41. S. H. Horn and L. H. Wood, "The Fifth-Century Jewish Calendar at Elephantine," *Journal of Near Eastern Studies* 13 (January 1954): 4, 20.

42. Ibid., p. 9.

43. Ibid., p. 4.

44. Richard A. Parker and Waldo H. Dubberstein, Babylonian Chronology 626 B.C.–A.D. 75, 2d ed. (Providence: Brown University Press, 1956), p. 32; and Herman H. Goldstine, *New and Full Moons 1001 B.C. to A.D. 1651* (Philadelphia: American Philosophical Society, 1973), p. 47.

45. Robert H. Gundry, *The Church and the Tribulation* (Grand Rapids: Zondervan, 1973), p. 189.

46. Young, *The Prophecy of Daniel*, p. 201.

47. Gundry, *The Church and the Tribulation*, p. 190.

48. John F. Walvoord, *Daniel: The Key to Prophetic Revelation* (Chicago: Moody, 1971), p. 234.

49. Payne, *The Imminent Appearing of Christ*, p. 151.

50. Gundry, *The Church and the Tribulation*, pp. 190–91.

51. Ibid., p. 191.

52. C. G. Ozanne, "Three Textual Problems in Daniel," *Journal of Theological Studies* 16 (October 1965): 446–47.

53. Robert C. Newman, "Daniel's Seventy Weeks and the Old Testament Sabbath-Year Cycle," *Journal of the Evangelical Theological Society* 16 (Fall 1973): 232–34.

54. Robert Anderson, *The Coming Prince*, 10th ed. (London: Hodder & Stoughton, 1915), pp. 67–75.

55. Jack Finegan, *Handbook of Biblical Chronology* (Princeton, NJ: Princeton University Press, 1964), p. 19.

56. *Encyclopaedia Britannica*, 14th ed., s.v. "Calendar, IV. Egyptian Calendar"; *Encyclopaedia Britannica*, 14th ed., s.v. "Chro-

nology, III. Egyptian"; Finegan, *Handbook of Biblical Chronology*, pp. 29, 32; Horn and Wood, "Jewish Calendar at Elephantine," p. 3.
57. *Encyclopaedia Britannica*, 14th ed., s.v. "Calendar, V. Hindu Calendar."
58. *Encyclopaedia Britannica*, 14th ed., s.v. "Calendar, VI. Babylonian and Assyrian Calendars"; cf. Horn and Wood, "The Fifth-Century Jewish Calendar at Elephantine," p. 5.
59. *Encyclopaedia Britannica*, 14th ed., s.v. "Calendar, VIII. Greek Calendar."
60. Anderson, *The Coming Prince*, pp. 119–29.
61. J. K. Fotheringham, "The Evidence of Astronomy and Technical Chronology for the Date of the Crucifixion," *Journal of Theological Studies* 35 (April 1934): 162.
62. See Goldstine, *New and Full Moons 1001 B.C. to A.D. 1651*, p. 87; Parker and Dubberstein, *Babylonian Chronology 626 B.C.–A.D. 75*, p. 46; Fotheringham, "Evidence of Astronomy," pp. 142–62; Joachim Jeremias, *The Eucharistic Words of Jesus*, trans. Norman Perrin, 3d ed. (London: SCM, 1966), p. 38.
63. Goldstine, *New and Full Moons*, p. 47.

Chapter 15

1. Robert Alter, *The Art of Biblical Poetry* (New York: Basic, 1985), p. 144 (italics his).
2. Many deny the authenticity of the oracles against Tyre (1:9–10), Edom (1:11–12), and Judah (2:4–5). Though it is beyond the scope of this chapter to present a lengthy, detailed defense of the text's unity, several observations are in order. Some scholars have questioned the originality of the Tyre and Edom oracles on historical and form critical/literary grounds. For example Hans Wolff points to structural differences between these oracles and others in chapters 1–2 (*Joel and Amos*, Hermeneia, trans. W. Janzen, S. D. McBride, and C. Muenchow [Philadelphia: Fortress, 19771, pp. 139–40). Wolff also contends that both oracles reflect the exilic period (pp. 158–60). However, Shalom Paul demonstrates the literary unity and artistry of Amos 1–2 in its canonical form, in the process exposing the methodological weaknesses of the form critical approach that denies this unity ("A Literary Reinvestigation of the Authenticity of the Oracles against the Nations of Amos," in *De La Tôrah au Messie*, ed. J. Dore, P. Grelot, and M. Carrez [Paris: Desclée, 1981], pp. 189–204). The historical allusions in the oracles are too vague to use for dating purposes.

Keith Schoville has proposed that the events in question are best explained against the background of Jehu's reign in the ninth century B.C. ("A Note on the Oracles of Amos against Gaza, Tyre, and Edom," in *Studies on Prophecy*, Supplements to Vetus Testamentum 26 [Leiden: Brill, 1974], pp. 55–63), while John H. Hayes has attempted to show that they fit into the period of the prophet (*Amos, the Eighth Century Prophet: His Times and His Preaching* [Nashville: Abingdon, 1988], pp. 55, 86–89, 90–93). The oracle against Judah has been denied on literary grounds. Wolff draws attention to its formal variations from the other oracles and to its so-called Deuteronomic style, which he associates with a supposed "Deuteronomic school" that worked much later than the time of Amos (*Joel and Amos*, pp. 139–40, 163–64). However, Paul shows that such arguments have been pressed too far, even if one were to assume the existence of a distinct Deuteronomic style characteristic of a Deuteronomic school ("A Literary Reinvestigation of the Authenticity of the Oracles against the Nations of Amos," pp. 194–96). The structure and language of the oracle are not determinative for dating.

3. Paul, "A Literary Reinvestigation of the Authenticity of the Oracles against the Nations of Amos," p. 197.

4. Paul points to several biblical and Semitic examples of a numerical pattern involving the numbers seven and eight in sequence. As he observes, the pattern is often employed to "express the concept of culmination or climactic finish" (ibid., p. 196).

5. Ibid., p. 197.

6. The New International Version is the translation used throughout this chapter.

7. Cf. Meir Weiss, "The Pattern of Numerical Sequence in Amos 1–2," *Journal of Biblical Literature* 86 (1967): 416, and the literature he cites in note 1 of his article.

8. In Psalm 90:10 multiples of 7/8 (i.e., 70/80) express the idea of completeness.

9. In Job 5:19–22 the accompanying list corresponds to the first number (6), unless one counts "destruction" (Heb. שׁד) in both vv. 21–22) twice.

10. For this translation of אֲשִׁיבֶנּוּ see Michael Barre, "The Meaning of *l' 'šybnw* in Amos 1:3–2:6," *Journal of Biblical Literature* 105 (1986): 622.

11. The translation of the second line follows the NIV margin rather than the NIV text. For a defense of this reading, see Michael Fishbane, "The Treaty Background of Amos 1:11 and Related

Matters," *Journal of Biblical Literature* 89 (1979): 313–18; and
Michael L. Barré, "Amos 1:11 Reconsidered," *Catholic Biblical Quarterly* 47 (1985): 420–27.

12. In this case the list of seven sins in verses 6–8 suggests completeness. The addition of two more formal accusatory statements in verse 12 dismisses all doubt that Israel is overripe for punishment (Hayes, *Amos the Eighth Century Prophet: His Times and His Preaching*, pp. 107–8).

13. Because of its very general tone, verse 7a supplements verse 6b by elaborating on the character of the crime described there. James Mays states that "7a is a parallel restatement of 6b" (*Amos: A Commentary*, Old Testament Library Philadelphia: Westminster, 1969], p. 46). The syntax of verse 7a supports this interpretation. The form translated "they trample" is a participle (הַשֹּׁאֲפִים), not a finite verb, and stands in apposition to the subject of the preceding line (cf. the third masculine plural suffix on מִכְרָם in v. 6b). To show the close syntactical relationship between verses 6b-7a one might paraphrase, "They (those who trample . . . and deny justice . . .) sell the righteous for silver, and the needy for a pair of sandals."

14. The precise meaning of the accusation in verse 7b is unclear. Traditionally the crime has been understood as sexual in nature, with the "girl" being identified as the son's lover or wife, a peasant servant girl, or a cult prostitute. However, the phrase translated "use" (lit. "go to," הָלַךְ אֶל) is not a technical expression for sexual intercourse (like the verb בּוֹא can be). Also if the crime is that of a man having relations with his daughter-in-law (cf. Lev. 18:15; 20:12), the son would be innocent. However, the tone of Amos 2:7 seems to implicate both father and son. The sexual exploitation of a girl from the lower servant class would fit well in the context of the social oppression described in verses 6–8. However, the term translated "girl" (נַעֲרָה) need not refer to a low-ranking servant or slave. Also the reference to profaning the Lord's name favors a religious violation such as idolatry (see Hans M. Barstad, *The Religious Polemics of Amos,* Supplements to Vetus Testamentum 34 [Leiden: Brill, 1984], pp. 17–21). Though perhaps fitting nicely with verse 8 (especially if the altar and temple referred to there belong to a pagan god), the view that the girl is a cult prostitute is unlikely since the word translated "girl" never refers elsewhere to a prostitute. More recently some scholars have identified the "girl" as a hostess at a pagan religious banquet known as a *marzeah*. (For this view see Barstad, pp. 33–36. On the evidence for the *marzeah* institution, see Barstad, *The Religious Polemics of Amos,* pp.

127–42, and Philip J. King, *Amos, Hosea, Micah—An Archaeological Commentary* [Philadelphia: Westminster, 1988], pp. 137–
61.) This view finds support from verse 8, where some type of
religious ritual is described, and from 6:4–7, where a *marzeah*
banquet is specifically mentioned (cf. מַרְזֵחַ in 6:7) and described.
(On the background of 6:4–7 see Gary V. Smith, *Amos: A Commentary*, Library of Biblical Interpretation [Grand Rapids:
Zondervan, 1989], pp. 193–94).

15. This analysis of the crimes essentially follows that of Duane L.
Christensen (though he sees v. 7b as referring to "promiscuous
intercourse"). See his "The Prosodic Structure of Amos 1–2,"
Harvard Theological Review 67 (1974): 436, and *Transformations of the War Oracle in Old Testament Prophecy*, Harvard
Dissertations in Religion 3 (Missoula, MT: Scholars, 1975), pp.
66, 71. Contrary to the analyses of many, verse 12 should not be
omitted when counting Israel's crimes. Though verse 12 is separated from the main list of crimes (vv. 6–8) by the recital of
God's benefits (vv. 9–11), it is literarily linked with the earlier
accusation (cf. the references to drinking wine in vv. 8b and
12a) and provides a fitting conclusion it. Its use of the second
person (starting in v. 10) makes its denunciation more direct
and highlights its culminating function.

16. Wolff, *Joel and Amos*, p. 138.

17. B. Kingston Soper, "For Three Transgressions and for Four: A
New Interpretation of Amos 1:3, etc.," *Expository Times* 71
(1959–60): 86–87.

18. Barre, "The Meaning of *l' 'šybnw* in Amos 1:3–2:6," pp. 621–22.

19. Weiss, "The Pattern of Numerical Sequence in Amos 1–2," pp.
418–19.

20. Ibid., pp. 419–20.

21. Hayes, who essentially follows Weiss's approach, suggests that
the 7/8 pattern is operative here (*Amos the Eighth-Century Prophet: His Times and His Preaching*, pp. 107–8). Verses 6–8 list
seven crimes, while verse 12 adds an eighth. However, if a
formal method is used to enumerate the crimes in verses 6–8,
then the same method should be employed in verse 12, in which
case the crimes would total nine, not eight.

22. Weiss, "The Pattern of Numerical Sequence in Amos 1–2," p.
421.

23. Christensen makes this point in "The Prosodic Structure of Amos
1–2," p. 436, and *Transformations of the War Oracle in Old
Testament Prophecy*, p. 71.

24. Israel might, of course, object that its sins were not nearly so bad

as the military atrocities of the surrounding nations. That is probably why Amos pointed out in the next pericope that Israel's elect and privileged position (3:2) made its crimes of oppression, paganism, and ingratitude—which on the surface might not seem as terrible as kidnapping whole communities, selling slaves, and ripping open pregnant women—far more heinous in God's sight than the cruel deeds of other nations. "From everyone who has been given much, much will be demanded" (Luke 12:48).

Chapter 16

1. K. J. Cathcart observes, "Although the concept of the Day of Yahweh has often been investigated, surprisingly there has not been any major study of it in recent times" ("Day of Yahweh," in *Anchor Bible Dictionary*, 2:84).

2. For example in his consideration of the concept Gerhard von Rad eliminates passages that do not expressly mention the day of Yahweh, contending that "they do not provide the interpreter with any sure exegetical basis" ("The Origin of the Day of Yahweh," *Journal of Semitic Studies* 4 [1959]: 97).

3. Richard H. Hiers is one recent scholar who recognizes that a wider range of terminology must be considered in order to understand the day of the Lord concept fully ("Day of the Lord," in *Anchor Bible Dictionary*, 2:82–83).

4. Hiers notes that on some 60 occasions the day of the Lord is said to be a future time of blessing (ibid., p. 83).

5. Gerhard von Rad, *The Message of the Prophets*, trans. D. M. G. Stalker (New York: Harper and Row, 1965), p. 97. In a related vein, Willem VanGemeren declares, "Zephaniah most extensively and dramatically developed the prophetic concept of the Day of the Lord" (*Interpreting the Prophetic Word* [Grand Rapids: Zondervan, 1990], p. 174).

6. Quotations from Zephaniah are the writer's own translations, and quotations from other Bible books are from the New Revised Standard Version.

7. Two recent scholars who reflect this linkage in their outlines of the book are Richard D. Patterson (*Nahum, Habakkuk, and Zephaniah*, Wycliffe Exegetical Commentary [Chicago: Moody, 1991], p. 289) and O. Palmer Robertson (*The Books of Nahum, Habakkuk, and Zephaniah*, New International Commentary on the Old Testament [Grand Rapids: Eerdmans, 1990], p. 266).

8. Greg A. King, "Recent Trends in the Study of Zephaniah," paper presented to the Society of Biblical Literature, November 1992. Elizabeth Achtemeier has called for a wholistic reading of

the book (*Nahum-Malachi*, Interpretation: A Commentary for Teaching and Preaching [Atlanta: Knox, 1986], p. 69).

9. This word is used in Zechariah 2:13 (Heb., 17) where it also sems to imply a coming encounter with Yahweh. Also see Habakkuk 2:20.

10. Robertson, *The Books of Nahum, Habakkuk, and Zephaniah*, p. 266.

11. Rich in meaning, it is difficult to communicate the nuances of פָּקַד with a single English word. In fact Harris quoted Speiser as saying that there is "no other Hebrew verb that has caused translators as much trouble." That is quite a tribute to the slippery nature of this word when one considers the many other challenging Hebrew verbs (R. Laird Harris, "פָּקַד," in *Theological Wordbook of the Old Testament*, 2:731).

12. Proof for a broader meaning than simply "to punish" for this word in Zephaniah is provided by the use of the same word in 2:7 in the context of restoration rather than punishment.

13. Carl-A. Keller, "Sophonie," in *Michee, Nahoum, Habacuc, Sophonie*, ed. Rene Vuilleumier and Carl A.-Keller (Neuchatel: Delachaux et Niestle, 1971), p. 193.

14. In fact, "epoch" or "era" might convey the meaning of the Hebrew word יוֹם more accurately than "day" in the phrase "the day of Yahweh." However, Stuart may be correct in noting that the phrase arose from the ancient belief that a sovereign could win his wars in a single day (Douglas Stuart, *Hosea-Jonah*, Word Biblical Commentary [Waco, TX: Word, 1987], p. 352).

15. Klaus Koch, *The Assyrian Period*, vol. 1 of *The Prophets*, trans. Margaret Kohl (Philadelphia: Fortress, 1983), p. 161 (italics his).

16. VanGemeren, *Interpreting the Prophetic Word*, p. 174.

17. Jeremiah 10:5 used the same two verbs—"do no harm" and "do no good"—in describing the complete inactivity of idols.

18. Achtemeier, *Nahum-Malachi*, p. 69.

19. David W. Baker, *Nahum, Habakkuk, Zephaniah*, Tyndale Old Testament Commentaries (Downers Grove, IL: InterVarsity, 1988), p. 91.

20. For example Ehud Ben Zvi, *A Historical-Critical Study of the Book of Zephaniah* (Berlin: de Gruyter, 1991), pp. 54, 134–36.

21. John N. Oswalt, "בָּטַח," in *Theological Wordbook of the Old Testament*, 1:101–2.

22. Achtemeier, *Nahum-Malachi*, p. 78.

23. Ivan J. Ball, *A Rhetorical Study of Zephaniah* (Berkeley, CA: Bibal, 1988), p. 46.

24. This is the term of M. DeRoche, "Zephaniah 1:2, 3: The 'Sweeping' of Creation," *Vetus Testamentum* 30 (1979): 106.
25. Ibid., p. 107.
26. Baker, *Nahum, Habakkuk, Zephaniah,* p. 91.
27. H. Haag, "חָמָס," in *Theological Dictionary of the Old Testament,* 4 (1980): 482.
28. Maria Eszenyei Szeles, *Wrath and Mercy: A Commentary on the Books of Hakakkuk and Zephaniah,* International Theological Commentary (Grand Rapids: Eerdmans, 1987), p. 96.
29. F. C. Fensham, "A Possible Origin of the Concept of the Day of the Lord," in *Biblical Essays: Die Ou Testamentiese Werkgemeenskap in Suid Afrika-9th Congress* (Potchefstroom: Rege Pers Beperk, 1966), pp. 90–97.
30. Robertson, *The Books of Nahum, Habakkuk, and Zephaniah,* p. 268.
31. Some scholars have attempted to connect the day of the Lord with a variety of concepts besides the covenant, such as holy war and the hypothetical enthronement festival of Yahweh. For a recent survey of scholarly positions, see Cathcart, "Day of Yahweh," 2:84–85.
32. This is true even though the book does not use the word "covenant."
33. This is in Joel's depiction of the day of the Lord in Joel 2:2. This may serve as evidence that Joel also saw the day of the Lord as related to the covenant.
34. Robertson, *The Books of Nahum, Habakkuk, and Zephaniah,* p. 282.
35. This is the sentiment of Victor Hamilton, *Handbook on the Pentateuch* (Grand Rapids: Baker, 1982), p. 388.
36. Patterson, *Nahum, Habakkuk, and Zephaniah,* p. 370. Patterson also observes perceptively that Zephaniah demonstrates "that because judgment is an integral part of God's teleological program designed to bless His people and His world, it is in a sense a veiled hope" (ibid., p. 369).
37. Greg A. King, "The Remnant in Zephaniah," *Bibliotheca Sacra* 151 (October–December 1994): 414–27.
38. VanGemeren, *Interpreting the Prophetic Word,* p. 175.
39. Eugene H. Merrill, *Kingdom of Priests: A History of Old Testament Israel* (Grand Rapids: Baker, 1987), p. 457.
40. VanGemeren, *Interpreting the Prophetic Word,* p. 176.